Donal Daly's *Digital Sales Transformation | In a Customer First World* should be on every business leaders' mandatory resource list, especially for those of us who know they need to boost their commercial team's organic impact ... but don't know how to practically tackle all that needs to be done in such a complex customer / competitor world. Donal gives practical advice, processes and metrics that you can adapt to your own business circumstances and his contemporary and extensive research into how today's customers are thinking and wanting to be served differently brings a critical mirror to reflect how well or not you are servicing your key and future accounts ... and what you should be doing about changing the way you manage your sales force's interactions with their customers. While much is talked about the data evolution and artificial intelligence, Donal breaks it down into a realism he coins as 'augmented intelligence' and again challenges us to apply these new tools in a smart way to overcome the tidal wave of overwhelming reports that fail to inform adequately or fast enough.

Patrick Hogan | Vice President Commercial Excellence | Honeywell

The customer of the future is not the customer of the past and sales organizations have to engage differently. At the core this book is a blueprint for the future of Digital Sales Transformation.

Tiffani Bova | Global Customer – Growth & Innovation Evangelist | Salesforce

Most people just assume the Digital Transformation is all about tech. I love that Donal sees what's always been at the heart of transformational change – people. That sounds philosophical, but this book is actually more strategic and execution-oriented: a must-read for anyone in sales and post-sales leadership.

Nick Mehta | CEO | Gainsight

Customer first. Donal reminds the reader of this important theme. As we navigate in this complex world, a seller must stay focused on the customer, in order to be successful and truly transform sales. This book provides a blueprint and is one I recommend to anyone working in a Sales or Marketing organization.

Sanjay Poonen | Chief Operating Officer, Customer Operations | VMWare

Digital Transformation is driving profound change in how customers engage. With the right balance of methodology, technology and a focus on the customer, *Digital Sales Transformation | In a Customer First World* is the blueprint for salespeople to make their customers successful and outpace their competition.

Mark Roberge | Senior Lecturer | Harvard Business School / former CRO | Hubspot

Outstanding food for thought in this book for modern enterprise B2B sellers. Donal provides great insights around how to select the right customers and then create value for them. A clear guide on how to balance Augmented Intelligence with human judgment to achieve success.

Chano Fernandez | Executive Vice President, Global Field Operations | Workday

The future, with all its anticipated marvels and challenges, is not just around the corner; it is already here. Digital Transformation is impacting every aspect of our lives. The everyday flow of information and the attention that it demands is only going to increase, and all of us have to adapt to it in order to deliver business success. This 'race for attention' impacts our customers as well. *Digital Sales Transformation | In a Customer First World* does a wonderful job explaining the details and the technological impacts of these changes, as well as dedicating a lot of space in the book to describing the inevitable changes in the way that customer relationships will develop. Donal delivers vital advice for any sales manager living in our new digital era, at the same time putting his finger on a key and ever-relevant point, saying that the basics of sales aren't gone. The first and perhaps the most important question a salesperson can ask himself is: "What problems does your customer have that you can solve better than anyone else?" This question is really timeless; business problems might be different, the way you solve them might be different, but the basic rules of selling are as relevant as ever.

Richard van Wageningen | Senior Vice President IMEAR | Orange Business Services

This book is thought provoking and inspirational. Donal explains with tremendous clarity how Digital Transformation can be used to get closer to customers. It is a must read for all sales leaders who value and aspire to a Customer First experience.

Jon Ireland | Business Change Executive | SDL plc

The world of selling (and buying!) is undergoing dramatic changes driven by Digital Transformation and most importantly, customer expectations. Donal provides a clear framework to assess these changes and enable leaders to adapt to extract value for themselves and their customers.

Avanish Sahai | Vice President Worldwide ISV and Technology Alliances | ServiceNow

Digital Sales Transformation is a recipe for collaborative customer success. Donal unveils his Customer Impact Architecture to explain how today's customers want to buy and clearly explains how to apply methodology, process and technology for sales success. This book is extremely valuable to both buyers and sellers.

Ingrid De Doncker | CEO | iDDea

Donal's book provides a comprehensive and thoughtful analysis of modern sales strategies, reflecting the twin dynamics of Digital Transformation and Customer Centricity. A must-read for those preparing for the future of selling, by one of the world's foremost experts in sales transformation.

Umberto Milletti | CEO | InsideView

Sales process automation has become table stakes for organizations looking to maximize growth. In *Digital Sales Transformation | In a Customer First World*, Donal expertly outlines how you can take the next step by leveraging AI. The potential to deliver near real-time actionable insight to buyers based on where they are in the process is game changing. That being said, this is more than a theoretical discussion on technology. It's a blueprint for how a company should run Sales. Any Sales Leader, CEO or Board Member would benefit from reading this book.

Don Soucy | Executive Vice President of Global Sales | Spok

The heart of digital transformation is the business model shift. In this post-sale, on demand, attention economy, we no longer sell products but deliver on a brand promise. This 'must read' book by Donal will help executives understand how the seller can start with empathy for the customer and build their transformation from this first principles design point.

R "Ray" Wang | Principal Analyst & Founder | Constellation Research, Inc.

DIGITAL SALES
TRANSFORMATION
IN A CUSTOMER FIRST WORLD

Donal Daly

OAK·TREE·PRESS

Published by OAK TREE PRESS
www.oaktreepress.com / www.SuccessStore.com

© 2017 Donal Daly, Altify Inc.

A catalogue record of this book is available from the British
Library.

ISBN 978 1 78119 328 0 (Hardback)
ISBN 978 1 78119 329 7 (Paperback)
ISBN 978 1 78119 330 3 (ePub)
ISBN 978 1 78119 331 0 (Kindle)
ISBN 978 1 78119 332 7 (PDF)

CONTENTS

FIGURES

ACKNOWLEDGEMENTS

At times like this I feel very fortunate. Writing for me is sometimes hard, but more often it is a joy. It is how I think and formulate my thoughts. I have never been one who has been able to outsource writing. I think and I start to write and then I interact with people who have lived in the world I am trying to improve, and then I think again. It is only through that process that the threads come together. Sometimes the hypothesis I present is flawed and I learn from many who are wiser or more experienced. Then there are those few enriching moments when I cause my collaborators to think, to question their perceptions, or exercise their imagination. In every case though, the conversations are inspiring and I am the beneficiary of wisdom more often than not. For that, and the genuine efforts many have made to make this book better than I could ever have managed on my own, I am eternally grateful.

Firstly, to you the reader, I want to express my appreciation that you have given of your time to read the book. Please let me know if it provided you with even a few thoughts to improve your sales performance, and let me know what else you would like to know. I will continue this story on my website at **donaldaly.com**.

Mike Rosenbaum is one of the most important leaders in the global Cloud industry. As EVP CRM Apps at Salesforce, his hand is on the tiller guiding the future vision for millions of the world's knowledge workers. I am fortunate to have known Mike for many years. Even as his role in Salesforce expanded to its current scale and scope, Mike has always remained gracious and generous with his time. He is one of the world's gentlemen. I am proud that Mike agreed, without fuss or hesitation, to write the *Foreword* for my book. A huge expression of gratitude is due to Mike, and also to Kate Wesson at Salesforce, who shepherded and supported this effort.

To the reviewers: thank you for your feedback and for your generous testimonials – Avanish Sahai, Chano Fernandez, Don Soucy, Ingrid De Doncker, Jon Ireland, Mark Roberge, Nick Mehta, Patrick Hogan, Ray Wang, Richard van Wageningen, Sanjay Poonen, Tiffani Bova, and Umberto Milletti.

Many of the early reviewers really valued the Practitioner's Perspective vignettes. For telling their stories and sharing wisdom, I want to thank Billy Martin, Glenn Davis, Haiden Smith, Janice Rapoza, Jon Ireland, Marc Parizot, Mat Singer, JP Knapp, and Thanhia Sanchez, for enriching the narrative.

Many others toiled selflessly to improve my work: the core content, the design, the methodology, the writing, the references, and of course the proof reading, the layout, and the flow.

Wendy Reed's advice on the kernel of the methodology ensured that I did not go astray as she constantly probed and questioned the structure and integrity of my thinking. I am indebted to her for her gift of time and energy to this project. Her vast experience and attention to detail greatly enhanced the methods and the flow of the overall book. The coalface experience of Phil Trapani, gained through multiple customer engagements (everyone loves Phil) and the decades of methodology wisdom from Greg Kiernan, further strengthened its coherence and completeness. This book is much improved by their contributions.

As this book is set in a Customer First world I was extremely fortunate to have the guiding hand of Ingrid De Doncker, making sure that the buyer's perspective was honestly reflected throughout. Ingrid's vision of the future of the buyer, and her expertise as a strategic procurement consultant, gave me an unfair advantage. I could look at the buyer / seller engagement though both sets of eyes at the same time. It is down to her frequent and good-natured interventions that I might appear somewhat knowledgeable about the buyer's perspective.

Looking at this book in its totality, I am delighted with the overall feel. That's due in no small part to the design talents and graphics flair of Rachel Quinn, Nigel Cullington, and Kelley Joss. They delivered their immense workload in an amazingly short timeframe, and always with a smile. I can't thank them enough.

And, then there is my indefatigable editor, Brian O'Kane. This is the fifth book on which we have collaborated. His ability to turn my sometimes convoluted writing into consumable reading, his patience and tenacity, and quite unbelievable productivity has been the solid foundation on which this project was built. I'm privileged to have Brian as my editor.

To Anthony Reynolds, the new CEO I was fortunate to hire at Altify, and his entire team, I want to express my sincere thanks. They allowed me the space to write this book and set out my thoughts and concepts that I hope will improve not just the lives of the sales organizations that Altify serves, but also others who choose to embark on the journey of Digital Sales Transformation.

As ever, my family supported me through the ups and down of this effort, and I am forever grateful to Cleona, Robin and Christian for putting up with me and who know that when I am writing a book it just means that Dad is spending a lot of time in "the box."

Thank you, Donal

FOREWORD

Mike Rosenbaum

EVP, CRM Apps, Salesforce

We are living in an era of unprecedented change. An obvious statement, sophomoric even, but it's true. Technology has had a sweeping impact on society and nothing has been left untouched. Business models have been indelibly upended. Communication is constant – our daily lives are punctuated with texts, emojis and videos that capture every moment, from the mundane to the magical. How we communicate, how we relate to each other and what we expect from each other has changed forever. It's also changed what we expect from companies, how we expect to relate to them and communicate with them, and what it means to be a customer.

At Salesforce, we call this the 'Age of the Customer.' In this book, Donal Daly calls it 'The Customer First World.' It's the idea that information technology advances (the cloud, mobile, social, artificial intelligence, and whatever we think of next) have ushered in a new type of customer expectation. And the businesses that succeed will reorganize to put customers at the center of everything they do. Customer centricity isn't radical. Family-run restaurants, neighborhood hardware stores and local coffee shops have practiced customer centricity for decades – they just called it 'good business.' But, the explosion of information technology has changed everything. Not just what's possible but what's expected and customer expectations are now sky-high. We want instant answers, fast customer service and effortless, frustration-free experiences that just work. We expect great service wherever we go – whether we're ordering coffee at our local independent coffee shop or using the Starbucks mobile app. And when we don't have a good experience, we're underwhelmed, we're annoyed, we tweet about it and we remember it.

The forward thinking companies that put customers first are setting a new standard that their competitors must compete with. Like 80 million others,[1] I'm an Amazon Prime subscriber and at least once a week, I order something that usually arrives within one or two days. There is hardly ever a problem and when occasionally there is, fixing it is as easy as opening my Amazon app. Now ordering something from anywhere else is a risk, because a high bar has been set. I'm very happy with that bar and anything below that bar is frustrating. On a rational level, I understand that Amazon has a world class distribution network and an incredibly talented information technology organization that smaller companies can't match. But on an emotional level, the bar has been set and I really want that consistently ideal experience. I am a demanding, exacting and somewhat irrational customer. We all are.

Amazon's not unique. It has embraced technology (and supply chain, distribution and logistics) to create an amazing customer experience, but so have many other companies. Warby Parker has reinvented the once-painful process of buying glasses. Casper has made it possible to order a high-end bed online, saving you (and your marriage) a Saturday of mattress haggling. Tesla has redefined luxury cars – everything from the manufacturing to the purchasing experience – making their dealerships like Apple Stores, a place where high-pressure sales don't exist and Tesla owners and enthusiasts are equally welcome.[2]

These brands and many others have digitally transformed so much so that they are actually technology companies. Information technology is such a disruptive force that every company today is a technology company, whether they want it or not.[3] Almost every company that I meet with wants to

---

[1] *BusinessInsider*, 'Amazon has around 80 million reasons to be excited for Prime Day,' July 10, 2017.

[2] *Fortune*, 'Elon Musk's Angry Customer Twitter Thread Is a Gold Mine of Customer Service Advice', September 18, 2017.

[3] CNBC, 'Every Company is a Tech Company now (yes, even Blue Apron),'

digitally transform but faces trade-offs: legacy systems, competing priorities, budget, change management, the list goes on and on. There are always countless reasons why it's hard to change. But I urge every single one of them – and you – to get started. Now. Today. Find a project where you can move and move fast. Do that one project, chalk up a win and then do another and another and another. You won't regret it. In fact, you'll be amazed by what you can accomplish.

Mike Rosenbaum

EVP, CRM Apps, Salesforce

August 10, 2017.

A Note from Anthony Reynolds, CEO, Altify

When I first met Donal I was excited about the company he had built. I was looking for a company to lead that could stake a claim, make a difference in a market, and solve an important problem. The vision, the product-market fit, the great customers were all the right core ingredients. So Donal and I got to talking.

Over a period of about five months I got to know Donal and Altify, and joined as CEO on February 1, 2017. Even though I had spent a lot of time before that doing diligence, talking to customers and getting to know the people at Altify, I still wondered a little about what I would find under the covers.

As a new CEO, you are always constrained by time and as a result you worry about two things when joining a new company. First, there's the product. If the product doesn't work, then it is really hard to grow a business and fixing product issues is often something that does not happen overnight. The reality at Altify is that I did not need to have any concerns there. This is the first time in my career as an executive where I have not had to give up a weekend to work on a customer's problem with the product. It just works.

The other thing that is hard to fix is company culture and from our first company kick-off in Dublin, Ireland in February 2017, I have been struck by the amazing collegial, collaborative and supportive nature of the team at Altify. People just love to come to work every day to help each other and help our customers. Our customers' success drives our operational priorities and is the bedrock of our culture. That is an asset I didn't know we had, and it is a tremendous accelerator for growth.

But beyond all of this I am excited to lead a company with such a great vision, constantly challenged and always evolving. The company started in 2005 with a vision, in

Donal's words: "to improve the lives of salespeople." I've seen so much evidence of that in my short time here.

So, I am delighted to introduce this book painting the vision, grounded in today's realities, and peeking just a little around the corner into the future. The re-imagined methodology, and the creative application of technology are very exciting. The book lays out clearly the fact that there are better ways to do what we do today, and Donal has helped us to visualize how we can drive value for and with our customers in ways that heretofore seemed impossible.

I am proud to be CEO at this great company, and I hope you find this book as helpful and inspiring as I did. I look forward to joining you on your journey to *Digital Sales Transformation | In a Customer First World*.

Anthony Reynolds
CEO, Altify

CHAPTER 1: INTRODUCTION

It was a day in July, in the middle of summer, and it was raining. Not just light rain, but that kind that bounces off the roof of your car doing its best impression of a Buddy Rich jazz drum solo, staccato one minute and almost harmonious the next. I shouldn't have been surprised. I was in Cork in Ireland, sitting in my car outside the Boole Library in my *alma mater* University College Cork (UCC). It rains a lot in Ireland, but that's why the country is so beautiful, and the people so imaginative. When it's raining all the time you need to be creative.

Now, a few decades after I graduated with a degree in Electrical Engineering, it was my daughter's turn to start her university life. As she was registering with the college I was performing my duly appointed role as chauffeur. As I sat in my car I reminisced about the things I had learned during my time in UCC. I enjoyed college a lot (I mean *really* enjoyed it) so I might not have been the world's most dedicated student of engineering. As I reflected on that time, it came to me that more than anything else, I discovered how to think and was taught how to solve problems. These skills have served me well. Thinking matters.

George Boole, he of the eponymous library, is famous not for spending time in Cork, Ireland – in 1849 he was appointed as the first professor of mathematics in UCC – but for the creation of Boolean Logic; you know all those ones and zeros that are the foundation of digital computing.[4] (It all started in Cork, so just to annoy my Dublin friends I claim that the Internet was invented in Cork.)

---

[4] Because of Boole all information can be represented as a series of ones or zeros. In computer language a 'bit' stores a value of one or zero. String eight bits together and you get a byte, a thousand bytes is a kilobyte, and so on to megabytes, gigabytes and so on, all the way up to exabytes and zetabytes – lots and lots of data, representing the world's information in a series of ones and zeros.

Once the rain stopped, and the sun started to shine – it shines most days between the rain showers – I got out of my car to explore the Boole Library, and came across this quotation:

> No general method for the solution of questions can be established which does not recognize the universal laws of thought.

> **George Boole:** *The Laws of Thought* **(1854)**

With the evolution of language in the 160 years since, this sentence may now seem a little cumbersome or convoluted. But the key message that I took away from it was that thinking matters if you are to solve any problem.

Seems obvious, right?

But I worry about it. I am concerned that critical thinking skills are diminishing now that Google seems to provide all of the answers and appears to many people to be the 'solution of questions.' In too many situations we race headlong into quick answers to slow, deliberate questions. In sales, as in many other business professions, this is dangerous.

As I was driving home, Buddy Rich once more invoking the rain gods to drum on my roof, I asked my daughter what she thought about this. Her response: "Don't you help people think for a living? Isn't that, like, what you do?" prompted me to write this book.

She's right of course. All great sellers are strategic thinkers first, adopting the maxim of 'measure twice and cut once' before they meet with a customer or embark on a sales pursuit. Now, with the rapidly changing dynamics in the market, it seems a worthwhile endeavor to help all knowledge workers – with a particular emphasis on salespeople – to amplify their critical thinking skills.

In 1934, T.S. Eliot, the poet and playwright wrote:

Where is the life we have lost in living?
Where is the wisdom we have lost in knowledge?
Where is the knowledge we have lost in information?

Eliot was in many ways presaging the Internet Age, the reality shared by Gen-Xers, Millennials and the upcoming Thumb Generation:[5] too much information – but too little insight. Millennials who are becoming an increasingly important force in the workplace are characterized by some as tech-savvy and proficient in applying technology to everyday problems efficiently.

But I wonder if the habits learned in an environment where the answer to everything is just a Google search away have in any way reduced their critical faculties, removed the need to develop ideas from first principles, or through that journey to nourish their own perspective. If that is the case with Millennials and indeed with an increasingly large proportion of Gen-Xers – the term 'Millennials' is representative much more of a mindset than an age group – then we need to be careful that this trend does not continue with the Thumb Generation.

We want our future sales leaders to leverage the wisdom of others. As they do, they will see the horizon more clearly if they stand on the shoulders of those who have gone before them. We want them to respect the value of lessons learned and to build on those lessons, and to stretch their minds, to extend those models, but we need them to seek insight, to learn the skills of primary research, to be inquisitive, curious and questioning.

We need to help them to think.

---

[5] Thumb Generation: This is a phrase that I came up with about three years ago watching my children and their friends exhibiting amazing dexterity with their thumbs as they texted and scrolled on their phones. I define this generation as those born between 1998 and 2010.

The Rise of Digital Transformation

The world in which we live is a world dominated by the race for attention. In the two minutes it has taken you to read to this point in this *Introduction*, the world sent 300 million emails, watched 15 million videos on YouTube, and searched 8 million times on Google. Salesforce customers processed 6 million transactions in that time, and together we managed to send 10 million emojis! The world is truly moving at Internet speed and it is only getting faster. I wonder though when we will realize that there is no deficit in information; there is a deficit in insight – and that insight is not solely the dominion of machines.

In case you hoped that one day things might slow down or you wouldn't have to worry about things changing all of the time, well, unfortunately, today is not that day. The future is not around the corner. It just passed you on the street. The world is being digitally transformed as we watch and wonder. Boole's ones and zeros are affecting every aspect of our personal and business lives:

- According to a September 2017 study[6] from BT, the $30B British telecommunications company, 40 percent of CEOs have Digital Transformation at the top of boardroom agenda, with many CEOs leading the projects personally
- The *Altify Business Performance Benchmark Study 2017*[7] has similar findings, placing Digital Transformation as the top priority for 47 percent of the study's 800 participants

---

[6] BT Study: *Digital Transformation Top Priority for CEOs*: **www.globalservices.bt.com/uk/en/news/digital-transformation-top-priority-for-ceos**.

[7] *Altify Business Performance Benchmark Study 2017*: **www.altify.com/benchmark2017**.

- McKinsey & Company, the worldwide management consulting firm, takes it one step further, saying[8] that expectations for growth are highest at companies that pursue digital to create new business.

The impact on business of Digital Transformation is clearly immense. Defining a Digital Sales Transformation blueprint to guide sales organizations to respond to this disruption as they struggle to catch up to their more digitally advanced customers is one of the core themes of this book.

---

[8] McKinsey Report: **http://www.mckinsey.com/business-functions/digital-mckinsey/our-insights/the-digital-tipping-point-mckinsey-global-survey-results**.

The Customer First Mandate

Everything starts with your customers, of course. It always has – and that's how it should be. But never before has the customer been under so much pressure, or so impatient. The business and personal productivity tools on their smartphones inform the mindset of digital business leaders, and they operate in a fast-moving attention-deficit economy. Wasting their time trying to sell them something they don't want or need is the worst crime you can perpetrate against these executives.

There are reasons why:

- Only 25 percent of executives want to meet a salesperson[9]
- Salespeople in the US spend $574B per year in meetings with customers that never progress[10]
- 41 percent of buyers say they do not prefer incumbent suppliers.[11]

And yes, there are reasons why just 53 percent of salespeople make quota.[12]

The role of the salesperson is not just to communicate value to their customer. It is to create value with the customer.

Consider the 'one third problem:'

- Only one third of buyers think meeting a salesperson is valuable[13]

---

[9] Forrester Research: *Executive Buyer Insight Study*.

[10] *Inside the Buyer's Mind: The Buyer / Seller Value Index Study 2016*: **https://www.altify.com/altify-buyer-seller-value-index/.**

[11] *Inside the Buyer's Mind*.

[12] *CSO Insights 2017 World Class Sales Practices Study*.

[13] *Inside the Buyer's Mind*.

- In the *Altify Business Performance Benchmark Study 2017,* one third of sellers admit to not being able to uncover the customer's problems
- In the same study one third of marketers say they do not understand their customers.

Customers need help. As the world increases in complexity, customers struggle to prioritize their growing list of business pressures. The imperative to make decisions and act quickly creates tremendous anxiety. There is extra-ordinary opportunity for the Customer First salesperson who seeks above all to solve the customer's problem, understanding that the impact on a customer of a poor buying decision is usually greater than the impact on a salesperson of a lost deal. Winning sellers who adopt this approach rise to the top in the ever-growing SaaS economy. But this time SaaS means 'Salesperson as a Service' – always on, always connected, on-demand, in service of the customer, reliable and secure. That's the path to recurring business.

Customer First is the second main theme of the book and I dedicate a large part of the book describing how to drive mutual value for seller and buyer.

Introducing *Digital Sales Transformation | In a Customer First World*

Digital Sales Transformation is not solely or primarily about 'digital sales.' It is about selling in a digitally transformed world. Ray Wang of Constellation Research defines Digital Transformation as more than just a technology shift:

> The digital disruption comes from both transforming business models and shifting how brands, enterprises, people, and machines will engage.

Digital Sales Transformation changes how you sell and transforms how you engage with your customer. Gone are the days when sellers use worn out sales methodologies to battle with their customers, 'deepen the pain,' 'burn the platform,' or 'drown them,' however rationally. (Rational Drowning is one phase in one of the methodologies!) It is now about innovative ways to deliver value to the customer with integrity and respect.

How customers perceive value from a seller is shaped significantly by the impact on their business of the product / solution they purchase. It all starts with the customer.

In *Chapter 2: Digital Sales Transformation | Part 1: Discover Impact*, I suggest that if, for example, a customer buys a CRM system from Salesforce, the impact will be significant. Buying copier paper from Staples, not so much. When you can categorize customers into levels of *Customer Impact* you can select the optimum sales engagement model and discover potential sales problems that may exist.

Knowing what's broken is one side of the coin, and is balanced in *Chapter 3: Digital Sales Transformation | Part 2: Customer Engagement Model* where I describe the technology components required at each level of Customer Impact to optimize the prescribed sales strategies and execution models. This is where our Digital Sales Transformation journey begins.

To ensure you are ready to begin the journey, in *Chapter 4: Digital Sales Transformation | Part 3: Capabilities Assessment*, I ask the question: "How do you know if you have a sales problem?" I suggest some symptoms that you might observe in your business and point to the underlying causes.

In a world responding to the Mega Trends of Digital Transformation and Customer First, companies are under pressure to act strategically, collaborate proactively and respond quickly, earning their customer's business month on month, time over time. *Chapter 5: The Ideal Customer Profile* invites you to answer three questions to make sure that you're selecting companies for whom you can best deliver value:

1. Is the company in your sweet-spot (industry, size, region, etc.)?
2. Are they likely to have problems that you can solve?
3. Will they be successful with your product / solution?

This is all about deciding what companies to call on so that you can ensure that you are playing on a field where you can deliver value and win.

The problem sometimes though is that, even when you identify the right companies, you struggle to build relationships with the right people. When I talk about building successful relationships, as I do in *Chapter 6: Relationships: The Buyer's Perspective*, I'm talking about mutual authentic engagement between buyer and sellers, founded on trust and respect, guided by shared values in pursuit of shared goals. While this is a high threshold to achieve, it is what your customers deserve, it is how the best customers want to engage, and it provides a safe-zone for constructive brainstorming, bargaining and building rapport.

This not always easy to do, so in *Chapter 7: A Structure for Building Relationships* I get down to the nitty-gritty, and provide a framework to uncover:

- Who matters?
- How do they think?
- What is your current relationship?
- What is the relationship gap?
- How do you bridge that gap?

Most deals are not lost because you don't have the best solution or the best price or the best terms and conditions. They are usually lost because you didn't understand the people or problems. I will get to the problems in a minute, but first I want to spend a little time on the secret weapon that you might not know you have.

In many sales organizations one of the most under-utilized assets is the executive management team. When deployed effectively and with precision, as described in *Chapter 8: The Executive Sponsor: Their Role in Large Accounts*, companies can achieve deeper strategic relationships and an uncommon level of value alignment with their key customers by leveraging their senior executives. This results in accelerated value creation for you and your customer.

An executive swooping in to help close a deal is not an Executive Sponsor Program – it goes much deeper than that. It's about the customer's business and it's about the long game. It comes down to knowing the customer's business. Whether you are pursuing a single strategic opportunity or building a strategy to maximize revenue from a large customer, we know that this matters.

Most customers don't care how much you know, until they know how much you care. The best way to convince customers that you care is to demonstrate you understand their business, their business issues, the cost of resolution, and the full implications of inaction. *Chapter 9: Know Your Customer First* explains how to get to know the customer's business, the cornerstone to maintaining long term business relationships and delivering value to your customer. It sets out seven steps in a repeatable method to know the customer's business and help them make progress:

1. Who is the customer (company)?
2. What goals matter to the customer and who are the key people that care?
3. Why do these goals matter to the customer?
4. What related projects or initiatives are in place?
5. What is broken that is stopping them being successful?
6. How can you help?
7. What is your gap in knowledge or solution?

Humans can be irksome creatures. When asked, they say they want to make rational decisions based on evidence and science. In practice that's never the full story. Emotion plays a critical role.

If math was the single arbiter of customer decisions then the role of the salesperson would be greatly diminished. Anyone can present the facts, and as long as those facts are correct and independently verifiable, the messenger is less important than the message. But math without magic is just math, a cold accurate guardian of rational decisions, but a poor custodian of personal connections. In *Chapter 10: Create and Communicate Value*, I show how to create true insights – honed from deep knowledge of the account, the buyer's persona, and their typical personal goals – to find the key to unlocking a connection that is both rational and emotional.

Customer engagement is a continuum with a constant focus: consistent delivery of value to the customer. *Chapter 11: Communicate Value at Scale: Account Based Marketing* introduces how you can begin to turn that value key for many customers at the same time. For any purchase, the customer goes through a number of phases, beginning with *Awareness* where they learn that you and your product exist. This is followed by *Interest* where they care about what you (and others) have. The next phase is the critical one: it's when they establish *Preference* for a given solution or supplier. The determination of what specific value you can provide to a customer better than anyone else is the fulcrum upon which successful customer engagement is balanced. Once you have targeted the right accounts using your Ideal Customer Profile, and identified the personas, your vehicle to communicate this value at scale is your Account Based Marketing (ABM) play – but only as part of a Customer First integrated Account Planning and Management solution.

The explosion of Artificial Intelligence (AI) solutions is a wonderful opportunity for practitioners of Digital Sales Transformation. I am particularly excited about the work that Salesforce is doing in this area, democratizing AI in the same way that it has revolutionized cloud computing for all businesses. The optimum solution is a combination of data, science and human judgment, the last based on knowledge and experience. For me the 'A' in AI stands for 'Augmented,' not 'Artificial.'

In *Chapter 12: The Role of AI in Enterprise Sales*, I talk about my AI journey and its pervasive role in all that we do to serve sellers. In 1988 I wrote my first AI book called *Expert Systems Introduced*. Its purpose was to demystify for the businessperson much of the enigma that was AI at that time, shrouded, as it was, in academic publications replete with inaccessible language. My goal back then was to deliver AI or expert systems for the *rest of us*. In hindsight that aspiration was perhaps a little premature. But now AI is exploding as a core part of Digital Transformation. My latest AI book *Tomorrow Today: How AI Impacts How We Work, Live, and Think*, published in late 2016, brings those concepts up to date.

Chapters 13: Sales Process, 14: Opportunity Management, 15: Account Management and *16: Sales Performance Management* bring all the concepts of the book together to set you off on your Digital Sales Transformation journey. Mapping process, methodology and technology to the Customer Impact Levels defined in *Chapter 2*, and the Customer Engagement Model in *Chapter 3*, these chapters outline the methods – a systematic repeatable series of steps – so that you can execute on the applicable strategies.

This is a time of great opportunity for sellers and customers alike. Technology has enabled an unparalleled velocity of innovation, collaboration and communication. There has never been a time like this. Individuals can do more with their minds than ever before. Innovation offers new ways to do the tasks that we struggle with today and exposes new possibilities that were heretofore impossible. How this plays out is yet to be determined, but the choices we make are important. The coin has been flipped towards the sky and, as it spins in air, we get to influence how it lands for sales professionals and their customers.

I am optimistic about the future of the sales professionals who take a Customer First attitude with them to work every day. This book is intended to be their companion on that journey, equipping them to pause to think about the customer, and to consider the important questions, lest they stumble towards accidental answers.

CHAPTER 2:
DIGITAL SALES TRANSFORMATION PART 1: DISCOVER IMPACT

Introduction

As Mike Rosenbaum said in the *Foreword*, we are living in an era of unprecedented change. Mike also acknowledges that saying this feels tired, worn, and perhaps obvious. We all know we are living in a whirlwind. We are feeling the wind in our faces every day. It feels like it has been that way forever – and we just work harder and dig deeper to get our jobs done.

But this time it feels different and this time there are facts, not just opinion, to support Mike's assertion – particularly when it comes to individual sales contributors, sales managers and sales executives who make their living in enterprise business-to-business sales.

The facts:

- The percentage of salespeople who make quota (53 percent) is at its lowest in more than seven years[14]
- Sellers are losing four out of every five deals they pursue[15]
- One million B2B sales professionals in the US will lose their jobs to self-service technology by 2020[16]
- The average sales win rate is 21.7 percent[17]
- One in five buyers say there is no need for sellers in the future[18]
- The direct cost to US sellers of meetings with customers that do not progress is $574B per year.[19]

---

[14] *CSO Insights 2017 World Class Sales Practices Study.*
[15] *Inside the Buyer's Mind.*
[16] Forrester Research: *Death of a (B2B) Salesman.*
[17] *Inside the Buyer's Mind.*
[18] *Inside the Buyer's Mind.*
[19] *Inside the Buyer's Mind.*

On the other hand, progressive companies who deploy Digital Sales Transformation outperform Nasdaq and NSYE by 11 and 14 points respectively. That's why I wrote this book.

If you are a sales leader, what do you see when you look around?

Stop. Look around.

What do you see?

Here's some of what I'm seeing around the world, right now:

- Longer times for new sales hires to ramp and become fully productive
- Extreme deal slippage and surprise wins and losses
- Declining win rate and poor ROI on sales investment
- Severe friction between seller and sales manager / sales executive
- Customers treating more suppliers as vendors, not partners
- Pressure on customer retention and higher customer expectations
- Insufficient and poor quality pipeline
- Poor return from existing accounts with increasing pressure on incumbents.

If you recognize your company in any of these observations, you're clearly not alone. (I address all these problems in *Chapter 4: Digital Sales Transformation | Part 3: Capabilities Assessment*.)

But why has it gotten so much harder than before? It's not as if the world's sellers have stopped working hard. I've not noticed a materially lower caliber of seller than I've seen in the past. It has always been hard to hire good salespeople. But now with such a low average win rate, companies need more coverage, and over-allocation of quota, just to standstill.

So, maybe Mike is right, at least in the world of sales. We *are* living in an era of unprecedented change. But what has changed? Well, the increasing pervasiveness of technology is obvious to everyone. Digital Transformation is knocking on your door, and tapping on your window. You can't ignore that.

But the seismic shift is a consequence of the pressure being felt by our customers, and the ensuing change in their behavior. Maybe we are seeing a change in how customers want to buy. Let's start there.

The Buyer's Problem

Like everyone else, B2B buyers are living in a more challenging and more complex world. Not all sellers think about it that way. The pace of change by itself brings additional complexity and risk. It drives a need for even more intricate and involved solutions that deliver increasingly impactful business solutions to resolve those more complex problems.

Figure 1: THE BUYER'S PROBLEM

As cost increases and the complexity (intellectual property) of products or services being transacted grows, the greater the potential impact on an organization. As frequency of purchase decreases, organizational impact tends to increase. As risk increases with cost and complexity or IP value – for example, in the case of business infrastructure projects or a CRM system – organizational impact goes up, along with the buyer's need to engage earlier and more intensively with sellers for guidance and input. The inverse is also true.

By extension, the opportunity for B2B sellers is to re-model their sales engagement, leveraging Digital Sales Transformation capabilities, to efficiently and effectively service the B2B buyer. Customers are already leveraging technology to optimize their buying activities. How a salesperson interacts with a customer to optimize the return from the sales effort ought to be informed by how the customer buys and the potential impact on the customer's organization.

In this chapter I introduce the Customer Impact Architecture model (**Figure 2**), a way to determine the impact on, or disruption to, a buying organization as a function of the complexity of the solution being purchased, the opportunity for organizational gain, and the potential organizational risk.

The model categorizes customer impact in four levels, easily identifiable by mapping Product Complexity and Buying Complexity.

Figure 2: THE CUSTOMER IMPACT ARCHITECTURE MODEL

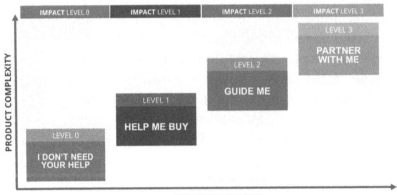

The Seller's Response

The challenges for the leadership of selling organizations are pretty clear. Firstly they need to embrace a Customer First approach and figure out how to map their sales engagement model to maximize customer impact. This is not about accepting that the customer's buying model is best for the customer, or that the customer always knows what is in their best interest. The seller's role continues to be about creating and communicating value, but doing so in a manner that is informed by the customer's buying process and how they want to buy. As customers have evolved, sales organizations have invested in more headcount to try to catch up with their more progressive customers. This is one of the main reasons why the percentage of salespeople who are making their sales targets has continuously declined for the last seven years to just 53 percent today.[20]

To catch up with their customers, sales leadership must apply a model that optimizes the engagement between buyer and seller. As we work through the Customer Impact Architecture model you will recognize that a seller's strategic value is directly proportional to the Customer Impact Level.

If the customer says: "Help me buy," the sales organization's complementary strategy should simply be 'Align with Buying Process to Accelerate Sales.' **Figure 3** shows how the seller's strategies correspond to the buyer's statements.

---

[20]   *CSO Insights 2017 World Class Sales Practices Study.*

Figure 3: THE BUYER'S STATEMENTS AND SELLER'S STRATEGIES

	Buyer's Statement	Seller's Strategy
Level 0	I don't need your help	-
Level 1	Help me buy	Align with buying process to accelerate sales.
Level 2	Guide me	Build relationships through value creation (to win).
Level 3	Partner with me	Create common vision to grow (in large accounts).

It makes sense, I think, that if the customer's perspective is "Help me buy," the seller's activities should help the customer buy. No rocket science there. This does not in any way imply that salespeople can abrogate their responsibility to create value for the customer, to understand their requirements and to prove how they can help solve the customer's problem; but by recognizing that different customers buy different things, in different ways, to solve problems of varying complexity and organizational impact, sales organizations can design optimal models of engagement to maximize value for the customer and the seller.

But, of course, the sales organization's response cannot be limited to just Strategy. In this evolved world of Customer First engagement and Digital Transformation, there are four components necessary for a complete Digital Sales Transformation:

1. Sales Strategy
2. Sales Execution
3. Sales Management
4. Digital Sales Transformation Technology.

Once the Customer Impact Levels are understood, the complete Customer Engagement Model incorporates strategy at a high level and technology underpinning everything else. Between strategy and technology, capabilities need to be honed by sellers to execute their sales processes, methodologies and skills, and by sales managers to instill a coaching culture and apply both an inspection and improvement framework.

Customers will continue to have more complex problems to solve. As they become digitally enabled they will expect their engagement with their B2B sellers to complement that capability. The disruption to sales organizations will continue unless sales teams understand and embrace AI and the other Digital Transformation technologies that can improve sales performance. They must also accept the need to continually self-educate to remain valuable to their customers and competitive in the market.

Digital Sales Transformation

The Digital Sales Transformation model below sets out three steps for sales leadership to understand how a customer wants to buy, how a seller should engage, and how to make sure the necessary capabilities are in place.

Figure 4: DIGITAL SALES TRANSFORMATION IN A CUSTOMER FIRST WORLD

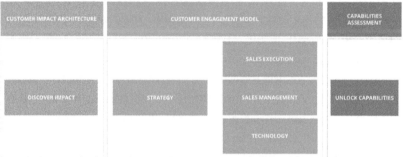

Using the Customer Impact Architecture will guide you to understand the degree of benefit, complexity and risk for the customer of a solution such as yours. It will help you to map your sales engagement to the corresponding customer impact.

After **Discover Impact**, we move forward to the next step. In the **Customer Engagement Model (CEM)** you will learn the strategy or strategies that are applicable to your sales business and appropriate for engagement with your customers. CEM suggests behavior and practices for salespeople and sales management and outlines the technology that you can apply.

By applying Discover Impact and CEM you will see a clear path for how to optimally engage with your customers, but you might also wonder about your capabilities and where there may be opportunities to improve your sales effectiveness.

In the third part, **Capabilities Assessment**, I present an easy way to see where your sales effectiveness might not be quite as effective as you would like. I map the symptoms of potential sales weaknesses to the underlying causes so that you can make the connection with the CEM.

Introducing the Customer Impact Architecture Model

To determine how best to engage with different types of customers, and to assess the right Strategy, Sales Execution behaviors, Sale Management practices, and Digital Sales Technology, consider the four levels of buyer / seller engagement – the Customer Impact Levels – as seen from the customer's perspective (the only perspective that really matters):

- **Level 0:** I don't need your help
- **Level 1:** Help me buy
- **Level 2:** Guide me
- **Level 3:** Partner with me.

The four levels of Customer Impact are:

- **Customer Impact Level 0 / I don't need your help:** For sellers currently at this level, represented primarily by sales of commodity products, the salesperson is just an order taker and the future is bleak. This is where the Internet is more convenient and more efficient. In this stratum, the seller does not matter. The buyer just wants her company to be served. Characterized by frequent purchases, low price and commodity products – think copier paper or other office consumables as examples – the Internet is the seller who wins: more efficient, always available, low selling cost, and equivalent or better service. As Andy Hoar, principal analyst at Forrester, said at the 2015 Forrester Sales Enablement Forum, *"So as technology gets better at explaining things, we don't need humans to explain anymore."* (Note: As my audience is primarily B2B Enterprise sellers who add value to their customers, I don't address Level 0 any further in this book – it's included here merely for completeness.)

- **Customer Impact Level 1 / Help me buy:** Where the product being purchased begins to adopt some complex characteristics, the buyer will usually have a buying process that, at an informal level, has more than a single buyer involved. The buyer will require detailed product knowledge from the seller and an ability to show the buyer how the product will meet her requirements and solve her business problem. Sales teams operating at this level will need to deploy a sales process, mapped to the customer's buying process and implement a framework to achieve accelerated sales velocity, through consistent visibility and management of the process.

- **Customer Impact Level 2 / Guide me:** As the complexity of the product and the buying process grows, the impact on the customer increases correspondingly. The cost of sale also rises. Sellers need rigorous qualification skills to ensure that they are applying resources to sales opportunities that they can win and that, by winning those opportunities, they can deliver significant positive impact on the customers. Proficiency in relationship development is a basic requirement but, to be most effective at this level, sellers need to have significant business acumen. They need to understand the customer's problems and aspirations and to project the impact their solution can have on the customer's business. While sellers are working to win a specific opportunity, they also care about what happens after the sale and they are developing future relationships and potential future sales pipeline.

- **Customer Impact Level 3 / Partner with me:** At Level 3, the sales organization, and supporting functions in the company like Customer Success and Marketing, collaborate to take a holistic view of the customer's company – not just the area of the business relating to a specific sales opportunity. Focus on creating, measuring and communicating value takes precedence in a 'long game' where the selling is a function of creating and delivering a common vision with the customer. Long term customer success, sustained relationships, and value creation are the tenets by which sales teams in Level 3 operate.

Discovering the Customer Impact Level

As you saw in **Figure 2**, customer impact generally maps to a combination of Product Complexity and Buying Complexity.

To determine the applicable Customer Impact Levels that will inform your customer engagements there are eight factors to consider – four from the buyer's side, and four from the seller's side.

Figure 5: CUSTOMER IMPACT LEVELS – DETERMINING FACTORS

Buyer	Seller
Buying Process	Revenue Opportunity
Buying Committee Size	Account Strategy
Buying Cycle Duration	Desired Relationship
Impact of Offering	Sales Engagement

I define these eight factors as follows:

Figure 6: CUSTOMER IMPACT LEVELS – DETERMINING FACTORS – DEFINITIONS

Buyer	Seller
Buying Process The series of steps that a consumer takes to make a purchasing decision. A standard model of purchase decision making includes recognition of needs and wants, information search, evaluation of choices, purchase, and post-purchase evaluation.	**Revenue Opportunity** The value of a single sales opportunity or the aggregate of opportunities related to a sustained sales engagement.
Buying Committee Size The number of people in a group of designated personnel informally gathered or formally established to review and evaluate suppliers and make recommendations and decisions on the most appropriate supplier, based on a set of informal or formal decision criteria.	**Account Strategy** The applicability of an Account Based Strategy to the interaction between the supplier and the customer. An account strategy – an approach that suggests that your perspective extends beyond a single opportunity – is more likely to be required when the Impact of Offering is more significant.
Buying Cycle Duration In some cases, a subset of the overall Decision Cycle and measured as the typical number of days from when a buyer initiates a project to purchase goods or services to when final contracts are signed. Buying Cycles can also include activities before a project is initiated and after contracts are signed, but excludes implementation.	**Desired Relationship** The level on the Business Relationship Pyramid (Vendor, Credible Source, Problem Solver and Trusted Advisor) required to optimize the value of the interaction between customer and seller.
Impact of Offering The measure of business improvement that the customer will experience by successfully deploying the supplier's solution.	**Sales Engagement** The extent of contact or engagement that the seller needs to maximize the Revenue Opportunity for each level.

In the next graphic you can see values of each of the eight elements for each of the Customer Impact Levels. These are guideline values based on my experience of dealing with a very large number of sales organizations all over the world – but need to be customized to your own situation. It's the relative values that matter – not the absolute values.

Figure 7: CUSTOMER IMPACT LEVELS – DETERMINING FACTORS – GUIDELINE VALUES

Indicator	Level 1	Level 2	Level 3
Buying Process	Informal	Probably Formal	Probably Formal
Buying Committee Size	1-3 members	4+ members	6+ members
Buying Cycle Duration	0-90 days	90+ days	120+ days
Impact of Offering	Low to Medium	Medium to High	Medium to High
Revenue Opportunity	$0-$50,000	$50,000+	$250,000+
Account Strategy	No (Opportunistic)	Desired	Required
Desired Relationship	Credible Source	Problem Solver	Trusted Advisor
Sales Engagement	Transient	Periodic	Continuous

An opportunity may not display all the factors for a specific level at the values shown in **Figure 7** so you may sometimes be a little unclear as to which impact level to choose. Sales is never completely black and white. Common sense should guide you as to which side of the dividing line your decision should fall. My advice is to err just a little on assuming greater impact than might at first be evident.

I recently had an insightful conversation with Mat Singer, a really nice guy, and a very experienced and successful sales effectiveness professional. I asked Mat to share his wisdom

31

and perspective for this book. Thank you, and over to you, Mat ...

A Practitioner's Perspective
Mat Singer, Level 3 / CenturyLink

Here at Level 3 Communications (soon to be CenturyLink) customers purchase many different types of services from us. A small retail store may just buy Internet access, but a regional bank is looking for a network solution that is reliable, secure, and can be managed by experts. The buying process for these customers is different and the sales process is different. We, Sales Effectiveness, have to prepare the sellers in each sales channel serving these customers with the process, tools and methodology so we help them, not burden them with administrative work. When calling on a retail store the seller's engagement is not the same as when calling on a regional bank because the buying process, decision makers, and buying timeline are different and we focus on how we help the customer meet their business objectives. We have to know how to have the right business conversation in each case. If you were to walk into a meeting with the bank CIO and start talking bandwidth and implementation time, you're out on your ear after the first meeting.

In our company we match our new or untenured reps to customers in the low 'buying complexity' and 'product complexity' part of the Customer Impact Architecture. They can get some repetition with the basics of sales before they graduate to solving for much more complex solutions and complex buying processes. The tools we provide them suit those engagements. For example, we don't push an account planning framework or tool on our reps selling more transactional, lower complexity solutions.

We then offer a different toolkit of best practices and tools for the more senior reps who are looking to drive more solution depth with existing large accounts or who are targeting large new logos. We are guiding the reps to deliver optimal value to their customer in each scenario.

We couldn't scale this approach without technology for two fundamental and game changing reasons.

First, we do our best to make it seamless for sellers and managers to do their job. When you incorporate the best practice framework right into the CRM system, it can really make it easy for a seller to qualify an opportunity the right way and make it easy for the sales manager to coach a rep on a deal. This removes inconsistency, the virus that plagues every sales organization.

The second game-changer for technology, particularly AI based technology, is that it can help a company move from antiquated means of monitoring sales performance to modern means. I like to use the book and movie *Moneyball* as my reference to the opportunity many companies have to use data to more effectively run a sales organization. *Moneyball* is a story about how the Oakland As baseball team used data and statistics to identify better players in the scouting process. Advanced analytical techniques are now used throughout professional sports teams these days. In the world of Sales, many companies still rely on a manual funnel review process, quota attainment levels, and average win rates as their core metrics.

Wow, what an opportunity to use AI to better predict outcomes of existing deals in the funnel. Imagine what kind of offensive or defensive adjustments could be made to squeeze out better performance for every single player (salesperson) on a team. Imagine what kind of improvements we could make to how we invest in tools and technology if we could better quantify the ROI. I know our sales organization at Level 3 / CenturyLink has so much opportunity to improve results as we can better define what it takes to be successful and better predict whether current actions are leading us towards the optimal results.

CHAPTER 3:

DIGITAL SALES TRANSFORMATION PART 2: CUSTOMER ENGAGEMENT MODEL

Customer Engagement Model

In the previous chapter I introduced the Customer Impact Architecture and set out a framework where you could determine how best to engage with customers of different profiles. The core premise is that based on the value that your solution would deliver – in other words, the potential impact on their business – your customer would have a preconceived idea about how they want to interact with suppliers. If that is true, and my evidence suggests it is, it follows that your sales engagement model should be informed by the customer's perspective.

You will recall also the customer's perspective regarding their desired engagement with the salesperson. As you can see in **Figure 8** below, the sales strategy lines up pretty nicely with what the customer says.

Figure 8: THE BUYER'S STATEMENTS AND THE SELLER'S STRATEGIES – 2

	Buyer's Statement	Seller's Strategy
Level 1	Help me buy	Align with buying process to accelerate sales.
Level 2	Guide me	Build relationships through value creation (to win).
Level 3	Partner with me	Create common vision to grow (in large accounts).

The purpose of the Customer Engagement Model is to go beyond strategy and to recommend an approach for each customer impact level.

I will now bring you on the journey towards Digital Sales Transformation.

Digital Sales Transformation Customer Engagement Model

There are four elements that we should consider as we work through each level of the Customer Engagement Model:

1. Sales Strategy
2. Sales Execution
3. Sales Management
4. Technology.

We have already defined the strategy for each level of customer impact in **Figure 8**. Now we need to map execution, management and technology for those levels.

Level 1 Sales Effectiveness Solution

You're engaged with a customer whose buying process is informal and there are one to three people involved on the buying side. That is because your product is not going to fundamentally change the customer's business. Your objective is to help the customer buy.

You need to uncover evidence that you are making progress so that you have some control of the process and you can anticipate and shape the customer's needs. As stated in the Sales Strategy, in order to accelerate sales (and win more) you need to align with the customer's buying process.

> **Strategy:** ALIGN WITH BUYING PROCESS TO ACCELERATE SALES
>
> Design sales process, mapped to the customer's buying process, and implement a framework for accelerated sales velocity, consistent visibility and management.

Level 1 Sales execution

Strategy without execution is hallucination. The five elements of sales execution for effective engagement when interacting at Customer Impact Level 1 are:

1. Targets mapped to Ideal Customer Profile
2. Buyer centric sales process
3. Evidence maps to customer outcomes
4. Business focused customer messaging
5. Effective sales call plans.

Targets mapped to Ideal Customer Profile: Using the Ideal Customer Profile (ICP) framework described in *Chapter 5*, you can ensure that you are playing on a field where you can win, and you spend less time working the wrong deals. This is all about deciding what companies to call. There are three core questions to consider:

1. Is the company in your sweet-spot (industry, size, region, etc.)?
2. Are they likely to have problems that you can solve?
3. Will they be successful with your product / solution?

These three questions are the foundation of the Ideal Customer Profile, described in detail in *Chapter 5: The Ideal Customer Profile*.

Buyer centric sales process: The implementation of a buyer centric sales process can be one of the most impactful initiatives for any sales organization. I have seen sales revenues increase by 33 percent solely as a consequence of such a project. The right sales process helps the seller see around corners. When designed well and implemented effectively it gives the sales organization (and all supporting functions) a common language and a repeatable process so that everyone is on the same page. Informed by knowledge of the customer's buying process, it reduces deal slippage and surprise losses by guiding sellers to do the right things at the right time.

Use the framework in *Chapter 13: Sales Process* to learn how to build and deploy an effective buyer focused sales process.

Evidence maps to customer outcomes: This is directly connected to your buyer centric sales process, but important enough to call out on its own. When you consider the sales engagement from the buyer's perspective, it is clear that the buyer has a different focus. If you measure progress by "Sent a proposal" or "Presented to the customer" you really don't know if you have advanced the sale. If, on the other hand, you calibrate progression by customer evidence like "The customer agreed that the proposal competitively or uniquely meets their requirements," or "The customer explained our competitive advantage after the presentation," then you know that you're getting closer to a deal. Build customer verifiable evidence or outcomes into your sales process. Doing this leads you to concentrate on the value you need to communicate and to take a Solution, not a Product, focus.

Business focused customer messaging: As a customer, I don't care if you have embedded leading edge battery technology in the electric car that you are selling. I care about the fact that I can drive 100 miles further with your technology. Only Apple can sell cool as a benefit (OK, maybe there are some other companies, but not many). All the rest of us have to show how the product delivers a business benefit that resolves a customer problem. Use the approaches described in *Chapter 9: Know Your Customer First*, and *Chapter 10: Create and Communicate Value* to develop messaging with business focused content that points to business value for the customer.

Effective sales call plans: If the Ideal Customer Profile framework informs whom you should call, by targeting accounts with your Ideal Customer Profile, you need to be sure that every call or customer meeting is effective. According to the research study *Inside the Buyer's Mind*, just 32 percent of first sales calls with a customer are valuable enough from the customer's perspective that they progress to a second call. In many cases the only preparation that some sellers do before meeting the customer is in the parking lot outside the customer's office. Clearly that is not working. On average sellers are wasting two thirds of their sales opportunities. Getting meetings with customers is hard, so you really need to have a strategic approach to your call or meeting preparation.

Some of the key elements of an effective call plan are:

- **Setting a strategy / agenda:** Why are you having the meeting? Why is the customer taking the time to meet with you? What do they expect to get from the meeting? Are you aligned on the meeting expectations?

- **Define objectives**: What you want to achieve on the call? What is the clear evidence that demonstrates that you are successful? What did the customer agree to do?
- **Information to convey:** What are three key messages that you want the customer to take away from the meeting? If there are multiple participants from your company at the meeting you will need to assign responsibility to deliver each message to someone specific, with a plan to ensure that the message was heard, making sure that all your key messages are covered.

Feels good, right? Feels like you should start now, doesn't it? However, there are still a few things yet to consider and we need to invoke the mighty power of the sales manager and the appropriate technology to bring it home.

Level 1 Sales management

The sales manager's role is the most critical role in the sales organization. I have never seen sales teams win if the managers did not do the job they were hired to do. The manager has to hire, develop and motivate the sales team. She must manage and own the sales forecast and pipeline for her team. She must assign and support opportunities and accounts, and she is responsible for the business development strategy for her team. It's a tough but critical role.

In the context of managing the team's engagement at this level, the five key elements managers must perfect are:

1. Manage team to the sales process
2. Collaborate on call plans
3. Use sales process stages for forecasting
4. Manage pipeline quality
5. Measure effectiveness and productivity.

Manage team to the sales process: Assuming that you now have a good sales process in place, it is the manager's job to use it as a framework for how she runs the business. The process should guide the sellers to take the right actions at the right time, and the manager, when reviewing a deal, should be asking the seller about the actions they are taking to advance through the next step in the process.

If the process is automated and integrated with the CRM, as it should be, that's where the manager should look to understand deal progress. Asking the sales team to use a process and then not managing to the process is both ineffective and demotivating. Asking the sellers to provide other updates outside of the process just means that the process will not stick. All the good work that was done to help the sellers know the customer's buying process and align their activities with that process will be wasted unless the manager manages to the process.

Collaborate on call plans: In most cases sales managers have a depth of experience that is greater than the individuals on the team. Helping a seller plan for a meeting with a customer before the meeting is much more valuable to the seller than getting a debriefing or post-mortem after the meeting. You can't impact the outcome after the meeting. This is one example of how the sales manager can bring her experience and objectivity to add value to the seller's next actions. Managers should challenge the salesperson (in a positive way) to set high goals for the meeting and then come up with a strategy on how to achieve those goals, and / or to consider the reasons why those goals might not be achieved. Each call plan can be a mini-deal review, where you understand the current state of the opportunity, define the desired state, and then develop a strategy to begin to bridge the gap, as much as possible, in the next customer meeting.

This is one of the surest ways I have seen to shorten sales cycles and increase win rate.

Use sales process stages for forecasting: With a buyer centric sales process in place, each stage of sales process should require certain customer evidence before you can progress to the next stage. With this objective measure in place, then you know with evidential certainty the likelihood of a deal being won. It then follows that, assuming the manager is managing to the process, the current stage of the deal is a reliable indicator of whether the deal should be forecasted to close – and when.

Manage pipeline quality: All the data that I have looked at tells me one thing for sure: if a deal is languishing in the pipeline for twice the normal length of a sales cycle, then it is almost certain that the deal has already been lost. Either the salesperson just has not updated the system or, with rose-tinted glasses, is holding out hope that the opportunity will raise from the dead and magically be closed. One of the roles of the manager is to guide the seller to manage inactive or stalled deals out of the system, or to consider an alternative sales strategy. Having a large pipeline stuffed full of dead or languishing deals makes everyone feel good about the future, only to be disappointed later. A pipeline that is smaller in value, but comprising valid opportunities that can viably be closed, is much more valuable than a big pipeline overflowing with deals that are either not qualified or are dormant. Managers should measure the seller's revenue (a lagging indicator) but must also assess the value of the qualified pipeline as a key indicator of the future health of the business.

Measure effectiveness and productivity: You should expect what you inspect. Only that which is measured is managed. These, and other such clichés, are clichés because they are true. There are lots of metrics that sales managers *could* measure. The problem, however, is that the sales manager is already really busy and running through reams of reports is not necessarily the most productive activity. I have highlighted below a few simple metrics that each sales manager should measure so that they know the relative strengths of the members of the team, and the overall health of the sales team's business:

- Revenue *versus* quota
- Win rate (by number and value)
- Sales cycle
- Pipeline value per stage
- Number of customer meetings and completed call plans
- Number of calls that progress
- Pipeline added per quarter
- Ramp time to productivity for new hires.

This is not an exhaustive list, but considering that we are managing sales engagements at Customer Impact Level 1, staying on top of these numbers can provide the manager with great insight into the business and performance of her team.

Level 1 Digital Sales Transformation technology

It doesn't matter what strategy, execution processes and methodologies, or management behaviors and practices you have in place, unless you can effectively make them part of how you run your business. That's the role of technology, and there are five elements you should implement to serve sales engagement for Customer Impact Level 1:

1. CRM
2. Automated sales process in CRM
3. Smart sales content
4. Sales forecasting and reporting
5. Guided sales call planning.

CRM: I don't expect that this needs a lot of explanation. Collecting and organizing actionable customer data is a full-time job, and one that isn't very forgiving of mistakes. As such, investing in a high quality tool for Customer Relationship Management (CRM) is a must for any business that wants to take revenue management and customer satisfaction to the next level. I have been an avid customer and partner of Salesforce for many years and I'm also happy to count them as a customer. I use Salesforce as my reference point when I say that the key benefits that accrue from CRM systems are:

- Improved information about your customers
- Enhanced communication across the sales team
- Collaboration with customer success and marketing
- Reporting to measure and manage the effectiveness and productivity of the sales team
- Ecosystem of software partners that provide specialist sales applications to improve sales performance.

There are many other features and capabilities that others care about – but, at the end of the day, you want to be sure that all your customer data is in one place and easily accessible at all times in the cloud and on mobile devices.

Figure 9: THE SALES PROCESS IN CRM

Automated sales process in CRM: If you have all your customer account and opportunity data in the CRM, that's where you need your sales process also. Intelligent sales process applications exist that live in the CRM, integrate fully with the CRM data, and make it easy for the seller to work their deal. There is no better way to introduce a repeatable sales process. That way you can leverage technology to make it easy to track sellers' progress through each stage of every deal. Because many of today's sales process software apps are inherently intelligent, you can quickly get insight on the deal and the technology makes sure that all sellers are speaking the same language, everyone is on the same page, and you have more control over deal slippage.

Figure 10: SMART SALES CONTENT

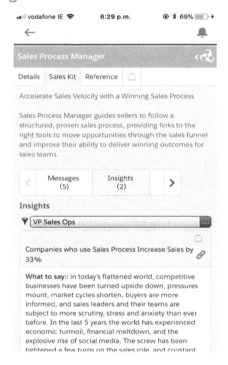

Smart sales content: When sellers can deliver the right business focused content to the customer at the right time in the sales process, it enables them to have confident business conversations. Content Management Systems have existed for many years and they have been somewhat helpful. Today, however, you can use technology that is context aware, knows where you are in a deal, can distinguish between different buyer personas, and automatically knows the typical competitors for each of your products. Then the appropriate customer messages, insights, and sales tools can all be made available consistently across the sales team, delivered intelligently as needed.

Sales forecasting and reporting: A sales forecast is an essential tool for managing a business of any size. It is typically a month-by-month revenue forecast. Sales forecasts must be based on evidence, not opinion. The only way to do that is to leverage technology that enables data-driven guidance on your forecast. If you combine the automated sales process in CRM above with the data in your CRM, you can quickly achieve an accurate outlook on the health of your sales business. Leveraging your CRM system you can also report on your customers, the sales team, pipeline, leads and all of the core elements you need to run your sales business.

Guided sales call planning: Smart call planning applications are available today that provide the underlying structure for collaboration between seller and manager to prepare for customer meetings. In some cases these applications will leverage AI to deliver insights on the people at the meeting and to provide coaching on the next recommended steps in the sale.

Figure 11: GUIDED SALES CALL PLANNING – EXAMPLE

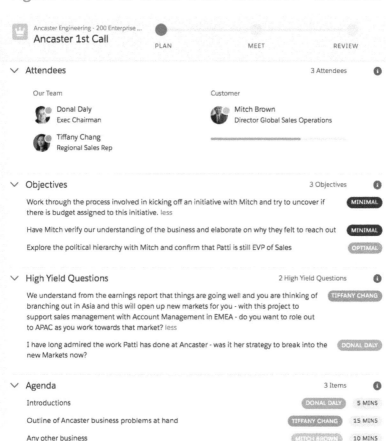

Level 1 Customer Engagement Model

Combining the solution components in *Sales Strategy*, *Sales Execution*, *Sales Management* and *Technology*, we now have a blueprint for sales success when in a sales engagement at Customer Impact Level 1.

Figure 12: CUSTOMER IMPACT LEVEL 1 – BLUEPRINT

Customer Engagement Model – Customer Impact Level 1

STRATEGY

ALIGN WITH BUYING PROCESS TO ACCELERATE SALES
Design sales process, mapped to the customer's buying process, and implement a framework for accelerated sales velocity, consistent visibility and management.

SALES EXECUTION

Targets mapped to Ideal Customer Profile
Buyer centric sales process
Evidence maps to customer outcomes
Business focused customer messaging
Effective sales calls plans

SALES MANAGEMENT

Manage team to the sales process
Collaborate on call plans
Use sales process stages for forecasting
Manage pipeline quality
Measure effectiveness and productivity

DIGITAL SALES TRANSFORMATION TECHNOLOGY

CRM
Automated sales process in CRM
Smart sales content
Sales forecasting and reporting
Guided sales call planning

Where to from here?

Thus far I have described a high level Customer Engagement Model to apply when dealing with customers at Customer Impact Level 1. These broad concepts will help you to execute on the strategy for this level. In *Chapter 13: Sales Process*, I detail a buyer centric sales process that encapsulates these concepts, and I show examples of where you might apply technology to support your efforts.

Level 2 Sales Effectiveness Solution

In a sales engagement at Customer Impact Level 2 the interaction with the customer has more depth. The customer has more to lose if they get it wrong, and we know that the impact on a customer of a bad buying decision is greater than the impact on a salesperson of a lost deal. The customer is looking for a solution to a real business problem and is looking to you to solve the problem for them. Your revenue opportunity with this customer is probably greater than $50,000 and, at this level of spend and customer impact, there will be many buying roles and people to consider. Each of the stakeholders on the buying side will have individual, different, and possibly competing, interests.

Your approach to a specific opportunity will shape future opportunities in the account, so how you sell, the relationships you develop, and the value you bring to the customer during the sales engagement set the stage for future engagements. The stakes are higher and you need to elevate your sales performance.

To be effective at Customer Impact Level 2, you need to know the customer's business and the particular problems they are trying to solve at this moment in time. As described in *Chapter 9: Know Your Customer First*, these problems may be Known, Unknown or Active and you should interact accordingly as prescribed in that chapter. With the many stakeholders you will need to develop many trusted relationships based on the value that you provide. Success will elude you if you just take a features / benefits approach to this sale. 'Seller as value-creator' is the mantle you should wear to win at Customer Impact Level 2.

Strategy: BUILD RELATIONSHIPS THROUGH VALUE CREATION TO WIN

Enable sellers to qualify opportunities, build relationships, connect solutions to customer business problems, create value and position competitively. Implement a deal management framework with increased visibility and collaboration for higher win rate and larger deals.

Level 2 Sales execution

I mentioned earlier that "strategy without execution is hallucination." Alternately attributed to Henry Ford and Thomas Edison, this quote captures neatly the actions needed in Level 1 but comes to life again here at Level 2. The main difference, however, is that at Level 2 the actions that you execute are a little more strategic.

First you need to be sure that you have all the Level 1 execution methodologies and processes in place and operationalized in software so that your sales engine is humming along nicely. Now it is time to shift up a gear.

There are seven more elements of sales execution for effective engagement when interacting at Customer Impact Level 2:

1. Structured opportunity qualification
2. Build relationships with key influencers
3. Uncover business problems
4. Business focused conversations
5. Develop competitive strategies
6. Collaborate with supporting functions
7. Execute strategies and actions to close.

Structured opportunity qualification: Deal pursuit is expensive. According to the research study *Inside the Buyer's Mind*, the annual cost of lost deal pursuit, for an enterprise

B2B seller with a $1 million quota, is $218,000. Selecting the right opportunities to work is one of the most effective ways to maximize your return on sales effort.

There are four Key Questions to consider:

1. **Is there an opportunity?** You need to assess whether the customer has a compelling reason to solve a business problem. You don't always need to have an identified budget for the project at this stage of qualification, but your customer must have access to funds if the project's ROI calculation merits the investment.

2. **Can we compete?** Can you provide unique business value to the customer with a solution that fits their needs – from the perspective of most of the key buying influencers?

3. **Can we win?** This is all about the relationships you have in the deal. You cannot win unless someone who matters in the customer organization is working on your behalf. That way you can assess the informal decision criteria and make sure you are aligned politically with the people that matter.

4. **Is it worth winning?** Is the return from the deal worth the effort? This can be determined by matching the cost of sale to the strategic value of the opportunity, the short term and long term revenue, and the likelihood of the customer being successful. Don't forget that last part – it's critical to long term repeat business.

Figure 13: STRUCTURED OPPORTUNITY QUALIFICATION

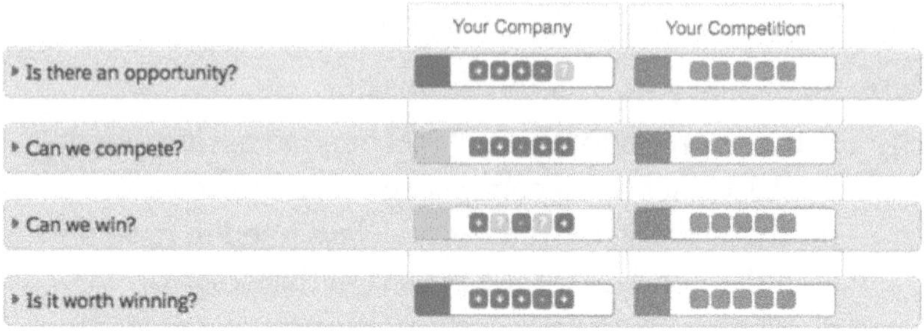

Build relationships with key influencers: In *Chapter 7: A Structure for Building Relationships* I describe how to determine the relationships that you need, and where there is a relationship gap, how to overcome that deficit. You know that you need to do that. Just speaking with the people who you can easily access and who are happy to talk to you isn't sufficient.

Uncover business problems: Customers are not focused on buying your product. They have problems they need to resolve or opportunities to grasp. Until you understand their problems you have not earned the right to sell your solution. It is essential to get behind their business goals and objectives and uncover the pressures they feel and the broken tasks or processes that they need to fix. *Chapter 9: Know Your Customer First* shows how to do that.

Business focused conversations: Business conversations beat product conversations every time. Buyers reward sellers who:

- Understand where they are starting from
- Expand their understanding of their business problem
- Provide valuable insights into the business and the market
- Connect the buyer's priorities to specific solutions.

Delivering value to the customer is not just a Sales function. It's not just a Marketing function either. *Chapter 9: Know Your Customer First* explains why an organizational approach to being Customer First is a strategic imperative for the whole go-to-market function of the company.

Develop competitive strategies: When you lose a deal, assuming it was a deal that you could win – that is, it passed *The Truth Test* as described in *Chapter 5*: if you were the customer, you would actually buy from you – then you were outsold by a competitor. You will only win if you set the ground rules of competition. In my mind 'No Decision' (which in fact is a decision, as the customer decided not to proceed) is always a competitor and your competitive strategy needs to account for that too.

Collaborate with supporting functions: One of my friends has a favorite saying: *"Never lose alone; make sure lots of others have their fingerprints on the weapon."* While that may at first seem a little cynical, in a 'cover your back(!)' kind of way, it is intended to say that you should leverage all the appropriate resources of your organization to help you to win.

A Deal Review – where sales peers and other supporting functions in your company collaborate on the opportunity, identifying vulnerabilities and making positive recommendations – is one of the best ways to strengthen your approach to a deal. And because a deal review takes place before a sales meeting with a customer, it is more useful than a post-mortem after the meeting. Separate to that, you may need your Customer Success team to demonstrate how the customer will be successful, your CTO (or Sales Engineer) to alleviate any technical concerns (if you are selling a technology solution), and you can benefit significantly from leveraging the marketing team to deliver Customer First messaging specific to this customer.

Execute strategies and actions to close: Winning a deal does not happen accidentally. Losing does.

Be strategic in your thinking about your approach to the opportunity, and relentless and urgent in the execution of the actions. Consider the most important deal you are working on right now: if it didn't move forward today, you have to assume it moved backwards. While you were busy doing something else, the customer's priorities were shifting, or your competitor was advancing up the hill. Time does not cure all ills. In sales, time is not your friend. Only the paranoid survive. Get on with it. Pick up the phone.

Level 2 Sales management

There is nothing more fulfilling than watching a sales manager collaborate with her team, coach deals, motivate and guide individual sellers to fill competency gaps to improve, and then celebrating with the team when together they make or exceed their targets. Well, maybe there are some things that are better, but I think you get my point: when the sales manager acts as more than a manager, but as a coach and guide, great things happen.

At Customer Impact Level 2, there are five behaviors and practices that the sales manager must master to be successful. These are, of course, in addition to those required at Level 1:

1. Coach to deal management framework
2. Collaborate in deal reviews
3. Use opportunity health / progress for forecast
4. Institute forecast and pipeline cadence
5. Collaborate with supporting functions.

Coach to deal management framework: Coaching is much more effective than management. Coaching is proactive, management less so. Coaching impacts 'what is going to happen.' Management reflects on the past.

If sales managers have a deal management framework in place, they can productively apply their expertise and experience to help the salesperson to win. Apart from coaching and developing the individual, a coaching framework should have two strands:

- Coaching the sales methodology or sales process
- Coaching to win.

The first makes sure that the seller is following the best practices and behaviors identified to be the winning formula for sales success – for example, the four key questions for qualification described in **Figure 12** above. Coaching the sales methodology is highly scalable with technology.

The second part of the coaching framework focuses on the specifics of a particular opportunity. The sales manager is helping the salesperson to identify risks and vulnerabilities and overcome challenges that are hindering their ability to move the deal forward.

To encourage you to coach:

- According to CEB, coaching can improve sales productivity by 88 percent
- Per Gallup, when sales coaching is effectively deployed, customer loyalty increases by 56 percent
- According to the Sales Management Association, most sales managers spend less than 5 percent of their time on sales coaching. Given all the time they spend on all their other activity, perhaps this is not a surprise. But it is still a real worry.

When you have a deal management framework, automated in smart software, the application can do a lot of the hard work to guide the sellers to follow the methodology. This frees up the manager to add value where it matters.

Collaborate in deal reviews: In *Collaborate with supporting functions* above, I described the Deal Review process. The sales manager's role is critical here. Remember though, it is a Deal Review. It is not a forecast call.

Use opportunity health / progress for forecast: In most sales organizations 'forecast accuracy' runs at about 50 percent. Just half of the deals forecasted to close at the start of a quarter make it over the finish line. Mathematically, you would be just as accurate if you flipped a coin.

If a sales opportunity is properly qualified, it is more likely to close than if it is not. When the customer can articulate your unique business value, you are making good progress. If you have evidence that someone (who can make things happen) in the customer's organization is working on your behalf, your chance of winning the deal is vastly improved. Use these (and other) tangible indicators of progress to decide if you should forecast the opportunity.

Institute forecast and pipeline cadence: When I observe great sales managers at work (Michelle, Craig, Tamika, you know I am talking about you), I see a regular rhythm. Every week the forecast call happens. Every month the pipeline call happens.

Early in the quarter they take out their deal management framework, open the aperture wide, and guide their teams to consider what might be possible for the quarter. Because weekly forecast calls often happen on a Monday, great sales managers will typically have looked through all the key deals over the weekend so that they have thoughts about how they can help.

Good forecast calls are not time wasted reporting the news:

"Hey John, can you bring me up to date on what happened with the JKHiggs deal last week?"

Not a lot of value transacts in those kinds of conversations.

The weekly cadence trains the sellers to come to the call knowing that they should be ready to ask for assistance as needed. Of course that also means that they (the sellers) know that they are accountable to do their work each week to progress the opportunity. Cadence drives behavior and good habits.

I recommend a weekly rhythm for forecast calls, and a monthly planning session on pipeline. The forecast and pipeline calls should be separate and distinct so that sellers know that just because they put an opportunity into the pipeline, it does not mean that the deal is part of the forecast.

Collaborate with supporting functions: I covered this in the *Sales Execution* section above, and all the same sentiments apply. One additional point to make is that the sales manager should be available to the salesperson to help nudge her peers in the other functions if needed. She should also be the guardian of the requests being made by her sales team so that the organization's resources are not being wasted.

Level 2 Digital Sales Transformation technology

I have often been asked to proffer an opinion as to the best sales methodology to improve the sales performance of a sales team. My answer is always: *"The one that is used consistently as part of how the business operates."* Technology's role is critical. Customers, aided by technology, are moving faster. Your competitors are competing more aggressively, propelled forward by smarter, always on, connected, data rich and AI powered systems. If you're not playing the game using all the appropriate smart Digital Sales Transformation capabilities, then you will inevitably fail. It is only a question of when.

Building on the foundation described at Level 1, there are five additional technical capabilities to leverage at Customer Impact Level 2:

1. AI based opportunity management system
2. Business conversation maps
3. Exception reporting and notifications
4. Forecast and pipeline management
5. Sales Analytics.

AI based opportunity management system: I have a fundamental belief that if any system has the data, adequate knowledge and an awareness of the user's context, it should be able to provide advice on what to do next. When you ask Google Maps for directions to a specific location (the data), it knows where you are (the context) and has available all the maps of the world (adequate knowledge), so it can tell you what to do next. The same applies to today's AI based opportunity management systems. The data is in the CRM, the context is where you are in the deal, and the knowledge is the embedded sales methodology. Combined, these elements can guide the seller on what to next.

The following paragraphs are real-life examples of advice for a sales opportunity from such a system.[21]

---

[21] This example comes from Altify's MAX Augmented Intelligence engine in the Altify Opportunity Manager application. The author was the founder of Altify, and is now Chairman of the company.

CONFIRM THERE IS AN OPPORTUNITY: This opportunity is at the 'Evidence' stage, but the assessment status does not clearly identify that there is an opportunity. Although there is a Customer Project and the Customer Business status indicates that you can demonstrate how this initiative addresses the customer's Goals and Pressures, Access to Funds is 'No' and Compelling Event is 'Unknown.' At this stage, it is important to identify where the funds are going to come from for this project and try to uncover the specific date by which the customer must act to avoid the consequence(s) of not acting to implement this project within that timeframe. Without this, you run the risk of spending time on an opportunity that will not progress and will end up rolling forward on your forecast quarter after quarter.

PROJECT IS NOT A PRIORITY: Assessment indicates you have no Access to Funds in this later stage but you are sure there is a project. This could indicate that the Customer Project is not a high priority project or that the project hasn't been approved and / or human resources haven't been assigned yet. If you have moved this opportunity forward a few times in your forecast already, you should consider qualifying out or moving this to an 'early develop' stage so that you can continue with discovery.

NO COMPELLING EVENT: You do not have a Compelling Event in your Assessment and you are well beyond the early stages. An opportunity that only possesses a compelling reason to buy and not a true compelling event is always at risk for a 'No decision' loss. It is essential at this stage to find out: "What is the date by which they need the pressure relieved?" and / or "What happens if they do nothing?" If the answer is not compelling, this might not be an opportunity you want to commit in your forecast at this moment. However, as you have rolled this opportunity forward more than 3 times already, you should consider if you should qualify it out. Remember, it is important to

61

assess the customers' motivation for change and their timing for doing so. Opportunities that do not possess a Compelling Event typically are not urgent or a priority for the customer. That might explain why the customer is not moving forward with you at this stage.

This is an example of AI (the Augmented, not Artificial, Intelligence variety) at work – guiding sellers, without any intervention from their manager, or sales coach, to achieve better performance.

Business conversation maps: The optimal flow of a conversation between the seller and the buyer might go:

> The seller teaches the buyer something valuable that they want the customer to know. Through that part of the conversation alone, the seller brings value to the customer and demonstrates his own pertinent business expertise. This enables the seller to reset the buyer's frame of reference, make an emotional connection, and finally point to the supplier's solution.

This is what experienced sellers do when they are working in a domain they understand and selling a solution with which they are familiar. But what happens when a new product is introduced, or when the company changes industry focus, or when new sellers join the team?

Technology exists today to accelerate the salesperson's experience in the business of the customer and the application of a (new) solution to solve that customer's business problem. Consider a solution like a Customer Insight Map, an intelligent visual representation of a 'typical' customer's business challenges to enable all the team, for all of your products, to have an engaging business conversation with the customer.

Figure 14: THE CUSTOMER INSIGHT MAP

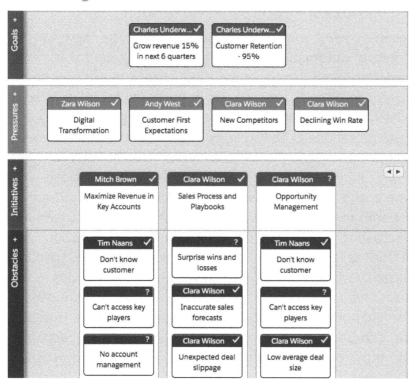

Buyers have been conditioned to expect insights, and by applying technology, Sales *and Marketing* can deliver. By putting the customer's business goals, pressures, and obstacles in the hands of the seller their path to a valuable conversation is shortened considerably. I describe this approach in detail in *Chapter 10: Create and Communicate Value*.

Exception reporting and notifications: Neither sales managers, nor sellers, have the time, nor in many cases the aptitude, to read, analyze, and interpret large amount of data. If you understand the key symptoms of success and failure, as described in *Chapter 2*, it seems obvious that you should report first on those items. That approach will enable you to respond to early triggers of success or failure.

Forecast and pipeline management: The key to the effective automation of sales forecasting is to use the evidence based data from the CRM system, based on a smart buyer centric sales process and opportunity health, to predict outcomes, and allow the seller or manager to query the system's rationale. That results in the quality of the forecasts improving over time as the system learns that a sales opportunity of Type X usually takes Y days to close, and where the system is wrong, the forecasting algorithm is updated to get closer to 100 percent accuracy. Because sales forecasting is ultimately dependent on human behavior, both of the seller and the buyer, the pursuit of 100 percent accuracy will be asymptotic. You will get closer and closer, but unless you are dealing simultaneously with thousands of homogenous opportunities you will never get there. However, you can achieve what I call material or directional accuracy and that's definitely better than good enough for most sales managers.

Pipeline management is a much easier problem to solve than forecast accuracy. Quality of deals, funnel velocity, pipeline mix (small, medium, and large deals) are the key factors to consider.

Figure 15: PIPELINE MANAGEMENT

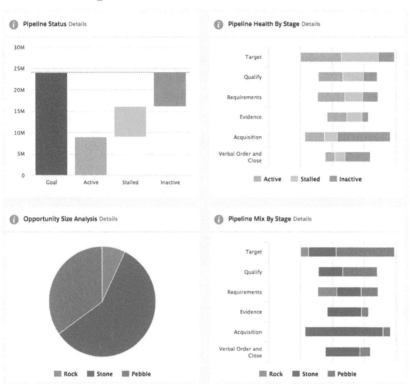

Where possible you should deploy a pipeline management system that is AI enabled so that you can be alerted to risks in the pipeline in time to take mitigating actions to remediate. The same applies to your sales forecasting system.

Sales Analytics: Sales Analytics is a little bit of a catch-all term. When trying to determine what you want to analyze, the answer starts with a question: *What are the Key Performance Indicators in my business?*

Where it makes sense to deploy a specialist application for forecasting and pipeline management (because the important questions are known and directionally common across all B2B sales organizations and therefore predictions and prescriptions can be automated), there are many

65

datasets that you will want to analyze that are particular to your business.

The first question to ask is: *What data matters?* Of all the data gathered by Sales, Marketing and Customer Success about your customers, there will be critical indicators of success and failure. Sometimes you can only determine those indicators by looking at the data. That's where a general purpose tool like Saleforce's Einstein Analytics can help.

Figure 16: SALES ANALYTICS

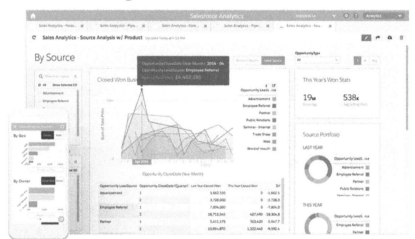

Level 2 Customer Engagement Model

Pulling together the *Strategy*, *Execution*, *Management* and *Technology*, we can define the blueprint for sales success at Customer Impact Level 2.

FIGURE 17: CUSTOMER IMPACT LEVEL 2 – BLUEPRINT

Customer Engagement Model – Customer Impact Level 2

STRATEGY

BUILD RELATIONSHIPS THROUGH VALUE CREATION TO WIN
Enable sellers to qualify opportunities, build relationships,
connect solutions to customer business problems, create
value and position competitively. Implement a deal
management framework with increased visibility and
collaboration for higher win rate and larger deals.

SALES EXECUTION

Level 1+
Structured opportunity qualification
Build relationships with key influencers
Uncover business problems
Business focused conversations
Develop competitive strategies
Collaborate with supporting functions
Execute strategies and actions to close

SALES MANAGEMENT

Level 1+
Coach to deal management framework
Collaborate in deal reviews
Use opportunity health / progress for forecast
Institute forecast and pipeline cadence
Collaborate with supporting functions

DIGITAL SALES TRANSFORMATION TECHNOLOGY

Level 1+
AI based opportunity management system
Business conversation maps
Exception reporting and notifications
Forecast and pipeline management
Sales Analytics

Where to from here?

In this section we have covered the Customer Engagement Model to apply when dealing with customers at Customer Impact Level 2. This is where the customer said: "Guide Me." The broad concepts discussed here will help you to execute on the strategy for this level. In *Chapter 14: Opportunity Management*, I explore the methods to be used in an opportunity management approach and you will see where you might apply technology to support your efforts.

Level 3 Customer Engagement Model

In the previous chapter when discussing Customer Impact Level 3, I pointed out that the *'Bad things that happen'* at this level are measured in BIG dollars. This is because you're engaged with a customer in a long game play. The aperture of the lens is open wider as you try to focus on a long term vision with your customer. Typically, at Customer Impact Level 3, the goal is to amplify the business relationship between your company and the customer's organization.

You must be careful not to forget why the customer bought from you in the first place and you must deliver on the promises that you made. From the customer's perspective, and as I said before, this is the *only* perspective that really matters. Customers expect significant impact on their business from their engagement with your company.

Multiple stakeholders are involved in a structured buying process that extends over many months or years as you collaboratively develop a common vision for their success. A strategic approach is essential and your execution must be flawless if you are to achieve the revenue growth to which you aspire.

> **Strategy:** CREATE COMMON VISION TO GROW IN LARGE ACCOUNTS
> Craft an integrated approach to elevate and expand relationships, understand the customer's business, create, measure and communicate customer success. Implement an integrated framework for the account team to build pipeline and close revenue in existing accounts.

Level 3 Sales execution

Execution at Customer Impact Level 3 is not solely the responsibility of one individual. There are too many strands of work, too many different personas in the buyer's organization, and too much thinking to be done to put it all on the shoulders of one person. As we walk through the sales execution for effective engagement at Customer Impact Level 3, you should consider the different roles that need to be performed by the account team.

In addition to the items described earlier in Level 1 and Level 2 the seven execution elements to focus on at this level are:

1. Structured account qualification
2. Create, measure and communicate value
3. Elevate and expand relationships
4. Know the customer's business
5. Create common vision for success
6. Identify whitespace
7. Execute account strategies and actions to grow.

Structured account qualification: This one is pretty straightforward. You should only be working with accounts where you and they will be successful. This is of course similar to *Targets mapped to Ideal Customer Profile* in Level 1. You should only be working with accounts that fit your Ideal Customer Profile. There are three key questions to consider to 'qualify' the account:

1. Is the company in your sweet-spot (industry, size, region, etc.)?
2. Are they likely to have problems that you can solve?
3. Will they be successful with your product / solution?

Chapter 5: The Ideal Customer Profile dives into considerable detail on each of these questions.

Create, measure and communicate value: The role of today's winning salesperson is not just to communicate value. Before that happens, they need to create value as part of the sales engagement or deliver measured value as part of a prior project. Remember at Customer Impact Level 3, your strategy is to create a common vision of success with the customer. That means you must understand their business, roll up your sleeves, and bring the expertise and experience of your company to guide the customer on the path that is best for them.

Chapter 10: Create and Communicate Value provides a detailed framework for how to approach this.

Elevate and expand relationships: To grow revenue in an account and become their strategic partner you must work in tandem with the key executives. It is unlikely that you will have access to all the key executives 'out of the gate,' and that's not necessarily a bad thing. Before you spend time with senior business leaders you will need to do your own research, gain insight from your supporters in the company, and consider the business issues that are top-of-mind for similar executives in other companies. As you develop your strategy for the account you must determine your desired relationship and deliberate on how to achieve that goal. Consider the methods described in *Chapter 7: A Structure for Building Relationships* and, if applicable, look to bring the power of your company's executive team to the account. See *Chapter 8: The Executive Sponsor: Their Role in Large Accounts*.

Know the customer's business: Similar to Customer Impact Level 2, and as stated many times already, your success will depend on how well you know the customer's business. Because, at Level 3 you are aspiring to operate as a Trusted Advisor, the threshold for success is higher. A framework to understanding the customer's business is set out in *Chapter 9: Know Your Customer First*.

Create common vision for success: Working strategically with an account is a long game. I recognize that with constant quarterly pressure, to close opportunities, to hit short term targets, that fact can dissuade you from spending time to truly align your activities with the customer's long term future success. But the reality is that if you do not take the time to work with the customer to create a common vision, you are operating as a Level 2 seller with a customer who wants to engage at Level 3.

Identify whitespace: In an account your ultimate goal is to discover how all your solutions can add value across the entirety of the customer's organization. If Division A has purchased and successfully deployed your Product X, then it seems not too much of a stretch that Division B might also get value from Product X. Division A might see potential in your Product Y, assuming that they address related business areas. To figure out your whitespace in the account for cross-sell and up-sell opportunities you will first need to understand the people and the problems, through relationships and knowledge of the customer's business. (See *Chapter 15* for a method to use to grow your pipeline through the identification of whitespace.)

Execute account strategies and actions to grow: It is most important when you have an account focus that all your activities are considered. Before you embark on any activity, consider which of the following objectives performing that activity will advance:

1. Documented customer success
2. Elevated or expanded relationships
3. Growth in pipeline
4. Growth in revenue.

It is important that you consider these objectives in the order listed here.

If this is an existing customer you better have delivered value in the past if you want to grow. If you have indeed been successful then you want to be sure that everyone knows that you have delivered value – hence the importance of documented customer success. That's one of the best ways to elevate and expand relationships. Elevated relationships is a path to increased pipeline and provides you the opportunity to close some of the pipeline to grow revenue.

Level 3 Sales management

At this level sales management can have a somewhat different shape, which will vary across organizations. In some companies large accounts will be treated as a separate and distinct revenue stream from the rest of the sales organization and the management structure will vary. If a company has instituted a global account program, it is frequently the case that matrix reporting lines come into play. The account manager, who has overall responsibility for the revenue from the account, may not be on the same team as the salesperson who is supporting the account strategy in a remote geography. When the customer account is very large it is important that it is viewed as a market, in and of itself, and the corresponding practices of prioritization and focus become relevant.

As I describe the key elements for a manager to perfect at Customer Impact Level 3, I have looked through many lenses to make sure that they are appropriate to most, if not all, scenarios.

The five key behaviors and practices for managers when supporting a customer engagement at Impact Level 3 are:

1. Collaborate on account plan and review
2. Measure customer success results
3. Engage executive support in formal program
4. Support relationship strategies
5. Measure pipeline and revenue growth in account.

Collaborate on account plan and review: In the same way that sales managers collaborate with sellers when developing their plan to win an opportunity, the manager's role in an account is similar. The core difference is that the scope of activity and revenue potential is usually much greater. There are multiple opportunities, many sets of business problems, and potentially different organizational structures in different divisions.

Sometimes I think that 'account planning' is badly named. (This is from the guy who wrote the book *Account Planning in Salesforce.*) The reason I worry about the label is that 'planning' may imply that it is something you can finish. The job of the manager, once they have reviewed the initial plan, is to make sure that in fact the account plan is a living, breathing, organism that changes over time as the circumstances evolve.[22] The best way to do that is with regular – I would recommend quarterly – account (plan) reviews.

Measure customer success results: This may be the responsibility of the account manager, the customer success team, marketing, or a sales operations function, but someone has to do it. I have seen too many instances where customers have achieved great results from deployment of a solution, but because no one measured the baseline data, it is hard to quantify the customer's return on the investment they made. Consequently the supplier cannot leverage that success to its fullest. This is an easy fix. It just requires a disciplined approach to the account and should be part of the account plan.

---

[22] Tim Berry, founder of Palo Alto Software, who 'wrote the book' on business planning (which suffers from the same task focused perception), hit the nail on the head in his comment: "'Business plan' is a verb."

Engage executive support in a formal program: In *Chapter 8: The Executive Sponsor: Their Role in Large Accounts*, I explain the tremendous benefit that can accrue from leveraging appropriate executives in an account. It is the role of the manager to determine whether the account is a good candidate for an executive sponsor and to lobby for that additional investment.

Support relationship strategies: There is a great opportunity in an account to have layered relationships. That means that the seller on the ground has one set of relationships and can be supported in the account by the manager and / or the executives, who can be used to create a different type of relationship, or a set of relationships with different people. This provides a mechanism to triangulate information, ask different questions of different people, and maintain greater overall coverage in the account.

Measure pipeline and revenue growth in the account: Large accounts should be treated like a market segment. For each market segment you will have pipeline goals and revenue goals. The same is true of a large account. The management role is to ensure that pipeline and revenue goals are set at the outset of the year (or whenever the plan is being developed) and that the account team is doing the work to build pipeline and close business. Of these two metrics, the one where I see most weakness is pipeline growth. Sellers tend to get focused on the deals they can close and don't spend enough time developing pipeline in the account. Remember we are at Customer Impact Level 3: it is a long game and pipeline is a critical measure.

Level 3 Digital Sales Transformation technology

At this stage you are probably clear on my opinion about the need for technology. At Level 1, technology is necessary to accelerate the sales velocity of the sales team. Technology provides the hub for managers and sellers to work together in a coach-first, manage-later paradigm at Level 2. But when it comes to the complexity that accompanies sales engagements at Customer Impact Level 3, I just don't know how you can survive for very long if you don't deploy the requisite technology. Because there are many stakeholders in both the supplier and customer organizations, a technology supported collaborative framework is simply a 'must have.' You are dealing, not with just one sales opportunity, but with many opportunities, each at a different stage in its lifecycle. You need a framework to manage that. Measurement of progress is essential to know whether you are on track to deliver on the vision for your customer. It is just too hard to engage at this level without some intelligent software system in place.

That's the role of technology, and there are five elements you should implement to serve sales engagement for Customer Impact Level 3:

1. Collaborative account management system
2. Account scorecard
3. Executive dashboards
4. Account reporting and dashboards
5. Market penetration insight.

Collaborative account management system: There are too many moving pieces in a large account not to apply technology. The whole account team needs access to the same information all of the time. Otherwise it is really not possible to have a common view of whitespace, relationships, customer's business and business problems, strategic objectives and assigned activities. Software is good at this stuff! It is good at sharing data, communicating and measuring, dynamically and visually representing complex constructs and doing so in a collaborative framework. If you are serious about engaging with companies who fall into the Customer Impact Level 3 category, then you have to leverage collaborative technology to support your account team.

Figure 18: COLLABORATIVE ACCOUNT MANAGEMENT

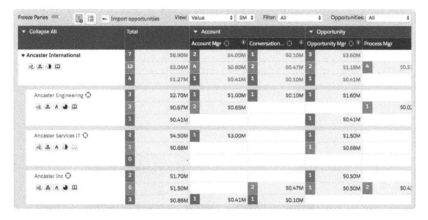

Figure 19: THE ACCOUNT SCORECARD

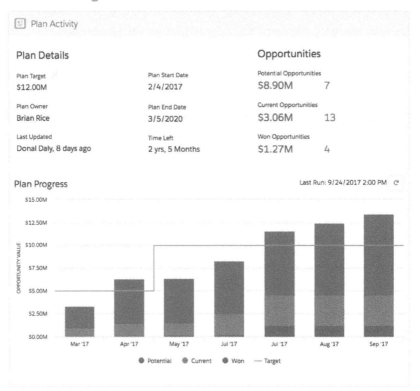

Account scorecard: An account scorecard is a simple mechanism to gauge the health of an account and to monitor the progress of your account planning and management activity. It should measure and present goals and objectives for the account and progress over time against those. It might also use simple measures like Net Promoter Score, customer satisfaction levels, solution deployment etc. It is not hard to do in software, but very valuable if you do it.

Figure 20: THE EXECUTIVE DASHBOARD

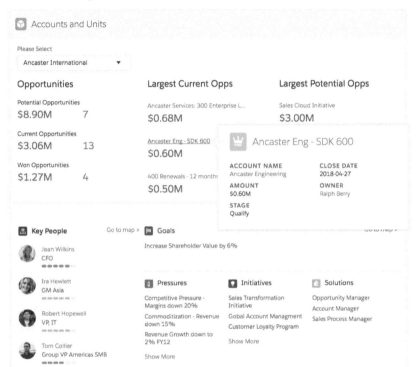

Executive dashboards: The next level of sophistication in measurement is the simplest of requirements. Your executives want to know what is going on in an account. They don't want all the detail, but they need to know the key people, the business issues they are facing and your history and current status in the account.

Account reporting and dashboards: This is really about reporting on the activity of the account team in the account and in the account plan. Accepting the maxim of *'you can't manage what you don't measure'* you need to report on the activity you want to see. If you are using a collaborative account management framework as a native application in Salesforce, it is very easy to deliver dashboards and reports that provide insight into that data.

79

Figure 21: ACCOUNT REPORTING

Market penetration insight: The last component that I recommend as part of your Digital Sales Transformation Technology Toolkit is a capability to stack all of your account plans one on top of the other to get a three dimensional view of your entire market.

For example, if you are the product manager for one product set that is included in many account plans, this view will provide you with a perspective on how your product is contributing to the large accounts initiative in your organization, and the future pipeline that you might need to be prepared to service.

Similarly, you may own a certain vertical market like technology. Then by combining all the account plans from the sales team for technology companies, you can get both a rear-view mirror and windshield view into your market.

Figure 22: MARKET PENETRATION

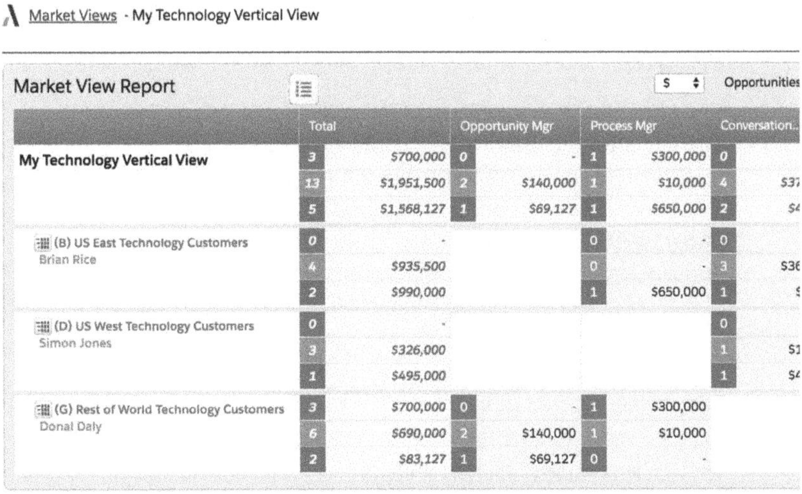

∧ Market Views - My Technology Vertical View

Market View Report				$ ⇕	Opportunities
	Total		Opportunity Mgr	Process Mgr	Conversation...
My Technology Vertical View	3	$700,000	0 -	1 $300,000	0
	13	$1,951,500	2 $140,000	1 $10,000	4 $37
	5	$1,568,127	1 $69,127	1 $650,000	2 $4
(B) US East Technology Customers Brian Rice	0	-		0 -	0
	4	$935,500		0 -	3 $36
	2	$990,000		1 $650,000	1 $
(D) US West Technology Customers Simon Jones	0	-			0
	3	$326,000			1 $1
	1	$495,000			1 $4
(G) Rest of World Technology Customers Donal Daly	3	$700,000	0 -	1 $300,000	
	6	$690,000	2 $140,000	1 $10,000	
	2	$83,127	1 $69,127	0 -	

Level 3 Customer Engagement Model

As before we can combine the components of *Sales Strategy*, *Sales Execution*, *Sales Management* and *Technology*, to come up with our blueprint for sales success when in a sales engagement at Customer Impact Level 3.

Figure 23: CUSTOMER IMPACT LEVEL 3 – BLUEPRINT

Customer Engagement Model – Customer Impact Level 3

STRATEGY

CREATE COMMON VISION TO GROW IN LARGE ACCOUNTS
Craft an integrated approach to elevate and expand
relationships, understand the customer's business, create,
measure and communicate customer success. Implement an
integrated framework for the account team to build pipeline
and close revenue in existing accounts.

SALES EXECUTION

Level 1, Level 2+
Structured account qualification
Create, measure and communicate value
Elevate and expand relationships
Know the customer's business
Create common vision for success
Identify whitespace
Execute account strategies and actions to grow

SALES MANAGEMENT

Level 1, Level 2+
Collaborate on account plan and review
Measure customer success results
Engage executive support in formal program
Support relationship strategies
Measure pipeline and revenue growth in account

DIGITAL SALES TRANSFORMATION TECHNOLOGY

Level 1, Level 2+
Collaborative account management system
Account Scorecard
Executive dashboards
Account reporting and dashboards
Market penetration insight

Where to from here?

We have now been through the Customer Engagement Model for each of the Customer Impact levels. Level 3 can be the most challenging. The customer said: "Partner with me," and through this last section you will now hopefully have a grasp on the broad concepts involved. In *Chapter 15: Account Management*, I dig deeper into the methods of an account management approach. You will also see where you can apply technology to support your efforts.

Conclusion

At the start of this chapter I said that the purpose of the Customer Engagement Model was to go beyond strategy and walk though execution, management and technology considerations for each customer impact level. Now that we have done that you know what you have to do, and you can visit each of the chapters I referenced for more guidance and help.

Before you begin that journey you may want to make sure that the requisite capabilities are in place so that you're firing on all cylinders.

In *Chapter 4: Digital Sales Transformation | Part 3: Capabilities Assessment* I help you diagnose any sales challenges you might have and understand the root causes underlying those problems. That's a good way to know where you might need to focus efforts to improve performance.

CHAPTER 4:
DIGITAL SALES TRANSFORMATION PART 3: CAPABILITIES ASSESSMENT

The Digital Sales Transformation Challenge

The first step to improve sales performance is to understand where you might be failing. If that sounds like a negative approach it is intended not to depress you but to highlight the areas in which you might have improvement opportunities. Before you can fix any problem, you need to be aware that the problem exists.

In truth there are ever only two reasons why you lose a deal. Either:

- You shouldn't have been there in the first place, or
- You were outsold.

There are no other reasons.

When you learn late in the sale cycle or after the deal is lost that the prospective customer has a problem you can't solve, or does not really have a project, or an incumbent supplier wrote the Request for Proposal (RFP), you know that you should never have applied your valuable sales resources to pursue the opportunity in the first place. This is where rigorous opportunity qualification matters.

If a real opportunity actually existed for which you have a viable solution to solve the customer's problem, but you did not win, then you were outsold. It is as simple as that. Some competitor did a better job of connecting their solution to the customer's business problem to win the deal, in which case the competitor outsold you.

Alternatively, when you lose to 'No Decision' it is because the customer perceives that they should not proceed, or should embark on an alternative project, solving a different business problem. Then the customer's organization outsold you. Your proposition was too weak to cause the customer to act or the alternative value proposition from inside the customer's business was stronger than yours.

I have the benefit of using technology to gather data about why deals are won or lost. Since 2005 I have gathered insight on literally millions of sales cycles: watching deals slip, seeing half of forecasted opportunities lost to a competitor, or lost to 'No Decision' where the customer didn't see a compelling reason to act. I have also participated in thousands of deal reviews and account strategy plans, and, supported by intelligent automation I have created or analyzed more than 3,000 sales processes. Deep analysis of all this data shines a bright light on the key reasons why sellers lose deals.

When I map deal slippage, lost opportunities, or poor account penetration to sales behaviors, there is a strong correlation of failure points to the complexity of the sales engagement. Understandably, customers conduct more diligence when the impact on the customer's organization of a purchase decision is greater. This sets a higher threshold of performance for the seller to be successful, and inevitably more areas where deal or account pursuit may go off track.

How Do You Know You Have a Sales Problem?

Mapping the common symptoms of ineffective sales execution or management to the different levels of customer impact makes it easier to see the competencies that need to be improved. Discovering the root cause is less obvious, so it is better to start with the symptoms. This provides a clear path to increased sales effectiveness, mapped to the complexity of the sales engagement (and the customer impact).

It is much easier to immediately observe the evidence, or symptoms, of a sales problem than it is to understand the underlying cause. For example, if a seller consistently loses to competition, it is patently obvious. The data shows you lost to a competitor and you don't need to interpret the data. On the other hand, it is not immediately obvious that the reason why there are frequent competitive losses may be because of a struggle to position the (competitive / unique) value of the solution in front of a customer. You can't know that unless you join the seller on the sales call, and that's just not a scalable solution in today's fast-moving world.

Let's look at the *observable* evidence of sales challenges for sales engagements that map to Level 1 Customer Impact, and then examine the most common reasons why these undesirable things (like deal loss, heavy discounting, etc.) happen.

Level 1 Sales Challenges

Whether or not your sales engagement maps to this level, you should still consider the problems that exist in Level 1, as Level 2 and Level 3 build on Level 1, so by definition you need to have all of the Level 1 issues nailed before you move on to Level 2 and Level 3.

So let's first restate the indicators of Customer Impact Level 1. You will remember that the buying process is probably fairly informal with a small number of buyers in the buying committee.

Figure 24: CUSTOMER IMPACT LEVEL 1 - INDICATORS

Indicator	Level 1
Buying Process	Informal
Buying Committee Size	1-3 members
Buying Cycle Duration	0-90 days
Impact of Offering	Low to Medium
Revenue Opportunity	$0-$50,000
Account Strategy	No (Opportunistic)
Desired Relationship	Credible Source
Sales Engagement	Transient

If the customer purchases your product it is not going to fundamentally change their business; the impact is fairly low and correspondingly the revenue opportunity relating to this transient sales engagement is less than $50,000.

You want the customer to believe that you understand what they need and that you know your product, so the desired relationship level is Credible Source.

You are opportunity focused, so you are not necessarily thinking about this account in a strategic way.

89

When you examine the list of *'Bad things that happen,'* you should bring the model to life for yourself. Think whether you see these 'bad things' in your sales organization and tick the appropriate box / boxes in **Figure 25** below.

Figure 25: CUSTOMER IMPACT LEVEL 1 – EVIDENCE OF SALES PROBLEMS

Bad things that happen		We have this problem
1	Small % of reps making quota	☐
2	Surprise wins / losses	☐
3	Inaccurate forecast / Deal slippage	☐
4	High rep turnover	☐
5	Long ramp time for new hires	☐
6	Low ROI on sales investment	☐
7	Loss to competition	☐
8	Price pressure	☐
9	Low integrity in pipeline	☐
10	Low CRM usage	☐
11	No verifiable evidence of progress	☐

There is unfortunately no end to the list of bad things that can happen in a sales environment. The list above is not exhaustive, and so far we are only at Customer Impact Level 1. There are many more bad things yet to come in the other levels – it's always good to know what to look for.

If you've not (at least mentally) gone through the list and checked off the items in the *"We have this problem"* column in **Figure 25**, take the time to do it now. It will make the next part more meaningful.

Ready?

Yes?

OK, let's move on.

In **Figure 26** I have mapped the evidence points above to the likely primary root causes – I call them Obstacles. Of course in many cases, each obstacle could be applied to most of the *'Bad things that happen'* list. For example, if a small percentage of your reps are making quota (#1 above), then you could argue that every obstacle contributes to that, and to an extent that is true. But I am trying to guide you to focus on the Obstacles that contribute most directly to the things you want to fix. If we don't allocate the *primary* causes we lose focus on what improvements we should prioritize.

You can see at glance that some of the Obstacles cause many bad things to happen. For example, if you have poor knowledge of the customer's buying process it is really hard to know whether you are focused on the right things. You can't possibly know when the deal will close – so your sales forecasts will likely be a bit of a guessing game. And, you probably can't really tell whether this is a real opportunity, so the value recorded in your pipeline management system is probably overstated.

The mere fact that there are more entries in the relevant *Bad Things* column for a particular obstacle doesn't necessarily mean you need to prioritize that obstacle. You need to examine the evidence in **Figure 25** to see where you have evidence of problems.

Figure 26: CUSTOMER IMPACT LEVEL 1 – OBSTACLES

OBSTACLES \ EVIDENCE	Small % of reps making quota	Surprise wins/losses	Inaccurate forecast / Deal slippage	High rep turnover	Long ramp time for new hires	Low ROI on sales investment	Loss to competition	Price pressure	Low integrity in pipeline	Low CRM usage	No verifiable evidence of progress
Poor knowledge of customer's buying process	■	■	■						■	■	■
Sales activities not aligned with buying activities	■		■		■						
No repeatable sales process	■			■	■				■		■
No common sales language				■	■	■					
Working the wrong deals	■	■	■				■	■	■		
Inability to present value			■					■	■		
Product not Solution focused		■						■	■		
No customer business focused content								■	■		
Ineffective prep for sales calls			■			■					■
Poor sales productivity	■			■		■					
Sales process disconnected from CRM			■			■				■	■
No productivity metrics	■		■			■	■			■	

If all your sales problems are covered in the Level 1 list, you can quickly move to other parts of the book. But because life (or the world of a salesperson) is not linear, nor fits neatly into a box, I would recommend first taking a look at the other symptoms of sales problems in Level 2 and Level 3. Perhaps some of the bad things described at those levels will give you food for thought too!

You will recall that the strategy to apply at Level 1 is:

> **ALIGN WITH BUYING PROCESS TO ACCELERATE SALES**
> Design a sales process, mapped to the customer's buying process, and implement a framework for accelerated sales velocity, consistent visibility and management.

You may now want to revisit *Chapter 3: Digital Sales Transformation | Part 2: Customer Engagement Model* to review the execution, management and technology components for this level.

Level 2 Sales Challenges

At Level 2, the impact on the customer of deploying a solution is increased over the previous level. The buying process is probably formal and the number of people in the buying committee has grown.

Figure 27: CUSTOMER IMPACT LEVEL 2 – INDICATORS

Indicator	Level 2
Buying Process	Probably Formal
Buying Committee Size	4+ members
Buying Cycle Duration	90+ days
Impact of Offering	Medium to High
Revenue Opportunity	$50,000+
Account Strategy	Desired
Desired Relationship	Problem Solver
Sales Engagement	Periodic

The revenue opportunity has grown correspondingly and is now probably greater than $50,000. The customer has problems to solve so the desired relationship level is Problem Solver.

As you are working an opportunity, you recognize that everything you do in this deal, the way you behave, the relationships you develop and the customer value that you deliver, all set the foundation for further opportunities with this customer, so as you periodically engage with the customer you have a strategic outlook as it relates to the overall account.

In this case, the *'Bad things that happen'* take on a richer texture and feel more 'strategic.' As you review the list in the following table, apply it to your company and ask yourself whether your organization has any of these problems in addition to the Level 1 problems you identified earlier.

Figure 28: CUSTOMER IMPACT LEVEL 2 – EVIDENCE OF SALES PROBLEMS

Bad things that happen		We have this problem
	Level 1 +	
1	Poor or declining win rate	☐
2	Low new customer acquisition	☐
3	Low average deal size	☐
4	Extended sales cycle	☐
5	Losses to 'No Decision'	☐
6	Seller's cite price as reason for loss	☐
7	Managers don't understand deal status	☐
8	Managers managing not coaching	☐
9	Customer treats you as a vendor	☐
10	Sellers don't believe in Marketing's value	☐

Once more I have mapped the evidence points above to the likely primary Obstacles below. Again, I have tried to keep the mapping tight so that you focus on the Obstacles that contribute most directly to your pain. Remember that some Obstacles from Level 1 may remain and you may need to blend the solution.

Figure 29: CUSTOMER IMPACT LEVEL 2 – OBSTACLES

OBSTACLES / EVIDENCE	Poor or declining win rate	Low new customer acquisition	Low average deal size	Extended sales cycle	Losses to No Decision	Seller's cite price as reason for loss	Managers don't know deal status	Managers managing not coaching	Customer treats you as a vendor	Sales don't believe marketing value
Inability to identify and access key influencers	■	■		■	■				■	
Struggle to uncover business problems	■	■	■	■	■	■			■	■
No competitive strategy	■	■				■				
No sales coaching culture							■	■	■	
Can't connect solutions to customer problems		■	■		■	■			■	
Can't create value in sales engagement			■		■	■			■	■
No collaboration with supporting functions				■						■
Can't create compelling reason to buy	■	■		■	■		■			■
No framework for deal management	■			■				■	■	
No sales management discipline	■			■	■			■	■	
Product, not business, focused onboarding			■		■	■				■

As before, you should examine the evidence, this time in **Figure 28**, to see where you have evidence of problems and prioritize the Obstacles that are causing you most difficulty.

You will recall that the strategy to apply at Level 2 is:

BUILD RELATIONSHIPS THROUGH VALUE CREATION TO WIN

Enable sellers to qualify opportunities, build relationships, connect solutions to customer business problems, and create value and position competitively. Implement a deal management framework with increased visibility and collaboration for higher win rate and larger deals.

You may now want to revisit *Chapter 3: Digital Sales Transformation | Part 2: Customer Engagement Model* to review the execution, management and technology components for this level.

You may have noticed that Level 1 and Level 2 address issues that pertain almost exclusively to opportunity pursuit. There is little coverage of account related sales strategies or activities.

However, you might ask yourself whether it is OK to have invested all the effort to open the door in an account, develop relationships, become an approved vendor, just to walk away from all that investment and move on to the next new account. If you answer that in the affirmative, then you don't need to consider the issues in Level 3. If on the other hand you truly have an account strategy and you have not sold all of your products to all of the divisions in the account, then it is worth considering the effort to solve the sales issues you may have in Level 3 and the potential return from doing so.

Level 3 Sales Challenges

At Level 3, the impact on the customer is high. The buying process is almost certainly formal and the number of people in the buying committee has grown again.

Figure 30: CUSTOMER IMPACT LEVEL 3 – INDICATORS

Indicator	Level 3
Buying Process	Probably Formal
Buying Committee Size	6+ members
Buying Cycle Duration	120+ days
Impact of Offering	Medium to High
Revenue Opportunity	$250,000+
Account Strategy	Required
Desired Relationship	Trusted Advisor
Sales Engagement	Continuous

The revenue opportunity has grown significantly and should exceed $250,000. The customer is looking for a partner to develop a vision with them so the desired relationship level is Trusted Advisor, where your engagement is almost continuous. This requires material investment of time and resource from your company and you definitely need a strategic approach with this customer.

The *'Bad things that happen'* at this level are measured in BIG dollars. Customers leave you, your profitability suffers, and you can't benefit from the work you have done – unless you execute strategically, continuously and flawlessly.

As you review the list in **Figure 31**, apply it to your company and ask yourself whether your organization has any of these problems in addition to the Level 1 and Level 2 problems you identified earlier.

Figure 31: CUSTOMER IMPACT LEVEL 3 – EVIDENCE OF SALES PROBLEMS

Bad things that happen		We have this problem
	Level 1, Level 2 +	
1	Customer defection / churn	☐
2	Poor customer satisfaction	☐
3	Few customer references	☐
4	No executive relationships	☐
5	Customer thinks you are hard to work with	☐
6	Increasing # of competitive deals in existing accounts	☐
7	Limited up-sell or cross-sell	☐
8	Poor return from existing customers	☐
9	Insufficient pipeline	☐
10	Declining profit	☐

If you checked more than a few boxes in the *"We have this problem?"* column in **Figure 31**, then there is a lot of money at stake. Items 1, 2, 8, 9, and 10 are bad things that you cannot sustain as a business. To relieve the pressure of these and the other items I have again mapped the evidence to the Obstacles to help you zone in on the problem areas to address.

99

Figure 32: CUSTOMER IMPACT LEVEL 3 – OBSTACLES

EVIDENCE

OBSTACLES

Obstacles	Customer defection / churn	Poor customer satisfaction	Few customer references	No executive relationships	Customer thinks you're hard to work with	Increasing # competitive deals in existing a/c	Limited up-sell or cross-sell	Poor return from existing customers	Insufficient pipeline	Declining profit
Poorly defined Ideal Customer Profile	■	■	■		■				■	■
No whitespace analysis						■	■	■	■	■
Cultural misalignment	■		■	■	■					
No strategic approach to accounts	■	■	■	■	■		■	■	■	
No common vision of customer success		■	■	■	■					
No framework to manage account						■	■	■	■	■
No account prioritization			■	■				■	■	■
Deal focus (v strategic account view)	■	■		■			■		■	
No Executive Sponsor Program			■	■		■				
Ineffective new product sales enablement						■	■	■	■	

You don't need to fix all the Obstacles at the same time. Nonetheless, these problems, if they exist in your company, are costing a lot of money. So use the evidence points in **Figure 31** mapped to the Obstacles to assess what Obstacles are causing most disruption in your business.

Disentangling the factors behind Level 3 sales challenges and moving towards a healthier position can be encapsulated in the following strategy:

CREATE A COMMON VISION TO GROW IN LARGE ACCOUNTS
Craft an integrated approach to elevate and expand relationships, understand the customer's business, create, measure and communicate customer success. Implement an integrated framework for the account team to build pipeline and close revenue in existing accounts.

You may now want to revisit *Chapter 3: Digital Sales Transformation | Part 2: Customer Engagement Model* to review the execution, management and technology components for this level.

Most of the hard work is done. You now have a better understanding of what is working in your sales organization and where you can improve. That's the toughest thing to do. If you don't know what is broken you can't fix it. It only gets better from here.

In the next chapter (*Chapter 5: The Ideal Customer Profile*) I will describe a framework to help you identify the customers you will want to select as your target.

CHAPTER 5:
THE IDEAL
CUSTOMER PROFILE

Introduction

In a world responding to the Mega Trends of Digital Transformation and Customer First, companies are under pressure to act strategically, collaborate proactively and respond quickly, earning their customer's business month on month, time over time. Selecting companies for whom you can best deliver value makes that a lot easier.

At the end of this chapter I suggest a framework that you might want to use to identify companies who you should select. In the same way that you qualify a sales opportunity you need to assess a company to clearly understand whether you can achieve the goal of delivering customer value while also uncovering a significant revenue opportunity. There are core elements that you should consider:

- **Firmographics:** Is the company in our sweetspot?
- **Customer Business Problem:** Are they likely to have problems that we can solve?
- **Positive Impact Potential:** Are they likely to be successful with our product?

These three elements point to your Ideal Customer Profile, the creation of which all starts with understanding the value that you can deliver to your customer.

I like to start with the **Customer Value Question**:

> What business problems does your customer have that you solve better than anyone else?

In order to answer that question, you first need to understand the profile of the customer that your business, its products, services, delivery and support capabilities have been designed to best serve. Because we also know this:

The impact on the customer of a bad buying decision is typically greater than the impact on a salesperson of a lost deal.

Defining your Ideal Customer Profile guides you to describe the customer that you can guide to make a good buying decision, when for that customer you can truthfully answer:

Yes, if I were that customer, in that account in that industry, with those business problems, then I would definitely want to buy what I have. It's the best thing for them to do.

That's the honest conversation that you want to be able to have with yourself about every customer, or account or department in an organization that you want to target. That's the *Truth Test*.

No one really wants to sell something to someone if they think it is not needed. It's harder to do that than sell to a real need that you can fulfill, and frankly it's also the wrong thing to do. To know whether every account you target will allow you to pass the *Trust Test*, you need to have a deep appreciation for the type of customer who will really benefit from your product or service. You need to be clear on your Ideal Customer Profile to ensure that you are selling to a customer who you can guide to make a good buying decision. With that conviction in your back pocket, you're going to have the courage to make bold statements, be strong in your presentation of value – knowing that: *"Yes, if I were that customer, I would definitely want to buy what I have."*

Conviction is a wonderfully powerful asset; it puts steel in your spine and the confidence that you know that you are in fact acting in the customer's best interests to help them make a good buying decision.

There are two things a seller (or sales organization) can control:

- Who they call on
- What they say when they get there.

In many cases, the irrational fear of potential missed opportunities (FOMO – the fear of missing out) drives otherwise rational sales and marketing professionals to adopt a scattergun approach to target customer selection.

Effective selling is about quality not quantity. High quality customer engagement happens when you engage with fewer buyers, selected by profiling your target buyer, and assessing your offering from the customer's perspective. If you are getting positive responses from only 10 percent of the targets you contact, you are wasting 90 percent of your time and have less resources available to add value to the customers that you can help. Spend the time on the right customers, by selecting them well, and you will need to contact fewer customers to get better results for both you and the customer.

Consider why sales transactions occur. A purchase is made when the buyer considers that the total cost expended is less than the total value received. The two easily identifiable aspects of this equation are 'total cost' and 'value received.'

The total cost is a combination of the product price and the cost of the implementation of the product to meet the needs of the buyer.

Xerox and other copier vendors express their product cost, not as the capital expenditure of the equipment, but as the per-page cost for each copy. Buyers of software applications include the software license fee cost plus internal resource usage, to determine the total cost of ownership (TCO) of the software solution. Air travelers, when looking at budget airlines, factor in flexibility and the potential extra travel time and costs if the airline does not fly into a major airport. Total cost is one side of the equation.

However, deals are rarely won or lost exclusively on cost. Until value and pain exist in the mind of the buyer, any price is too high. Value is not just the list of product features and benefits. For every overt need stated by a buyer, there is pain and consequential impact if that need is not met, or the pain is not cured.

Customers value vendors in a multitude of ways. You have features and capabilities customers don't care about or put on their purchase decision criteria. Just because Microsoft Excel has the Kurt function to enable you to establish the kurtosis (the sharpness of the peak of a frequency distribution curve) doesn't mean that most users care about it. (In fact that is probably true for about 90 percent of the 461 functions that Excel 2013 supports.) People still buy Excel for several other reasons.

Some things your product does, or how it operates, users will find irritating, but not terminally so. I like to use WordPress for my personal blog at **DonalDaly.com**, though some days the performance is not what I would like it to be – but I still use it and pay for it because it allows me to build and manage my website very easily.

There are basic features or capabilities in the product that you provide that are expected as table stakes. If you are selling a car, the buyer expects it to have four wheels, reasonable fuel economy, and seatbelts. Online hosting suppliers are required to provide a secure, reliable hosting infrastructure that doesn't fail. These are the basic capabilities – your price of entry – that are assumed by the prospective buyer. You don't get any credit for these fundamental features.

Then there are the few specific needs that the customer cares about deeply. If you can satisfy those requirements with your complete solution, the customer sees real value and cares less about the competitor's feature-laden 'über-product.' If you understand and can focus on the value that you can uniquely and competitively deliver – from the customer's perspective – then the profile of customer to whom you deliver that value will self-suggest. As you redesign your efforts to make it as easy as possible for a customer to buy, you must consider the specific profile of that customer – your Ideal Customer Profile. Otherwise, you will fail to meet his exacting needs.

Choosing who not to do business with is as important and sometimes easier than choosing those with whom you should engage. Where prospective customers operate in markets that require all products or services used to be available in the local language and your product is English language only – move on to the next account. Don't be swayed by the future possible foreign-language capabilities that you might deliver in the next few years. There are probably sufficient customers elsewhere who can operate in English only. If customers are married to traditional practices and your offering promises advantage through discontinuous innovation – look elsewhere. If your product is leading edge, your customer must fit the profile of an early adopter; so you should prioritize companies whose outlook maps to the early adopter profile.

Value must be expressed and value expression implies that you understand the position you want to occupy in the mind of the buyer. Positioning is not about you, your product or your company, but about the place in the customer's mind that you want to inhabit. If, from the broad expanse of the world's companies, you have selected your customer targets well – customers chosen to meet the inherent value of your product, and pruned by profile to meet the competitive advantage you bring – then your positioning should self-suggest. It will encompass an expression of value that sets you apart as the preferred supplier or customer partner. And this is where well-directed, strategic marketing travels side-by-side with effective selling. The determination of what specific value you can provide to a customer better than anyone else is the one silver bullet that is crucial to the sales role. Successful companies are not concerned about marketing activity to win marketing awards; they are focused on providing a compelling expression of value that helps them win sales with customers who fit their Ideal Customer Profile.

Coupled with your unique differentiated value, clearly understood and articulated, this consistent approach can be the catalyst for unparalleled revenue acceleration in your chosen market. You won't always get the deal – but you can rest assured that you will be in the right place, at the right time, with the right offering, more of the time.

Selecting your target customer with restraint and accuracy will shorten your sales cycle. Your time is spent where it counts. Disciplined customer selection will increase the ROI for sales effort, reduce the marketing and support expenditure associated with the sale and, as a result, deliver greater profits. A single professional salesperson will be more effective addressing a market or territory armed with a well-aimed rifle, than an army of marketing folks wielding shotguns.

How can you apply your solution to a customer's problem, unless you have focused on the needs of that specific customer? It's not possible.

Is it more likely that you will succeed if you identify the ideal candidate, before you start your selling exercise? Without question!

Therefore you need to understand the profile of the customer to whom you can uniquely and competitively deliver the most positive impact; concentrating your efforts on those customers whose needs mirror the advantages and benefits you offer. This is your 'sweetspot' or your Ideal Customer Profile.

Creating Your Ideal Customer Profile

People sometimes forget that they can actually make choices about the customers they want to pursue. Creating an Ideal Customer Profile sets out the framework for everything else that you do: how you market, what messages you want to deliver, who you call on, and what you say. In fact it's important to remember that, if you don't choose the customers, then they will choose you and that might be less than ideal, as the type of customers that choose to engage with you might not be the ones to whom you can deliver unique business value. This will ultimately result in wasted effort as your win rate will be suboptimal. Rather than suffering from FOMO (fear of missing out) on all those companies you are not pursuing, defining your Ideal Customer Profile isn't limiting at all, it's empowering! You get to control your destiny.

Consider why he would buy your product, and mull over why he might not. Analysis begins with understanding the ideal profile of a prospective customer. If every sales or marketing activity began with one question, what should that question be? It's not *"What's our return on investment, or ROI?"* It should never be *"What can we sell to this market segment?"* Before anything else is considered, you must determine what profile customer can benefit best from what you've got. What's your 'sweetspot'? Where does your offering mesh so smoothly with the customer's business requirement that he would be foolish not to consider purchasing your product, in preference to anything else?

The Ideal Customer That You Have Today

Take the time to stroll through your customer's mind, gain a picture of their company, industry and business challenges, and you will uncover what a good customer looks like. This is the most obvious place to start determining your Ideal Customer Profile.

Though there will be similarities across your customer base, not all of your customers are the same. It is probably fair to say that the revenue that you receive will differ from one customer to the next. Of course, certain customers will be more successful with the adoption of your product than others: in other words, they get more value – but I will come back to that later in the *Positive Impact Potential* section of this chapter.

You need to determine which of your current customers deliver most value to your business. By value I mean both financial metrics like revenue, profit, low support overhead, cost to acquire, and payment terms, and market value metrics like reputation and advocacy. For example, if you are selling a product that helps SaaS companies manage their recurring revenue accounting policies Salesforce might be an ideal customer. Not only would Salesforce be a large opportunity in terms of revenue, there is probably no better lighthouse reference account. While you might get equal revenue from another company, Salesforce's influence in the market as a thought leader and innovator reflects well on you if they have chosen your product.

The 80 / 20 Rule: Many companies find that 80 percent of their revenue comes from the top 20 percent of their customers, and that the cost-to-serve for each customer rarely increases in direct proportion to the revenue you receive. Your investment to acquire and support a $40,000 account in terms of cost-of-sale and cost-to-serve is possibly similar to the required effort for an account that is worth $500,000. It's almost certainly not a linear relationship between effort and revenue.

Figure 33: PARETO IN PRACTICE

Your ideal customer, the one that you want to use as a model for your Ideal Customer Profile, probably sits in that top 20 percent of customers that deliver 80 percent of your revenue; more return, less effort. Therefore you first need to establish which of your customers fall into that top 20 percent and then forensically identify the characteristics that describe these companies.

I was involved in a project with a SaaS software company to establish their Ideal Customer Profile. We first conducted some analysis based on the Annual Recurring Revenue (ARR) received from each customer. Because this was a SaaS business, ARR correlated to number of users in the account, which in turn usually correlated to the size of the company. As you can see in **Figure 34**, this company's revenue profile mapped to the 80 / 20 rule.

Figure 34: COHORT ANALYSIS: REVENUE BY CUSTOMER SIZE

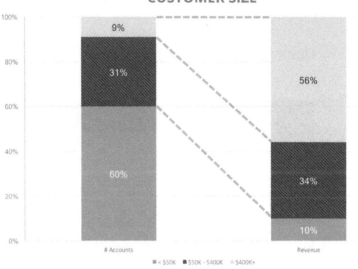

In fact in this case, 90 percent of the company's revenue came from 40 percent of the company's customers, but more interestingly 56 percent of the company's revenue came from just 9 percent of the customers. Clearly a deeper focus on the larger customers was needed. Further analysis, comparing customers who paid on average less than $50,000 per year with customers who paid $50,000 or more per year, demonstrated a wide divergence in future value.

Not only did the larger customers start from a larger base ($103,000 on average) but over the period of their first six quarters as a customer their average spend grew 125 percent (to $232,000) – compared with a growth of only 15 percent for all of the 'under $50,000' customers.

Figure 35: COHORT ANALYSIS: GROWTH IN ANNUAL RECURRING REVENUE

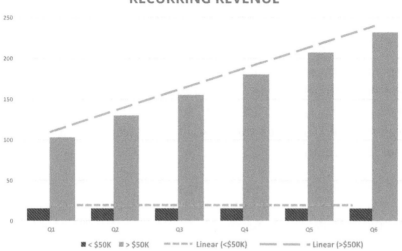

This analysis guided the company to focus exclusively on companies that fitted the profile of their larger customers – the Ideal Customer Profile.

Of course, you can't just eyeball an account, and say: "This account will grow to $200,000 ARR." Or at least you can't do it consistently without a common understanding across your organization. The first step is to determine, through desk research, and interviews with the customers, the attributes that describe this profile.

If you don't have a broad base of customers from which to choose you will need to develop a hypothesis of your Ideal Customer Profile and interview prospective customers that you think fit that description.

The attributes of your Ideal Customer Profile can be separated into the three categories noted earlier and reprised here:

- **Firmographics:** Who should you call?
- **Customer Business Problem:** What problem do they have?
- **Positive Impact Potential:** Will they be successful?

Separately these three ICP Categories can be used to provide reference points for the Marketing Communications, Product Management, and Customer Success functions in your organization. Together they provide a powerful definition of your Ideal Customer.

ICP Category 1: Firmographics

> **DEFINITION:** Firmographics (also known as emporagraphics or firm demographics) are sets of characteristics to segment prospect organizations; a method of identifying customers and developing customer profiles based on qualities that apply to businesses, not individuals.

It is important to understand that there is usually a difference between Total Available Market and Total Addressable Market. Your Data Analytics application may have appeal to potential customers all over the world, but if you're based in North Carolina and your go-to-market team only covers the United States, the market in South Korea or Australia that is available to local purveyors of solutions similar to yours is not open to you today. You can't serve that market – so you can't consider it to be addressable. If your Data Analytics application is not HIPAA (Health Insurance Portability and Accountability Act) compliant it is unlikely that you will be able to address a market segment where your software touches sensitive patient data. ERP vendors will typically sell to companies that have reasonably complex enterprise resource planning requirements. That means that the majority of the 28 million small businesses in the US – small bakeries, flower shops, and other 'mom and pop' businesses with simple business operations – are not part of an ERP software supplier's addressable market. In reality, the aggregate value of your opportunity from all of the companies who fit your Ideal Customer Profile is your Total Addressable Market.

The following firmographic factors describe your addressable market and set boundaries for your Ideal Customer Profile:

- Industry
- Size
- Geography
- Job Titles
- Business Maturity.

Industry: Some companies will have a product or service that has broad attraction, appealing to all industries and sectors. Suppliers of office stationery, IT services or hospitality services can usually find a need for their offering somewhere in most industries. Others market a niche product designed only for a very particular industry or sub-segment within an industry. Software suppliers who provide accounting capability for legal firms will typically have very little market opportunity in manufacturing or retail industries.

The list of industries you *optimally* serve is possibly the easiest filter to apply to arrive at your firmographic profile. It is certainly the first. Choose the industries, or industry sectors, in which you will specialize, by considering their propensity to buy.

EXAMPLE: My ideal customer is typically found in industries like professional services, high-end manufacturing, technology and telecommunications or where intellectual property management in contractual arrangements with customers is important.

Size: Is your ideal customer a large corporation with thousands of employees, billions in revenue, and multiple locations around the world? Usually selling to these companies means a long sales cycle, needing lots of resources, with arduous vendor approval, procurement and legal processes. On the other hand, perhaps the company that fits your ideal customer profile is a small business where you're dealing directly with the business owner. If you consider Exxon or Microsoft good examples of your ideal customer, then it is unlikely that Bob's Grocers or Jill's Flowers will make the list.

If you're selling a HR software product that has a $50,000 implementation fee to get started and a $1,000 per user license fee, you've pretty much excluded yourself from the small company with five users. The customer would need to pay $55,000, an average cost of $11,000 per user. In a larger organization with 500 users, the total price works out at $550,000, an average of $1,100 per user.

A video-conferencing solution that links multiple offices together for better company communication only makes sense for companies that have multiple office locations. HR management software is not really needed if you only have five employees.

Your cost to acquire and service a customer should inform the size of your ideal customer. If it costs $25,000 to acquire and implement a customer then each sale must provide a profit margin of more than that. Cost of customer acquisition is often a factor that determines the minimum size of a sale, which usually correlates to size of the company to which you are selling.

So yes, size matters. Total company revenue, number of office locations, size of customer service team, number of legal staff, energy consumption, number of business travelers, and annual advertising spend are all indicators of size.

> **EXAMPLE:** My ideal customer has more than 10 Intellectual Property specialists on staff or spends more than $500,000 each year in legal fees on Intellectual Property related issues.

Geography: This one should be self-explanatory. The factors that determine which continents, countries or regions that you sell to are more than just proximity and ability to serve. You also need to consider legislation, currency, language and culture. Business is conducted very differently in Tokyo, Tel Aviv and Toronto. Selling to and serving a customer in Paris, Texas is very different than selling to and serving a customer in Paris, France.

> **EXAMPLE:** My ideal customer is headquartered, or has a registered corporate office, in Quebec.

Job Titles: One of the easier, perhaps obvious, ways to identify whether a company fits your Ideal Customer Profile is to establish whether certain job titles exist in the account. For example, if you are selling a Data Analytics solution to solve a problem usually encountered by Sales Operations professionals, you can check the number of people in the company with Sales Operations in their title. Selling a corporate legal solution to a company that does not have in-house counsel will probably be difficult.

EXAMPLE: My ideal customer understands the importance of Sales Operations and has five or more FTEs in the Sales Operations function.

Business Maturity: To further help you identify the Ideal Customer Profile you can consider the four phases of the business life cycle:

- Start-up
- Growth
- Maturity
- Decline.

If *Company A* is in the *Start-up* phase, its business goals and pressures are different to the challenges faced by *Company B* that is in *Growth* mode. It follows that your products and services might be more applicable to one company and less valuable to the other.

I have started five different businesses. The wonderful thing about the very early days of a business is that it is crystal clear about what needs to happen: the product needs to be built and someone needs to buy it before you run out of money. It's fun and frenetic.

When a company moves into the *Growth* phase, things change. It's no longer just about getting customers. Growing the company requires a focus on building the business to scale. In addition to finding new customers, continually recruiting and hiring, the company needs to be concerned with keeping and growing existing customers, optimizing production, refining go-to-market processes, finding new channels to market etc. If you are selling a HR software system, a *Growth* company will definitely be closer to your Ideal Customer Profile than a *Start-up* company.

When the business comes out of *Growth* mode and enters the *Maturity* phase, the business drivers change again. Managing the cost side of the business starts to take on more importance and companies in the *Maturity* phase will more likely be in the Ideal Customer Profile for companies who are selling solutions focused on cost savings and efficiencies, or related to repositioning for a new phase of growth, or supporting acquisitions or divestitures.

The last phase is *Decline*. This sets in when the company loses the ability to change or adapt. Think Kodak or Nokia. They quit investing in new products or missed innovation trends. Instead they are just trying to maintain their position. Some, like Nokia, will look to reposition or restart their innovation cycle. In this phase cutbacks, downsizing, and efficiency become the focus.

> **EXAMPLE:** My ideal customer is in Growth or Maturity phases where the business operations are sufficiently sophisticated to support investment in infrastructural projects.

ICP Category 2: Customer business problem

Subject to meeting the firmographic test it follows naturally that, if a company has a business problem you can address, the company will likely fit your Ideal Customer Profile. Assuming you are clear on the top three or five business problems that you can solve, then you need to identify companies that are likely to have those problems.

At a high level, all companies are focused on growth. That may be measured by revenue growth, profit growth or market share. If everything was working well in all businesses then there would be no business problems to solve and the world of B2B commerce would grind to a halt. The reality though is that there are usually factors that create pressure on a company, causing them to act or react in order to meet their growth goals. These pressures are either *external* macro-factors like market trends, demographic shifts, economic volatility, evolution in technology, new competitive threats, or *internal* factors such as shareholder pressure, poor revenue performance, sub-optimal production facilities or employee attrition. When these pressures exist, there are business problems. The key therefore is to target companies that are likely to have the business problems that you can solve.

The majority of companies that I speak with all stress that one of the biggest challenges for their sales organizations is to shift from selling products to selling customer focused solutions. This is a direct consequence of increasing demands for customers to take an approach that is more about them than ever before. Our expectations as business professionals have been heavily influenced by our experience as consumers. While not every consumer is a businessperson, every businessperson is a consumer. The experience we have in consumer-land shapes our expectations in business-land. Our customers expect us to partner with them to solve business problems with a focus first on their needs.

The good news is that the number of desired outcomes your customer has is endless. Life in large corporations today is an endless struggle to improve, increase, transform or reduce. Your task is to determine which one, or two, of these outcomes you can facilitate, and what value you can deliver.

Here are some possibilities:

- Increased revenues
- Increased sales per customer
- Reduced cost of goods sold
- Improved customer retention
- Faster time to market
- Improved operational efficiency
- Increased differentiation
- Decreased employee turnover

- Improved asset utilization
- Decreased costs
- Faster response time
- Increased market share
- Additional revenue streams
- Improved time-to-profitability
- Reduced cycle time
- Faster sales cycles
- Decreased operational expenses
- Reduced cost of sales
- Faster collections
- Minimized risk
- Increased inventory turns
- Reduced direct labor costs
- Increased market share
- Increased billable hours

The question you want to answer is who wants what you've got. Your first task is to clearly understand, why someone should care about your offering. You need to ask yourself what benefit your product delivers. Does it make an existing process more effective, thereby increasing revenue for the customer? Will it deliver cost-efficiencies? It must do one or the other. Based on your current market knowledge, will it be an urgent purchase for the customer in the short term? The last thing you want is to spend your time promoting something that the customer finds interesting, but doesn't feel the urgency to act on now.

It is useful to think about the value you deliver by distinguishing what I call *measurable value* from *ambient value*. Measurable value is tangible: *reduce response time by 30 percent, increase market penetration by 10 percent*, or *reduce labor costs by half* are all examples of measurable value, easily identified and easy to explain. Ambient value is hard to explain and harder to sell: *improved image* and *stronger morale* are examples of ambient value.

Sellers often fall into the trap of describing their measurable value as ambient value. *Better customer satisfaction* and *increased productivity*, unless quantified, are perceived by customers as ambient value and are hard to sell. But *better customer satisfaction* means a reduction in customer churn that typically results in a quantifiable lift in revenue, while *increased productivity* brings lower production costs or greater output for the same effort. Do the work, and run the numbers to quantify the benefit, and turn perceived ambient value into real measurable value.

Mega trends and business pressures

As has been said before, the only constant is change, and with change comes opportunity. Change is the single greatest indicator of pressures to which industry needs to respond, and the catalyst for business opportunity. In 2017, and for the foreseeable future, Digital Transformation and Customer First are two of the most significant developments that all companies need to acknowledge and design strategies to counter or leverage. I call these the Mega Trends.

Amazon, Airbnb, Uber, Netflix, and Apple all entered markets with innovative customer centric approaches that embodied Digital Transformation, and the retail, hospitality, taxi, video rental, and music industries were forever changed.

As a consequence of these Mega Trends, companies will face pressures or disruption in several different areas:

- Financial
- Customers
- Competition
- Operations.

Financial: The Customer First demand may put pressure on the cost-to-serve, which will inevitably translate to a pressure on profit. Digital Transformation may dis-intermediate the value chain for commodity products where customers can transact online eliminating the middleman and his

124

opportunity to charge for services, consequently reducing his revenue. An example of this is the travel industry. A further example might apply to a provider of HR software. If a company has a profit problem, then a HR solution might increase employee engagement and drive better productivity. Productivity of course will also impact a company's ability to drive top-line revenue, so the provider of a HR solution has two distinct connection points – revenue and profit – with the customer.

> **IDEAL CUSTOMER PROFILE QUESTIONS:** What trends are happening in the company's industry that might be placing pressure on their financial goals? How does your solution help a company increase revenues or reduce costs? What specific problems are you solving? Where would you find information that tells you that the company has those specific problems? (See *Finding the Information* below.)

Customers: Customers are a different source of pressure. If a customer expects everything to happen at Internet speed (Digital Transformation) and in a personalized manner (Customer First) tremendous pressure will be placed on a company's supply chain and all customer engagement functions. This will potentially make demands on product and service features, functionality, and cost. For example, if a bank does not provide online and mobile banking capability, their customers will defect. As the bank goes through this metamorphosis, each of their Sales, Marketing and Customer Service functions needs to be re-imagined. This provides an opportunity for suppliers who can help the bank through the change.

> **IDEAL CUSTOMER PROFILE QUESTIONS:** What customer demands are being placed on companies in your target market? How does your solution help a company meet the requirements of those demands? What specific problems

125

are you solving? Where would you find information that tells you that the company has those specific problems?

Competition: Does Digital Transformation allow new competitors to enter the market? Are there new competitive arrivals in the market that are more customer centric? Is the company losing market share to competitors as a consequence of either of the Mega Trends?

> **IDEAL CUSTOMER PROFILE QUESTIONS:** What competitive threats are facing the companies in your target market? How does your solution help a company help them respond to those threats? What specific problems are you solving? Where would you find information that tells you that the company has those specific problems?

Operations: There has never been a time where the opportunity for companies to re-imagine their business operations has been so extreme. The mandate for speed (Digital Transformation) and flexibility (Customer First) impacts everything your customer must do from product idea through to cash collection. Product design is increasingly collaborative. Productivity is a key measure for all Sales Operations professionals. HR systems must cater for remote employees and on-demand workers. More companies are supporting distributed payment systems for customers.

> **IDEAL CUSTOMER PROFILE QUESTIONS:** What operations challenges do the companies in your target market have to address? How does your solution help a company help them optimize their operations? What specific problems are you solving? Where would you find information that tells you that the company has those specific problems?

126

And there may be other more specific trends or disruptions that are more directly or obviously applicable to your target industry that you might want to consider:

- Increased customer engagement
- The rise of the subscription and sharing economies
- Industry consolidation
- Currency volatility
- Growth in Mergers & Acquisition
- Artificial Intelligence
- Changes in globalization.

Finding the Information

The question you might now be asking yourself is how to find the *ICP Category 2: Customer Business Problem* information. Much of the available information from sources like Hoovers (**www.hoovers.com**) or Dun & Bradstreet (**www.dnb.com**), tends to provide the data to help with *ICP Category 1: Firmographics.* To understand the customer's business problems, you might have to dig a little deeper. The following approaches will help:

- **Corporate Reports:** Corporate reports are a treasure trove of information for investors: they tell you whether a company is making money or losing money – and why. You'll find this information in the company's quarterly reports on Form 10-Q, annual reports (with audited financial statements) on Form 10-K, and periodic reports of significant events on Form 8-K. Outside of the US you will generally find similar sources to discover information on public companies. It's usually easy to find information about large companies from the companies themselves, newspapers, brokerage firms, and the SEC. For smaller companies, some of the later approaches here will be more useful.

- **Earnings Calls:** An earnings call is a conference call between the management of a public company, analysts, investors and the media to discuss the financial results during a given reporting period such as a quarter or a fiscal year. In the earnings call, the company leadership will often discuss their strategic direction and where they plan to focus. The interaction with analysts can uncover gems of information as the analysts probe on issues that have proven to be a struggle to the company. A great information source is Seeking Alpha (**www.seekingalpha.com**) where you can get the complete transcripts of earnings calls, including the audio and slideshow presentations.

- **Investor Relations:** Most public companies have sections on their website dedicated to Investor Relations. In addition to their financial filings, you will often also find a copy of the annual report, or presentation to shareholders, or a 'Letter from the CEO' that highlights their strategic imperatives and commentary on the business broken down by functional or geographic areas.

- **Analysts' Coverage:** In the technology sector companies like Gartner (**www.gartner.com**) and Forrester Research (**www.forrester.com**) produce reports on companies' capabilities, and their strengths and weaknesses relative to their competition, also highlighting the areas that they (the analysts) deem to be important.

- **Press Releases:** Company press releases, whether they are announcing executive leadership appointments, new customers, product release or partnership agreements usually point to the reason why the news matters – from the company's perspective. These announcements provide further insight into what the leadership in a company thinks is important.

- **Competitor Activities:** When Amazon announced the acquisition of Whole Foods, the stock price of Walmart declined substantially. When one of your target companies' competitors makes a strategic move, it usually foretells a reaction. Knowing that the company needs to make a move helps you to understand what might be important to them.
- **People Who Bought This Also Bought This:** There are thousands of companies in the Salesforce ecosystem who provide products built on the Salesforce platform. Typically, customers of Salesforce buy their CRM system and subsequently add other capabilities from the ecosystem. When Salesforce announces a new customer (on an earnings call or in a press release) it makes sense that software companies in the ecosystem should look at that company as a potential Ideal Customer. Another example: if Caterpillar, the American corporation that provides machinery and engines, is awarded a large contract by one of its customers, providers of embedded analytics solutions might see this an opportunity to help Caterpillar customers monitor and optimize their fleets more effectively.

ICP Category 3: Positive impact potential

Your Ideal Customer Profile doesn't just point to companies that are easy to acquire. You also want to keep them for life. You know that the impact on a customer of a bad buying decision is typically greater than the impact on a salesperson of a lost deal. You also know that selling to customers for whom you can deliver value is an easier thing to do than trying to persuade a customer who is not a good fit to buy your product. This applies for new divisions in an existing customer, new products to an existing customer, as well as for new customers. When you adopt the buyer's perspective and take the time to consider the positive impact that you can provide, then you're on a path to mutual success.

Caring about the customer adopting your product successfully means that you care about keeping them as a customer, investing more with you over time, and being an active advocate. If all of this makes sense it follows that you shouldn't try to acquire customers that don't have Positive Impact Potential.

If you knowingly pursue customers without Positive Impact Potential, nothing that your Customer Success team does will ever have the result you're hoping for – and even worse, the customer will never achieve their expected or required results (and they will tell their friends and peers in other companies).

A *Good Fit* customer is one that maps to all your criteria for Positive Impact Potential. They are likely to have a successful experience with your product. It is also probable that they are more ready to consume what you have to offer.

If you are selling a software application that is built on the Salesforce platform, and the customer has just recently deployed Salesforce, it is probable that they will need some time to bed down that implementation before they take on another connected software implementation project. They will need to get the first project out of the way before they have capacity to deal with the next one.

It's great if you have found a supporter in the customer's organization who is willing to purchase your solutions, but depending on where they are on their journey, they may not yet be either ready or able to buy from you. If you ignore the fact that customers will occupy different positions on the spectrum of Positive Impact Potential, and instead you normalize targeting or support across all customers, you will fail to unlock that Positive Impact Potential for at least some of those customers. A Good Fit customer that you lose as a customer (but is still in business themselves) is the worst kind of churn. It means you failed them.

To determine if a company will fit your Ideal Customer Profile you should consider:

- **Is there evidence that the company has the requisite internal expertise and competence to adopt your solution successfully?** Example: Where a data analytics solution is being deployed, the company will need technically competent personnel with existing expertise in data analysis, or personnel who can be trained to effectively deploy and use your solution.

- **Does the company have the necessary resources available to deploy and sustain successful use of your product?** If they do not have the resources to invest (money, time, energy) into everything required to be successful, they are a bad fit. The budget (in financial and / or human resource terms) that a customer has deployed historically for the business area to which your solution applies is a good indicator of the company's match to your Ideal Customer Profile.

- **Where your solution has a technology component (in a product or related service) is the customer's technical environment compatible with your offering?** Example: If you have a software application that integrates with the Enterprise or Unlimited Editions of Salesforce.com, and your customer only has the Professional Edition, then this company does not fit your Ideal Customer Profile.

- **Does your offering include the level of support and reliability required by the target customer?**
  Example: If you are selling to organizations that respond to and deal with emergencies when they occur, especially those that provide police, ambulance, and firefighting services, it is likely that they will require 24 / 7 support and availability. If your support is available only from 9 to 5, Monday to Friday, then emergency services organizations will not fit your Ideal Customer Profile.

- **Is the company culturally aligned with yours?**
  Companies with similar values tend to work better together. Companies, like people, tend to cluster around the same set of values, beliefs, intent and behaviors. Cultural fit – the extent to which the customer's culture resembles that of your company exhibited by how it operates its business and its behaviors, practice and values – often foretells the length of relationship you can expect to have with that company and how likely it is that they will succeed with your product or solution.

This last point is important. The culture of a company is usually a reflection of the values of the leadership team or the person at the top. The values at Apple were a reflection of Steve Jobs' drive for perfection. Marc Benioff at Salesforce has instilled a set of customer centric and socially conscious values throughout his company. At Bang & Olufsen, designers rule the world: products are not designed based on extensive market research or focus groups – but on the gut-feel of the designers. At UPS, all process is implemented with militaristic precision. At Cirque de Soleil, each theatrical presentation still bears the critical and creative mark of the founder's unique perspective. At Nordstrom, customer service reigns supreme.

Where your company's values and culture align with that of your customer, all interactions will be easier. If the manner in which a customer engages with its suppliers maps to how you want to do business, that company is more ideal for you. A circle of trust is easier to develop between people with similar perspectives. Recognizing the rainbow of perspectives will guide you more effectively to the pot of gold.

Selling to the Trump administration would be very different than selling to the Obama administration. If one administration maps to the Cultural Fit element of your Ideal Customer Profile, it is likely that the other will not.

There are many ways to describe culture. I have used four categories of culture in the next chapter, *Chapter 6: Relationships: The Buyer Perspective*, to help you decide what best fits your customer engagement.

In summary, when the culture is Bureaucratic, everything will be very structured, and very controlled. Whoever dictates policies and procedure will be the source of power and that's where you need to focus. The Entrepreneurial culture is fast moving, and revolves around the leader. Unless you're aligned with the visionary one, your chances of success are slight. When the culture is Collaborative you need to be too. Committees rule; individuals make very few decisions in isolation; and process is across teams with clear measurements. The Individualistic culture is hard to sell to because there's little centralized decision making. It's like an amalgam of multiple fiefdoms.

As I said earlier, in a world responding to the Mega Trends of Digital Transformation and Customer First, companies are under pressure to act strategically, collaborate proactively and respond quickly, earning their customer's business month on month, time over time. Selecting companies who are more likely to be successful with your product, those with a strong Positive Impact Potential, makes that a lot easier.

Pulling It All Together – The Ideal Customer Profile Model

The following tables describe the Ideal Customer Profile Model, separated into the three categories: Firmographics, Customer Business Problem, and Positive Impact Potential. To make it more real I have completed the model using an example company that sells software to help companies improve the performance of their sales organization.

When you have assimilated the model you can use this framework to compile your own Ideal Customer Profile model.

ICP Category 1: Firmographics

In this section, the attributes that describe companies who absolutely fit your firmographic criteria should be listed in the *Ideal Customer* column. Others that might fit, but with some caveats, can be listed in the *Caution* column, meaning that further consideration might be required, and finally, the *Off Strategy* column contains attributes that indicate a bad fit – attributes that describe companies with whom you should not engage.

ICP Category 2: Customer business problem

In this section, list the identifiable Internal or External pressures that impact your prospective customer that might give rise to problems that you solve.

ICP Category 3: Positive impact potential

In this section, in the *Attribute* column in the table, list the attributes that point to Positive Impact Potential for the company. In the *How Do You Know?* column describe the situational proof-points that indicate the company's ability to be successful.

Figure 36: FIRMOGRAPHICS – ATTRIBUTES

Attribute	Ideal Customer	Caution	Off Strategy
Industry	High-tech, High-end manufacturing, Communications and media, Bio-tech, Professional services, Healthcare	Financial services (requires complex customer engagement)	Retail, Pharma, All B2C, Legal
Size	Between 100 and 5,000 sellers	More than 5,000 sellers	Fewer than 100 sellers
Geography	North America, United Kingdom, Ireland, Australia, New Zealand	Companies in EMEA or South America whose primary business language is English, but are remote from support centers	All other countries, and non-English speaking companies
Job Titles	Both VP Sales, VP Sales Operations (or similar) required	-	-
Business Maturity	Growth, Maturity	-	Start-up, Decline

Figure 37: THE CUSTOMER BUSINESS PROBLEM

Pressure (Indicator of Problem or Opportunity)	Problem / Opportunity
Sales expense as percentage of Revenue or of Total Expense growing, or higher than industry average Substantial new Sales hires (due to growth) Change in business model No technology deployed in Sales team	Sales Productivity
Recent M&A Less than 60 percent of Revenue from existing customers New Product introduction New disruptive entrant threatening installed base	Maximize Revenue in existing accounts
New Business Revenue per seller declining or less than industry average New Sales leader	Suboptimal Win Rate
No / few executive case studies / references	Build relationships
Traditional company business shifting to new economy model Commoditization of offering	Customer First selling
High rep turnover Large number of reps per manager	Balanced Sales rep performance
Missed market guidelines Lower than average gross margins	Inaccurate Sales forecast

Figure 38: POSITIVE IMPACT POTENTIAL

Attribute	How Do You Know?
Is there evidence that the company has the requisite internal expertise and competence to adopt your solution successfully?	Company has previously adopted similar solutions successfully.
Does the company have the necessary resources available to deploy and sustain successful use of your product?	Company has learning, project management and change management personnel on staff, and has CRM admin capability on staff, or normally engages a system integrator to support technical implementations.
Where your solution has a technology component (in product or related service) is the customer's technical environment compatible with your offering?	Company uses Salesforce (Enterprise Edition or greater).
Does your offering include the level of support and reliability required by the target customer?	Company has track record of engaging with companies who provide support cover Monday to Friday.
Is the company culturally aligned with yours?	The company culture is not Individualistic.

Conclusion

Early in this chapter I started with the **Customer Value Question**:

> What business problems does your customer have that you solve better than anyone else?

Use the ICP as your guide to answer that question. It will direct you to the right profile of customer, to whom you can bring optimal value today, as you solve the problems that you solve better than anyone else. When you consider the Positive Impact Potential you're investing for the long term with your customer. As you seek to develop relationships as outlined in the next two chapters, you will approach conversations with your potential customer confident that, just as you selected this customer, the customer should select you. That's a good place to start.

CHAPTER 6:
RELATIONSHIPS:
THE BUYER'S
PERSPECTIVE

Introduction

There is no success in business without business relationships. There is no success in sales without impactful *connections* between the right people in the seller's organization and the right people at the customer. I am purposefully using the word *connections* here to differentiate from what has been traditionally been called *relationship based* sales. I want to remove from your mind the image of the traditional salesperson trading solely on his customer relationship based on golf outings and expensive dinners. Social events can be very helpful to get to know the person behind the customer, uncovering the values, attitudes and perspectives that shape decision making and priorities. But today's buyers have problems to solve. They might accept your invitation to a golf outing or a football game, but they will forge connections with suppliers who partner with them to solve their business problems.

From here on in, when I talk about building successful relationships, I'm talking about mutual authentic engagement between buyer and sellers, founded on trust and respect, guided by shared values in pursuit of shared goals. While this is a high threshold to achieve, it is what your customers deserve, it is how the best customers want to engage, and it provides a safe-zone for constructive brainstorming, bargaining and building rapport.

The Scale of the Problem

I have worked with talented sales professionals around the world and I have found that failing to access the key people, or to influence them effectively (by demonstrating value), is one of the most frequent reasons cited for failure in a sales campaign. This holds true whether the sellers are in pursuit of a new customer, or seeking to expand in an existing account. How many times have you, or one of your sales team, spent weeks with an existing customer, or new prospect, only to learn that one of the key influencers that you did not connect with had sent the sale in another direction? Well, you're not alone.

According to the research report *Inside the Buyer's Mind*, while most salespeople think that they get to decision makers 'Almost Always,' only 38 percent of buyers believe that sellers get to the decision makers most of the time.

Figure 39: SELLERS' INTERACTION WITH KEY DECISION MAKERS

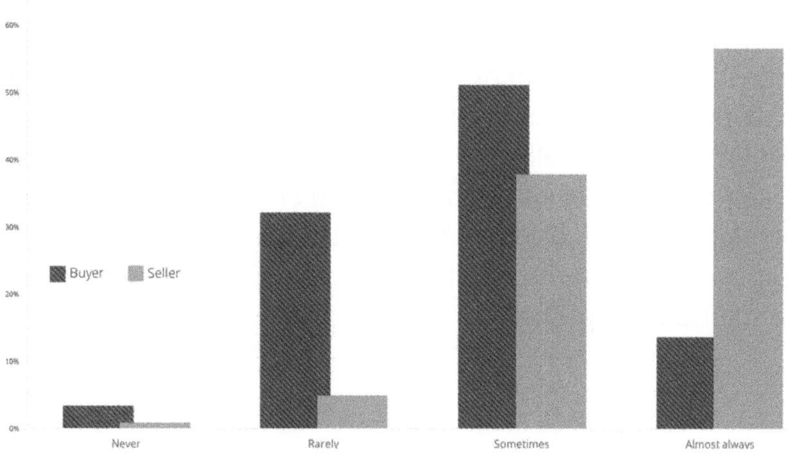

Even where a seller has an existing relationship with the account, the buyers believe that the sellers only 'Almost

Always' get to the decision makers less than half of the time (42 percent). The sellers themselves think this is the case 68 percent of the time.

The data is fairly clear: sellers are not as good accessing the key players as they think they are. The challenge for sellers often is to know how to access the right people, how to bring value that earns them the right to get those meetings. At the same time some sellers will be satisfied spending time with those on the buy side who are willing to spend time with them. While this activity may seem productive, it is often not the case.

Since *Inside the Buyer's Mind* was first published in 2016 there has been a lot of commentary about the increasing number of stakeholders involved in every buying decision. A study from Gartner correlates the likelihood of a sale closing with the number of people involved in the buying committee, highlighting that, as the number of buying roles increases, the probability of any deal getting done diminishes. In these situations, 'No Decision,' the nemesis of salespeople, becomes the primary competitor. Gartner's study suggests that there is a material impact even when the buying group moves from one to two buyers and that, when it grows to five or six buyers, the probability of a deal happening reduces to 30 percent. The reality, of course, is that the causal factor driving the number of people in the buying committee is the complexity of the solution being purchased. The number of people involved in the purchase decision is a consequence of the solution complexity.

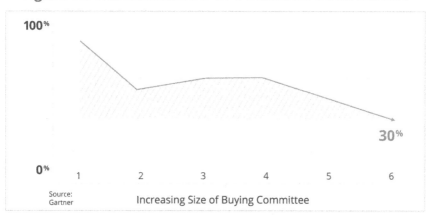

Figure 40: THE LIKELIHOOD OF PURCHASE COMPLETION

According to *Inside the Buyer's Mind*, the average number of stakeholders involved in a buying decision varies dramatically by the complexity of the solution being purchased. What we know for sure is that the old paradigm of top-down, single decision maker, directed purchases are increasingly rare – so it is important to be able to access all the key influencers in any deal. Based on the 2016 *Inside the Buyer's Mind* research project, we know that there are more than five buying decision makers involved much of the time.

In a typical enterprise purchase you're not going to have a one-call sale. Multiple meetings (~ five) with the key influencers will be needed. That's a lot of meetings. Clearly the buying team is not going to allocate the time to each supplier to meet with each of his people up to five times. That would require 125 (5 x 5 x 5) engagements between seller and the individuals in the buying team. Even if some of the meetings are with many people at the same time – where there will be multiple representatives from both buyer (see **Figure 41**) and seller – there will be many cases where specific people who are running the project will engage 20 to 30 times throughout a typical enterprise sales engagement.

Figure 41: THE RELATIONSHIP MAP

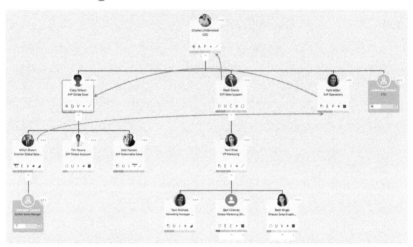

The overhead this places on the buying organization is extreme; and the perceived value of multiple generic meetings is low. So the natural sequence of events is that the facilitator of the buying team – either a business leader or a professional buyer (not mutually exclusive) – quickly whittles down the potential number of suppliers to a shortlist and then to the preferred vendor. Clearly getting access to all of the decision makers early in the buying cycle is clearly important.

The results from the *2017 Business Performance Benchmark Study* suggest that 61 percent of sellers believe they are effective at gaining access to key buying influencers. In either case, there are a material number of sellers who can't get to the people who make the decision. That study goes on to show that those who are effective have a 28 percent greater Win Rate (materially similar to the results from *Inside the Buyer's Mind*) and a Sales Cycle that is reduced by 21 percent. The performance delta is not surprising.

Figure 42: SELLERS' ACCESS TO KEY BUYING INFLUENCERS

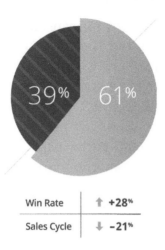

Win Rate	⬆ **+28%**
Sales Cycle	⬇ **−21%**

Those who are successful at accessing the key influencers and building relationships are more successful and quicker at achieving quota. They are granted return access, of course, because each time they visit they bring gifts of valuable insight born of continuous research and consideration of the customer's perspective.

It is not just about accessing people; it is equally important to understand clearly what each influencer wants to achieve. Personal motivation is as important as company motivation. When you can tap into the personal dreams or aspirations of the individual and connect on a more intimate level you get to understand what is really important to him. Then your actions can be more effectively directed.

When Customers Engage Sellers

Contrary to some current misconceptions, B2B buyers are not in fact conducting much of the buying cycle unaided by sellers, evaluating solutions on their own, and only reaching out to suppliers in the late stages of their process. According to *Inside the Buyer's Mind,* which researched over 1,200 buyers and sellers, over two-thirds (67 percent) of the buyers seek input from suppliers before they begin to evaluate solutions. More strikingly, more than one-third (35 percent) work with suppliers even before a project is identified; and nearly half (48 percent) look for assistance prior to working on their business requirements.

Figure 43: WHEN BUYERS AND SELLERS FIRST ENGAGE

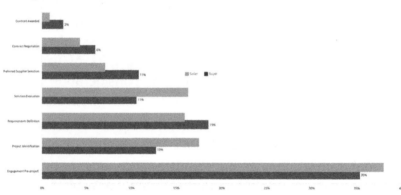

The results directly contradict an often-quoted statistic that buyers are 57 percent of the way through their buying process before engaging a supplier.[24] As evidenced by the data, buyers need sellers early. This does not mean that buyers are not more educated, or that the world has remained the same, but that today's crazy busy buyers need sellers to help them, to create, not just communicate, value.

---

[24] CEB: *The End of Solution Sales.*

148

That's a wonderful opportunity for mutual authentic engagement between buyer and sellers, in pursuit of shared goals.

According to the McKinsey *B2B Customer Decision Journey* survey, customers find it helpful to speak to someone 76 percent of the time when buying a completely new product or service, and 52 percent of the time when buying a previously purchased product or service but with different specifications.

Figure 44: WHEN BUYERS FIND IT HELPFUL TO SPEAK WITH SOMEONE

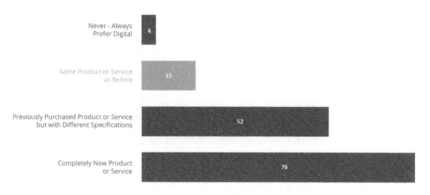

It is important to remember that not all sales or purchases are the same. As cost increases and the complexity (intellectual property) of products or services being transacted grows, the greater the potential impact on an organization. The Kraljic Matrix described in *Chapter 8: The Executive Sponsor: Their Role in Large Accounts* adds further depth to this analysis. This usually means that buyers need help from sellers earlier.

Two other important factors that need to be considered from the buyer's perspective are risk and frequency of purchase. As frequency of purchase increases, organizational impact tends to decrease. As risk increases with cost and complexity or IP value — for example, in the case of business infrastructure projects or a CRM system — organizational impact increases, along with the buyer's need to engage earlier and more intensively with sellers for guidance and input.

Figure 45: THE BUYER'S PROBLEM – 2

The results from *Inside the Buyer's Mind* also shows that sellers who engage early have a 30 percent greater win rate. When a buyer contacts a seller earlier, the win rate increases. But sellers can't wait for the buyer to call. They need to add value when no one is buying. They need to devise strategies to encourage this early engagement from the buyer and make sure they are building the right relationships.

Once the problem or opportunity is understood, objectives and requirements are determined. In the past the customer might move straight to the RFP (Request for Proposal) stage. In today's Internet centric world, customers may look to online sources, social networks, or peer recommendations to further inform their next steps. At some point, suppliers are invited to provide information in the form of an RFP or other mechanism, and the customer evaluates the different offerings. Clearly, the earlier you are involved in the cycle, the better position you are in to shape the requirements, and to influence the progression along the way.

The customer will choose the product or service that meets their requirements and negotiate contracts with the chosen supplier. The chosen product or service is then implemented. Finally, the solution is measured for return on investment (ROI) against metrics established earlier in the Customer Decision Cycle (see **Figure 47** below).

Level of Relationship

A better understanding of your customer's business can improve your level of relationship and assist you in entering the customer's decision process earlier. Often, at the start of your relationship, you may find yourself at the bottom of the pyramid – the Vendor level, where the width indicates the extent of competition. As you move up the pyramid, the competition thins out – Trusted Advisor is a rarified space.

Figure 46: THE BUSINESS RELATIONSHIP PYRAMID

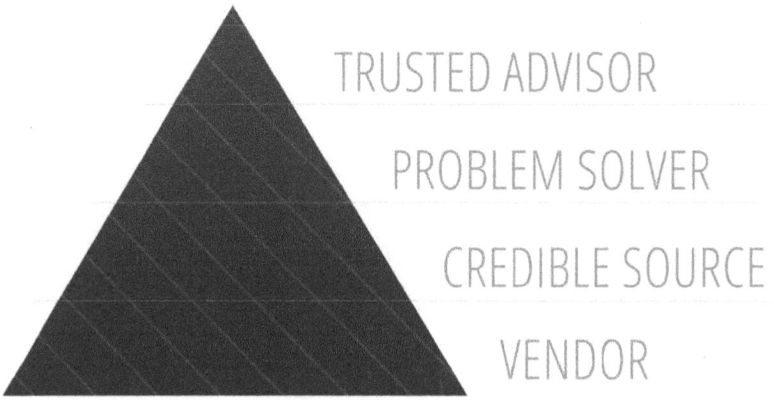

TRUSTED ADVISOR

PROBLEM SOLVER

CREDIBLE SOURCE

VENDOR

Changing the way you view your target account can help you to improve your relationship with the customer. Consequently, you change the way your target account views your relationship. If you view the account from the perspective of the customer's business, you can begin to see the drivers that move and shape their strategies and actions. Once you identify those drivers you can add more value by addressing the customer's specific needs. Better understanding and identification of your customer's needs directly correlates to improving your relationship with the customer.

Take a look again at the Business Relationship Pyramid in **Figure 46**. I'd like you to think about your current relationship with your customer. What level are you at today?

The Business Relationship Pyramid shows four levels:

- **Vendor:** At the Vendor level, your relationship is based solely on your product and your company's ability to deliver. Generally you become aware that your customer has a specific need only when you receive an RFP or a call from the customer. So you are reactive in responding to the customer's needs. As an example, for a customer who has a project to automate their manufacturing facility, even though you don't know anything about their business, you might be asked for a quotation to supply widgets. You are basically being asked for a price for a product that meet predetermined specifications.

- **Credible Source:** As a Credible Source, you consistently meet or exceed the customer's expectations – but your value is not necessarily appreciated at the highest levels in the customer organization. Your contact or coverage in the account is with lower level managers across multiple functions. You are not involved early enough in the cycle to materially shape an initiative with the customer. While you have some lower level relationships, and might think that you know what is going on in the account, you might still be surprised by an initiative that is sponsored from a higher level, so you are still mainly in reactive mode. Following the previous example, you are still being asked for a price for a product that meets predetermined specifications to help with automating the manufacturing facility, but you may have been put on the list of potential vendors because of your relationships with the lower level managers, and you can use those relationships to better understand the requirements and possibly suggest alternative approaches. The key however is that at this point the sponsor of the project has already shaped in their mind what they think the likely solution will look like.

- **Problem Solver:** As a Problem Solver, your relationship with the customer becomes more proactive once they have identified their problem. However they have not yet identified the shape or specifications of the potential solution. You may help the customer create an RFP for a solution to solve a problem that the customer has identified or for an initiative they have just sponsored. You are aware of existing problems and develop solutions for them. You also have contact with the customer at higher management levels within multiple functions and across multiple units.

- **Trusted Advisor:** At the Trusted Advisor level, you and the customer explore emerging needs and new directions on a confidential basis. Therefore, your role in the customer's organization is similar to that of a consultant. The watchword for value in this relationship is co-creation. A consultant, by this definition, means someone who will give unbiased advice that does not always lead to a purchase from the consultant. You should be both identifying potential problems that they have not recognized and suggesting solutions or approaches to solving problems that they have not yet considered. Your contacts within the company are at the executive level throughout the enterprise. Your outlook will be much longer term and you will have an opportunity to create initiatives through your understanding of both the customer's business and other trends in the customer's industry.

The Customer's Decision Cycle

In order to improve your relationship with the customer, you first have to understand where you're starting from – in the context of the customer's decision cycle. Typically, when a customer is making an investment, they are doing so in response to a problem they need to solve, or an opportunity that they can see.

Business needs drive the customer's decision process. Ideally you are helping them shape their needs and crafting an initiative with them to meet their requirements. Whether you are involved or not, the decision cycle will follow a similar pattern, and understanding that cycle will inform your activities.

The stages of the Customer's Decision Cycle are:

1. Define the goals and assess the pressures
2. Establish initiatives
3. Initiate project
4. Evaluate products
5. Prove concept
6. Negotiate and sign contracts
7. Implement
8. Measure results
9. *(Start all over again).*

Depending on the relationship you have with the customer, you will engage with the customer at different stages of the Customer's Decision Cycle.

Figure 47: THE CUSTOMER'S DECISION CYCLE

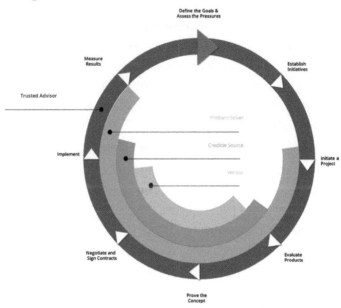

From the definitions of the Levels of Relationship, mapped to the Customer's Decision Cycle, you can see that as a *Product Vendor* you only enter the process when the customer is ready to evaluate products – and then you are out of there. You are generally not involved in measuring the results of your work. In this scenario, either relationships are not needed for the product you sell, or you have not managed to establish even a modicum of relationship success. Price will be the single arbiter of success. Some people refer to the salesperson in this situation (perhaps pejoratively) as a 'drive-by seller.'

Moving up the relationship pyramid, notice that your role in the customer decision making process expands. At the *Credible Source* level, you are now entering the process just before the customer is ready to evaluate products or solutions to address their needs. But you exit before the results of the project come to light, so you're still not viewed as a business partner.

As a *Problem Solver*, your involvement expands further. Now you enter the process just before the customer has initiated a project and you are involved in the measurement of the results. You have the opportunity to communicate the value that you delivered and you are in a position to work with the customer post-sale as well as pre-sale.

At the *Trusted Advisor* level, you really don't ever enter – or exit – the process. Your involvement with the customer is more cyclical. You may recommend areas that the customer should investigate and develop. Or, when the customer has a need, they come to you and together you assess the problem.

A *Trusted Advisor* has extensive knowledge of the customer's business. Often, you will identify opportunities for the customer to improve their business even before the customer has identified those needs themselves. Understanding the customer's business, uncovering needs and requirements, and defining solutions for the customer differentiates you in the account and permits you to gain a large measure of influence over the decision process.

What do you suppose happens to the number of competitors when you enter the decision process earlier? Clearly, if you are doing your job well, and are helping the customer uncover their needs, you have a distinct competitive advantage, and the customer will see less reason to go to the market to look for alternative suppliers. That way the number of competitors is reduced and the pressure on price is correspondingly decreased. A clear measure of your *Trusted Advisor* status is the number of non-competitive opportunities in which you are involved.

Operating at *Trusted Advisor* level with your customer is certainly a desirable goal. But, if your customer is not willing to invest with you at this level then you are wasting your resources and potentially endangering your relationship with the customer. Conversely, if your customer does want to work with you at the *Trusted Advisor* level and you are operating at the *Product Vendor* level, you are opening yourself up for competitive vulnerability and risk.

Part of your mission is to deliver value. To do this you must clearly understand what your customer values and how, based on your available resources, you can deliver upon that value.

As I reported in my 2013 book, *Account Planning in Salesforce*, Marc Benioff, founder and CEO of Salesforce, has been a great example to his company of building relationships with customers, founded on mutual authentic engagement in pursuit of shared goals. One such example is the relationship developed between Salesforce and Burberry. In June 2012, Angela Ahrendts, then CEO of Burberry, appeared on the cover of *Fortune* magazine. As *Fortune* told the story:

> Last May, Burberry CEO Angela Ahrendts flew to California from her London headquarters to introduce herself to an executive she thought could be critical to the future of her business: Salesforce.com CEO Marc Benioff.
>
> When the two met at the Ritz-Carlton in Half Moon Bay, they stood in the hall batting around ideas for 15 minutes before even sitting down. Ahrendts explained her vision: to create a company where anyone who wanted to touch the brand could have access to it.
>
> She just needed a digital platform to make it happen.
>
> Benioff sketched a diagram of how Burberry could become a 'social enterprise,' overlaying technology like Salesforce, SAP, Twitter, and Facebook atop the entire company. (Benioff signed the drawing "Angela + Marc = LIKE," and Ahrendts reportedly keeps the framed original in her office.)

"I told him, 'I think I finally met someone who talks faster and has more energy than I do,'" she says. "We just connected."

Figure 48: MARC BENIOFF'S SKETCH FOR ANGELA AHRENDTS

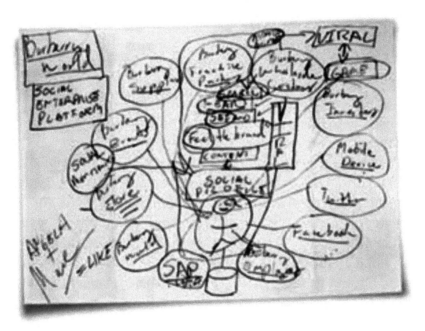

The Burberry / Salesforce story is a great example of how a supplier took the time to create value for his customer by taking the customer's perspective. In this case, Salesforce is viewed as a co-traveler on Burberry's journey, the apogee of the supplier / customer relationship.

As you take the time to adopt your customer's perspective, you will have arrived at a place where you can take out your own napkin with your customer, and sketch your joint vision as you build your relationship with your customers and develop your mutual success plan.

You don't have to be a CEO to make this work. While this story is about the relationship between two high-flying CEOs, similar stories, albeit with less media-worthy protagonists, are happening every day between great salespeople and their customers.

But staying with this story: When Marc Benioff sat down with Angela Ahrendts to paint his vision of the Burberry Social Enterprise, you can be sure that he first learned about her vision for Burberry. He focused on making Burberry successful, and making Ahrendts a hero through multiple public appearances at Salesforce events. In 2014, she went on to become SVP of Apple's retail and online stores, overseeing online retail and Apple's 478 high-earning bricks-and-mortar stores. Collecting an annual compensation package of $25 million, Ahrendts is the first woman on Apple CEO Tim Cook's executive team. Announcing her appointment in 2014, *Forbes* credited her with righting 'the sinking fashion house.' It's probably a stretch to say that Marc Benioff was responsible for Angela Ahrendts' career progression, but he certainly cared about her success. That's one of the core elements of a trusted business relationship.

Inside the Company's Mind

There is an old adage that says: 'Companies don't buy, people buy.' The message is that, in order to get a company to buy something from you, you have to get the people in the company to buy. Of course, this is true, but I don't subscribe to the notion that the two are disconnected.

A company, its personality, culture, business outlook, market position, business pressures and consequent buying proclivities, are in fact an attribute of the company itself as well as of the people in the company. There is a 'chicken and egg' situation here. Companies have personalities and culture. When someone joins an organization, they are influenced by those attributes; on the other hand, a company is made up of people, whose personalities and attributes are themselves influencers on the overall personality of the company. It is not sufficient to consider just one or the other.

One of the biggest mistakes made by some sales professionals is assuming that all customer companies are created equal. It's as if they expect some alchemist to stir a magic potion and to serve up cookie-cutter customers, each with the same level of technical savvy, common approach to risk, and similar awareness of their need. But, of course, it isn't so. If you have done your work to define and assimilate your Ideal Customer Profile in *Chapter 5*, you will know that this is not so – and you are ahead of the game.

One of the best things that can happen to a salesperson is when their satisfied buyer moves from one company to another and invites the seller into the new company to supply the same solution. I have a good friend Mark (you know who you are) who first became a customer in 2006 when he was at one of the world's largest software companies. After a very successful career at that company where he oversaw a tremendous evolution in the sales organization, he was recruited to one of the top five hardware and services companies about four years later. I was delighted when we got the call to once again partner with Mark in what was possibly the world's largest sales transformation at that time.

In 2015 Mark moved companies again – this time to what I would call a New Economy company. This company was early stage, almost Start-up but on the cusp of Growth. It was moving fast, growing fast, hiring and firing fast, and burning through lots of cash fast. The company had just gone public in a frenzied IPO market. Mark was recruited by one of the board members to bring some discipline and process to the sales organization. When Mark called me to tell me he was moving I remember him saying: "We are really going to need your help again. This company is all over the place and this will be our greatest challenge yet."

I was delighted that we would be helping Mark again and of course also pleased that we would be putting another significant customer logo on the board.

Unfortunately, this time it didn't work out. We fell at the culture hurdle. When we looked at what the company wanted to achieve, its practices and procedures, we decided that there were several foundational practices that they first needed to put in place before they would be ready to benefit from our solution. The Positive Impact Potential was low so we decided to not engage until the company was ready. After 18 months of frustrated effort, Mark left the company. He had made progress on the business processes that he knew were required at a company in the Growth stage. The company was very entrepreneurial – which in itself wasn't a problem – but it also had a lot of attributes of the Individualistic culture described below. It just was not a good cultural fit.

While it's reasonable to expect that companies of similar profile might make parallel purchases of similar products, specific peculiarities of the culture in one company – in this case relating to company maturity – may mean that the fit is not right. Customers are different, and you need to embrace the buyer's perspective. It's his money after all, and sitting at his side of the table will help you get it.

Mark's new company was a better fit for him – and for us – and we are delighted to be helping him now on our third sales transformation project together.

A company's culture – the combination of practices, behaviors, and values that drive the organization – impacts how the company buys, and therefore how you should determine how you might sell to it.

There are four types of culture you should consider: Bureaucratic, Entrepreneurial, Collaborative and Individualistic.

Each requires a different selling approach, so you need to assess the prevalent culture in your target customer to correctly position yourself, your company, and your value proposition.

Understanding your customer's culture is key to helping you recognize how decisions are made. Culture is a bit like an iceberg. What you can't see is often greater than what you can. Look beyond the obvious to ascertain the culture – then adapt your approach accordingly. Once you understand how the organization thinks, you are ready to build relationships with the people.

Let's consider how to recognize the culture and how to position accordingly.

When the culture is **bureaucratic**, everything will be very structured, and very controlled. Whoever dictates policies and procedure will be the source of power and that's where you need to focus.

Figure 49: A BUREAUCRATIC CULTURE – ATTRIBUTES

Decision making	Highly structured, formal
Work Structure	By function in silos
Communication	Controlled and deliberate
Control Mechanism	Policy and procedure
Source of Power	Who dictates policy & procedure?

Recommended Approach:
> Pay attention to detail
> Learn the system
> Look for help to navigate the system
> Use formal written communication
> Follow the chain of command

The **entrepreneurial** culture is fast-moving, and revolves around the leader. Unless you're aligned with the visionary one, your chances of success are slight.

Figure 50: AN ENTREPRENEURIAL CULTURE – ATTRIBUTES

Decision making	Centralized and fast
Work Structure	New opportunities
Communication	Rapid, externally-oriented
Control Mechanism	Leader's vision, extreme loyalty
Source of Power	Who is connected to the leader?

Recommended Approach:
> Act fast
> Align with the visionary
> Focus on projects easily connected to the vision
> Be open and prepared for change

When the culture is **collaborative** you need to be too. Committees rule. Individuals make very few decisions in isolation. Process is across teams with clear measurements.

You need to respect the customer's team process and align with project initiators.

Figure 51: A COLLABORATIVE CULTURE – ATTRIBUTES

Decision making	Consensus-driven
Work Structure	Business Unit or cross-functional
Communication	Open
Control Mechanism	Process / Objectives measurement
Source of Power	Who initiates projects and measures results?

Recommended Approach:
> Sell to the team
> Cover all members of the team
> Focus on common ground
> Show respect for the team

Figure 52: AN INDIVIDUALISTIC CULTURE – ATTRIBUTES

Decision making	Decentralized
Work Structure	Projects and expertise
Communication	Only when essential
Control Mechanism	Individual self interest
Source of Power	Who can perform? Who has expertise?

Recommended Approach:
> Focus on the top performers
> Be prepared to build many relationships
> Respect their time
> Don't expect conformity
> Bridge communication gaps

The **individualistic** culture is hard to sell to because there's little centralized decision-making. It's like an amalgam of multiple fiefdoms and you will almost never get consensus across the company.

A Customer Culture Story

In the next chapter, I will outline a five-part framework on how to effectively build the right relationships with the right people. Before I get into that, I want to tell a story about how investing time to learn about the person behind the buyer helped me in a very large sale.

It was April 2015 and I participated in a Deal Review – at Altify, we call it an Opportunity Test and Improve – for a multi-million dollar deal with a Fortune 500 company. I will call this company XCo. The purpose of the Deal Review was to assess where we were in the sale, help the seller to identify risks and vulnerabilities, and come up with a plan of action to mitigate those risks. This deal passed the *Truth Test* – we were convinced that it was in XCo's interest to purchase our solution.

As the salesperson went through the methodology and presented the deal, on the surface it felt like we should win. The opportunity had been qualified, budget was allocated, and we had been selected as one of the two finalists. We clearly had a great solution fit, a combination of enterprise sales methodology and intelligent software that would uniquely meet the requirements of the customer. There was no question that we had product superiority. Our team had studiously examined their business, worked out XCo's return on investment, and provide an ROI framework that helped the customer understand how our solution would provide greater return than the alternative. However, with that clear advantage, it was unclear as to why XCo had not yet made the decision, and made it in our favor.

I remember looking at all the people in the evaluation team – there were 15 people involved that would make the decision that then had to be approved by the CEO. Clearly XCo's evaluation team was taking this project very seriously. Their goal was to dramatically change the way in which XCo's sales and support organizations would interact with their customers. They wanted to develop long term partnerships with their customers, increase the value that XCo would deliver by better understanding their customers' goals, and make sure that the solution offered was optimally matched to their customers' needs. The Relationship Map for the opportunity looked something like **Figure 53**. (Names and photos changed.)

Figure 53: THE RELATIONSHIP MAP FOR XCo

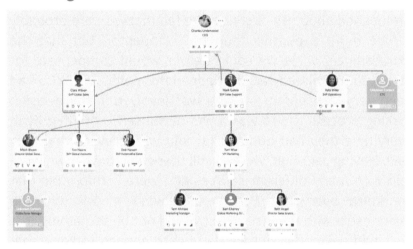

Most of the people on the map were favorably disposed to our solution, but Clara, the Decision Maker, and a few other key influencers remained Neutral. We looked at all of their Formal Decision Criteria and could honestly say that we were equal or better in all areas. We collated all the Informal Decision Criteria that we had gathered though our interactions with XCo, and we felt pretty good about that too. We provided stellar customer references. But, even though it all looked pretty good, there had to be a reason why we had not already been selected. The other company on the shortlist was the incumbent, but we had learned that XCo was not overly pleased with them and that this was why this particular project had been initiated.

Applying the tried and tested adage of 'Only the paranoid survive,' we assumed we were losing, and went back though all of the factors in the opportunity to answer that critical question: "If we were to lose, what would be the top three reasons?" When you do that kind of exercise, openly and honestly, it prompts some deep critical thinking. The obvious answers of price, some unknown decision maker, or competitor's relationship, always come to the fore. We felt pretty good about the first two. We felt that we were probably a little more expensive than the competitor, but that the extraordinary value we could deliver would compensate for that. XCo had already acknowledged this point. Also, XCo had been very transparent on who was involved in the decision making process. There was a wonderful sense of integrity in everything they had done so far and we believed what they said. Having said that, we had still triangulated what we were told with many different sources and were comfortable that we knew everyone. There was always a risk that the relationship with the incumbent would not be something that we could overcome, but we had heard enough to know that that door was open.

After all of the analysis we came down to one thing: XCo was sincere about developing long term partnerships with their customers. Were they convinced that we were prepared to hold ourselves to the same standard? Did they in fact believe that our two companies could work together over the long term? Even though we had a clearly superior solution, and had delivered benefit to our other customers, were we people they felt they could depend on? We knew that we were – but accepted that, if they did not believe that we were culturally compatible, then they would likely not choose us.

I can remember it now as if it was yesterday. We went 'social sleuthing.' We needed to find out more about the people on XCo's evaluation committee to determine for ourselves whether we were culturally aligned. Looking on LinkedIn, for each of the people, we discovered from their activities some of things that interested them: What did they publish or post? Whose posts and shares did they share with their own followers? Were there LinkedIn groups in which they were active, or particular influencers or companies that they followed? People might follow Richard Branson for a different reason than they would follow Sheryl Sandberg or Bill Gates, Steve Jobs or Warren Buffett. If they followed their current or past company it indicated a level of engagement in their work. We looked at their work history. It turned out that many of the buying committee had worked together in a previous company over the span of a decade. These people were close, loyal, and a tight-knit group. Almost all of them followed Salesforce, a fact that was not overly surprising given that they had recently had made a very significant investment in Salesforce's CRM solutions.

Where LinkedIn gives a great sense of someone's professional perspective, their activities and posts on Twitter and Facebook tend to paint more personal pictures. Without bringing you through a blow-by-blow of our investigation, we learned that the majority of our buying group were politically slightly left of center, family was very important, they cared about the environment in a socially-conscious way, and long term relationships were important. There were many sports fans and dog-lovers among them.

Overall, we got a picture of a group who had worked closely together, were passionate about many things, cared about doing the right thing, and, from a business as well as personal perspective, cared about long term trusting relationships.

If I annotated the Relationship Map for XCo, it would look something like **Figure 54**.

Figure 54: THE RELATIONSHIP MAP FOR XCo – ANNOTATED

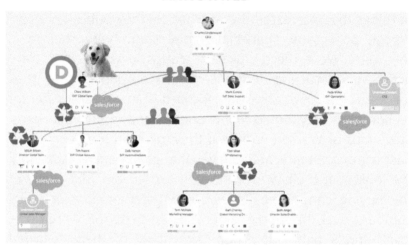

We decided to change our approach. XCo definitely had all of the attributes of a Collaborative culture. The 'bake-off' between our company and the competitor was coming up and, in addition to being asked to present our solution and show how it met their needs, there was a segment at the end where we were asked to highlight our five key differentiators.

The reality was that even though we knew we had a superior solution – our technology was the gold standard (because we had about a 10-year start on everyone else in the industry), our methodology was stronger – 20 years of sales process and methodology innovation, and our supporting services were best-in-class – we also realized that if we focused only on those items we were going to lose. The key differentiator that mattered in this situation was our approach to long term customer relationships. This is a core value of everyone in our company, was something that we had dramatically undersold, and in fact was probably the most significant thing that they, the customer's buying committee, should care about.

Having already demonstrated that we understood their business problem and shown how we could help XCo rapidly grow their business with a new Customer First model, we presented our five key differentiators in this order:

1. Our Employees
2. Our Customers
3. Our Customer Success Team
4. Our Methodology
5. Our Technology.

What made this easy was that it was a reflection of who we are as a company. The employees come first, because if they are not engaged and excited to come to work every day, they would not be enthused about helping our customers succeed. We spoke about our customers: Matt, Helen, Bob, Sarah, Jeff, another Jeff, and Michelle. These were individuals from our customers that we had come to know well as we supported their efforts to transform their company's businesses. We used photos of the people, not company logos. The relationships we had (and still have) with these people were a testament to the long term partnerships that we build, sincerely and in a sustained manner.

Most of the time was spent on these first two topics. Then we went on to talk about the Customer Success team, our methodology and our technology.

I am not exaggerating when I say that Clara's eye welled up. She cared so much about doing the right thing for her company and her customers that her passion shone through in that extra twinkle in her eyes.

Later that week we learned that we had won a multi-million dollar, multi-year relationship with this great company. Three years on, our business with XCo has grown. XCo has been phenomenally successful with our solution, and I couldn't be happier for them.

So, that was a happy ending!

Cultural alignment matters, not just in theory, but in practice too.

CHAPTER 7:
A STRUCTURE FOR BUILDING RELATIONSHIPS

As I've said earlier, most deals are not lost because you don't have the best solution or the best price or the best terms and conditions. They are usually lost because you didn't understand the people or problems. In *Account Planning for Salesforce* I defined the purpose of Account Planning as:

> Building long term business relationships in a complex marketplace that enable us to create, develop, pursue, and win business that delivers mutual value.

This definition holds true whether you are pursuing a single strategic opportunity or building a strategy to maximize revenue from a large customer. Building long term relationships matter, and to do that you need to understand how the company works, the relationships between the people, and the politics of the organization as it relates to your short term or long term goal. You must be clear on the different dimensions of hierarchy and influence, as well as the difference between organizational structure and political structure. This helps you to answer these five key relationship questions:

- Who matters?
- How do they think?
- What is your current relationship?
- What is the relationship gap?
- How do you bridge that gap?

Who Matters? (Who are the Key Players?)

Everyone, of course – everyone matters. That's the first point to make and something to always remember. Respecting everyone and being open to how you can help them and they can help you is a good place to start from. Whether you are speaking with the CEO or anyone in the C-suite, the manager who has been charged with implementing the project you are working on, the administrative assistant (especially the administrative assistant) who helps organize meetings, or the security officer at the door of the company's office, everyone matters. They might not help you today to close the deal you are working on, and maybe they will never matter in the context of growing revenue with this customer – but everyone matters and it doesn't take a lot of effort to treat them respectfully. I have seen business relationships terminally damaged when a senior decision maker observed a potential supplier treating one of their employees poorly, assuming the 'girl' in the room was the person who should make the coffee or book the taxi, being dismissive of a junior person in a meeting, or behaving in some other disrespectful manner. Apart from the fact that everyone deserves respect, irrespective of seniority or station, treating people appropriately is the right thing to do, and it happens to be good business.

Notwithstanding all of this, there are specific people in the customer's company who can influence decisions and make things happen. The organization chart is just one guide and frequently not one that points to the real power base in the company. Think of it like this. If someone is high in the organizational hierarchy, it doesn't always mean that they are also high in influence. Conversely, even though someone lacks a big title, or does not report directly to the C-level in the company, they may still have significant influence over the outcome of a buying decision or the company strategy.

To determine 'Who matters?' in the context of your deal or account strategy, you need to understand the impact that person can have. We can call this their *Level of Influence*. It's partly a function of their Rank – their position on the org chart, the formal part of the equation – but also, more importantly their Influence – the informal part, but the element that indicates the say they might have over the eventual outcome.

Figure 55: THE LEVEL OF INFLUENCE MAP

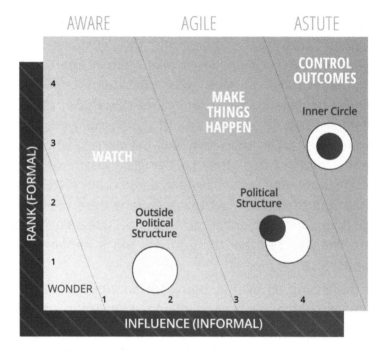

Most people start in a new organization at the bottom left and move up in rank and out in influence. Eventually they cross a threshold: they become aware of how the business operates – the politics of the organization. People to the right of the awareness border begin to see how the game is played.

When a person learns how to avoid the political traps and become agile enough to dodge the inevitable political conflict, they cross a second border: agility. This is the ability to anticipate events and respond quickly. This is characterized as the *Political Structure* of the organization.

As a person becomes astute at using their rank and influence to build power, they cross another boundary. People to the right of this line not only can respond to events and take advantage of opportunities, but they also understand how to create opportunities. This is the *Inner Circle* of the organization. People in the Inner Circle control what happens within the organization. They have a group of lieutenants in the Political Structure who execute their ideas and make things happen.

Key Players are people in the Inner Circle or in the Political Structure. People outside of the Political Structure – well, they just watch and wonder about what just happened.

Measuring Level of Influence: The following 10 questions will help you to assess the impact an individual might have:

1. Will there be a significant impact if this person says "Yes" or "No" to new initiatives and projects?

2. Is this person responsible for overall business strategy, or do they have business responsibility for solving a critical business problem (that you can solve)? Another way of asking this is: "Will this person get fired if this project / strategy / initiative fails?"

3. Do the end-users of your products report to this person, or does he represent their interests?

4. Is this person the functional leader of the team, business unit or division, with profit / loss responsibility?

5. Do people seek out this person's endorsement or expert opinion in areas that pertain to what you sell?

6. Is this person's influence greater than you might expect, given his position?

7. Can this person work around the company's policies or procedures to make things happen if he desires?

8. Is this person's support critical where important initiatives are considered?

9. Does this person sign-off on the financial justification for your project?

10. Will this person be measured on the success of your products?

Conventional wisdom says call high – try to get to the C-suite – but this isn't really always good advice, at least not as your sole relationship strategy. You need more information than someone's title to determine whether in fact they have influence. Rank does not equal influence and it is influence that you should care about.

Increasingly, particularly in large enterprise B2B commercial transactions, purchase decisions are made by buying committees. All of the individuals who are impacted by the purchase will likely have some say in the adjudication of who is the best supplier to meet their needs, and each vote will matter – though, of course, some will matter more than others.

In a Customer First world, the customer is not the company; it is the aggregate of the people who will be impacted by a buying decision. Each of these individuals will likely have an opinion based on personal experience, as well as on information they gather from the Internet and their peers in other companies. Because top-down decisions are decreasing in frequency, you will need to establish the 'what's in it for me?' for everyone on the buying committee. Then you must consider how you can make sure all their interests are aligned as you uncover their needs and how your solution can add value to their role.

In organizations where Procurement is a strategic function, the alignment of interests of the buying team falls within their remit, and in those cases they are often the facilitators of the compromise of the competing objectives of all of their internal stakeholders. This makes it easier for you – but cannot be relied on. Do your own research.

The important thing to remember though is that your customers, even those in the Inner Circle of their organizations, are increasingly looking to build consensus in their teams and they will look to those in their organization's Political Structure to guide them.

A good way to visualize this is with a Relationship Map (**Figure 56**), which helps you to track attributes of the individuals, including their power and Influence.

Figure 56: THE RELATIONSHIP MAP – 2

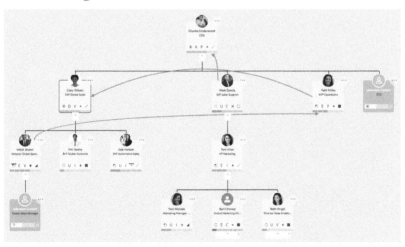

In **Figure 57** below you can see that I have highlighted that your focus area should be with the people on the right of the map (overlaid) because these people are those who influence the Decision Maker (Clara Wilson) and the Approver (Charles Underwood).

Figure 57: THE RELATIONSHIP MAP – 2 – FOCUS AREA

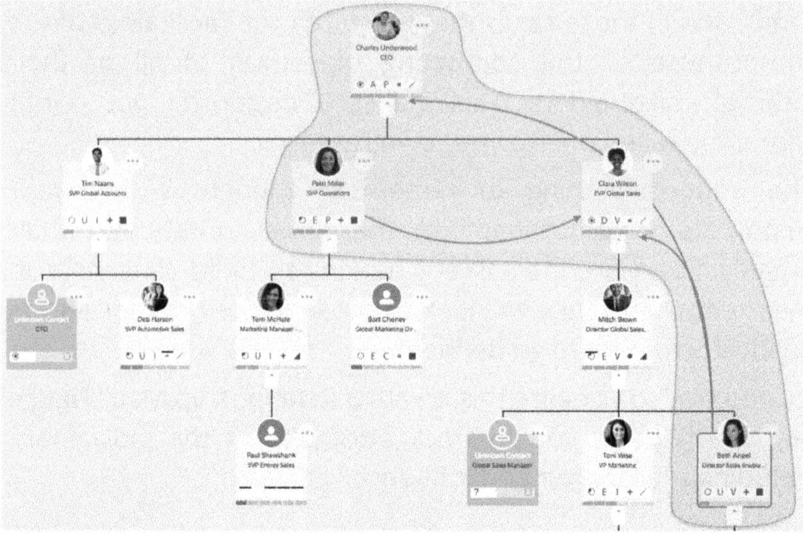

How Do They Think?

Once you have determined 'Who matters?" by assessing their Level of Influence, you next want to get a sense of the individual. As I related in *The Customer Culture Story* in the previous chapter, once you have a better understanding of a company's culture – as demonstrated by the aggregate behavior and perspectives of the individuals you engage with – your approach will be much more informed. Before you can change someone's mind, you have to look inside it.

I have found it useful to have a framework to know what to look for when assessing an individual's personal perspective. As you learn about each of the individuals on the buying committee, the framework provides you with a guide to determine what that means to your relationship strategy. You should determine *Decision Orientation* and *Adaptability to Change* from the personal perspective of each of the individuals.

Decision Orientation: The view you see is always dependent on where you are standing. How people make up their minds, come to a conclusion, and make a decision is shaped by their backgrounds, experiences and knowledge. In business, decision orientation is determined by the roles people play in a company as well as their personal backgrounds. Understanding an individual's decision orientation is critical to being able to relate to them, and build sustainable business relationships.

Anne is a good friend of mine. She is President of her company and has broad business experience. She understands and likes technology. She works a lot in supporting the sales and marketing activities in her business and can hold her own in most areas of business. At the core though, she is a finance person. She trained as an accountant, has worked as CFO, and is a master with Excel and financial analysis. While her perspective is broad, the primary lens though which she evaluates business propositions is a financial one. Knowing that is important to anyone looking to enter a business relationship with her. Even if your technology is amazing, and you've built a good personal relationship, at the end of the day, unless the numbers stack up and the ROI is clear, Anne is unlikely to support your business proposition.

Jim is another good friend of mine. He cares deeply about getting along with the people he works with and the customers and suppliers with whom he engages. Jim's ability to maintain contact with everyone he has worked with is second to none. His network is very expansive. Most people who have worked for him will say that he was the best boss they ever had. But if you let him down or behave in a way that he feels is unprofessional, or just not right, he will never want to work with you again. Jim doesn't have much interest in technology, and financial considerations in a deal are just guardrails. His personal perspective will always be governed by whether he wants to work with you. He cares deeply about the relationship aspect of any commercial engagement.

There are four types of decision orientation you should consider: Financial, Technical, Relationship and Business:

- A **Financial** orientation implies a primary focus on price, cost, and economics. While your product must be viable, numbers and negotiations will be key.
- A **Technical** focus is about product functionality and capability. Such individuals are often analytical and detail-oriented. Product demonstrations, benchmarks, and careful deliberation will be key.
- Someone with a **Relationship** orientation believes they are forming a business partnership and that you and your company are important to them. While your

product must be viable, support, trust, effort, and responsiveness will be important.

- A **Business** orientation takes a big picture view and this person can properly balance the technical, financial, and relationship issues. Their vision often extends beyond their company to include their customers, and their competition.

If you want to develop a strong relationship with your customer so that you can work collaboratively with them, knowing their inherent decision orientation bias is essential. That knowledge helps you understand what's important to them and guides how you present value.

Adaptability to Change: Merriam Webster defines change as: "to make different." It also categorizes the word 'change' as a verb. This of course implies motion, and we know that change is constant in the world of business. When you are solving a business problem for a customer you are in fact facilitating or creating change and, for your customer, that entails new actions, objectives and processes for a group or team of people. Each of the individuals with whom you are engaging will respond differently. The more you understand their personality the better you will understand what motivates them and whether the fear of change will be a barrier to progress.

As with Decision Orientation, having a framework to model Adaptability to Change helps categorize the people with whom you are working, and guides you to take the right actions to help them on their change journey:

- **Innovators** love to be first with the latest ideas. They are attracted to new solutions and products and will experiment with the solution. They are enthusiasts for NEW. But, innovators, while usually influential, rarely have budget. They can also be fickle – looking for instant gratification – and if you don't deliver quickly, they will lose interest and move on to the next shiny object.

- **Visionaries** are revolutionaries. They expect to achieve significant competitive advantage by being among the first. Visionaries are early adopters and often have funds that they can allocate to buy new solutions or products. However, often they will demand special modifications or improvements to a new solution, tailored to their specific needs.

- **Pragmatists,** sometimes called the 'early majority,' believe in evolution not revolution. With a low risk threshold, they adopt products and services with a proven track record of success including references from people they trust.

- **Conservatives** are pessimistic. They tend to question gaining value from investments in new solutions and to change only when pressed – when the only alternative is to be left behind.

- **Laggards** are the last to implement new solutions. They generally will do so only when there is no alternative. Laggards tend to doubt that new solutions or products will provide any value. I'd recommend selling around them if possible.

The ability to categorize each buyer into one of these discrete groups may seem difficult at first but should become obvious as you examine their:

- Track record for implementing new solutions
- Conversations with you and your team
- Interactions with your peers
- Office / technology environment.

Figure 58: BUYERS' ADAPTABILITY TO CHANGE

	What they want	What they buy	What to sell
Innovators	State-of-the art	Trials Tests	Product excellence Innovation
Visionaries	Revolution Recognition	Customized solution	Future competitive advantage
Pragmatists	Evolution Solve problems	Total solutions	Proven expertise in solving similar problems
Conservatives	Not to be left behind	Industry standards at low price with no risk	Return on Investment
Laggards	*Status quo*	Enhancements or extensions of existing systems	Investment protection

Figure 58 is a good reference to use to shape the conversation with each of the influencers in your target account. By understanding a buyer's adaptability to change, you will know what you should emphasize and where to seek support if your proposition doesn't quite gel.

What Is Your Current Relationship?

Now that you have figured out who matters (the Key Players) and how they think (their Decision Orientation and Adaptability to Change), you next need to assess whether they will be on your side and supportive as you work to build a relationship between your company and theirs. Do they have preference for you or an alternative provider?

This is where it gets a little tricky. To understand your Current Relationship, and the Relationship Gap as illustrated in the next section, you need to consider the context. You need to differentiate between the relationship that you have as it pertains to the overall account, and your relationship as it pertains to a specific opportunity. They might be the same, but there are reasons to consider why they might be different.

In the previous chapter I discussed the Level of Relationship. With the exception of the Trusted Advisor status, you only engage with Key Players after the customer exits the *Establish Initiatives* stage of the Customer Decision Cycle, and is at the *Initiate a Project* stage or later. This means you are primarily involved in opportunity pursuit at each of the other Levels of Relationship.

If a Key Player perceives you as a Problem Solver on the Business Relationship Pyramid, then he is doing so only in the context of the problem domain in which he believes you have capability and competence. For example, even though you have demonstrated expertise in deploying a CRM system, and the customer values your ability to help solve problems in that specific area, you might not even make the list of potential suppliers when the customer kicks off an initiative for a HR management system. If you have not communicated your value in that area, there is no reason to believe that you will still retain the *Problem Solver* badge.

Because of your constant access as a Trusted Advisor you never exit the Decision Cycle and consequently the Trusted Advisor relationship status is the only position on the Business Relationship Pyramid that definitively transcends both opportunity and account activities. To faithfully record your Current Relationship, you need to understand your *Preference with Key Players* in an opportunity pursuit as well as your position on the Business Relationship Pyramid.

Preference is from the customer's perspective and describes whether the customer has a greater liking for you than for alternatives. It can be defined as:

> Subjective assessment by the customer of you as a supplier *versus* alternative providers.

Preference with Key Players can be classified into the five categories listed in the table below.

Figure 59: PREFERENCE WITH KEY PLAYERS

	Description	Behavior
Mentor	A person who believes that your success is critical to their company or to them personally. A mentor will work to help you win by giving feedback, guidance, political insight, or competitive information. A mentor takes a personal interest in your success and will sell in your absence.	Works with you to develop and test your plan. Shares confidential company information. Actively sells in your absence. Links personal success with your success. Willing to be held accountable for implementing your solution. Openly states that your solution or company is superior.

	Description	Behavior
Supporter	A person who prefers your solution and thinks that you should win. A supporter will typically provide you with information or assistance, if you request. However, they may not be vocal in their support.	Works with you to develop a plan to adopt your solution. Provides you with information about other key players and about the competition's plan. Privately admits your solution or company is superior.
Neutral	A person who shows no preference. They could be ambivalent, or they may have chosen not to display their true feelings. They may not have decided, or you may not have demonstrated sufficient value to gain their open support.	Agrees that your company or solution is a potential fit. Invests time and energy to understand the capabilities of your solution and company. Understands / explains the Compelling Event. Provides information on the key business issues. Thinks a need or problem exists and agrees that a solution or change is desirable.
Non-supporter	A person who believes you shouldn't win and / or prefers an alternative to your solution: your competitor, an internal solution, or nothing at all.	Works with your competitor to develop a plan to adopt their solution. Provides your competitor with information about other key players. Provides your competitor with information about your solution and your plan. Privately admits that your competitor's solution or company is superior.
Enemy	A person who believes that your success will hurt their company or them personally. An enemy will make a special effort to cause you to lose. They may be a mentor to your competition.	Works with your competitor to develop and test their plan. Shares confidential company information with your competitor. Actively sells your competitor's solution, even in their absence. Links personal success with your competitor's plan. Willing to be held accountable for implementing your competitor's solution. Openly states that your competitor has the best solution.

The following 10 questions will get your brain working to assess the level of support you might expect from an individual and to determine whether they are friend or foe. (Hint: You are looking for a lot of *"Yes"* answers)

1. Does this person talk to others about the value your company can bring to their organization?
2. Has he been a willing reference for you with other customers?
3. Has he introduced / supported you in meetings with other senior influencers in his company?
4. When speaking with others in his company does he refer to you as his chosen business partner?
5. Does he share internal or competitive insights that can help you to strengthen your position?
6. Does he proactively advise you when issues arise in his organization that might affect your position?
7. Do you consider him a partner that you can count on to help you develop the value proposition for his business area?
8. Does he speak with Key Players about the value that you have brought to his company?
9. Does he look for your input on general issues that are not specifically related to your products?
10. Does he proactively come to you with ideas that might help you win?

Documenting your current relationship

To chart a path to your desired destination it is always good to know where you are. Documenting your *Current Relationship*, both in the context of the account and any active opportunity, provides clarity on the current state. If you have selected your account well, using the Ideal Customer Profile framework, you know the typical roles or titles in an organization with whom you need relationships.

As you assess your current Level of Relationship in an account it is important to consider that the aggregate of the Relationship Status that each person on your team has with his or her counterpart in the customer's organization is a representation of the Relationship Status between the two companies. For example, if you have just taken over an account, but the history between the two companies has been fractious because the customer perceives that your company has not delivered on its previous promises, then it is extremely unlikely that your initial Level of Relationship can be anything greater than Credible Source at best. This means that the account will only look to you as a source of information as it pertains to an opportunity that is already underway and will not look to you for strategic account advice. Conversely, if there is a Trusted Advisor relationship between someone in your company and a Key Player in the customer's organization, then you will benefit somewhat from the halo effect. That gives you a better place to start and you can build on that foundation. **Figure 60** – based on roles identified in your Ideal Customer Profile – provides an example of how to describe the current state.

Figure 60: RELATIONSHIP AND PREFERENCE – CURRENT STATE

ROLES	Current State (Example)	
	Relationship with Key Players	Preference of Key Players
VP Sales	Problem Solver	Supporter
Sales Operations	Trusted Advisor	Mentor
IT	Vendor	Non-Supporter
CMO	None / Vendor	Neutral
Customer Success	Credible Source	Neutral
L&D	None / Vendor	Neutral
Account Managers	Credible Source	Supporter
Sales Managers	Vendor	Neutral
CRM Admin	Vendor	Neutral

What Is the Relationship Gap?

Now that you have figured out your Current State you can map that to the Desired State. Your Desired State describes what you need to do to be successful in the account – which is dependently primarily on your Relationship, and also on the opportunity – which is influenced by Relationship, but more directly impacted by Preference.

Figure 61: RELATIONSHIP AND PREFERENCE – DESIRED STATE

RELATIONSHIP	Current State	Desired State	Gap
VP Sales	Problem Solver	Trusted Advisor	**1 Level**
Sales Operations	Trusted Advisor	Problem Solver	**-1 Level**
IT	Vendor	Credible Source	**1 Level**
CMO	None / Vendor	Credible Source	**1 Level**
Customer Success	Credible Source	Credible Source	-
L&D	None / Vendor	Credible Source	**1 Level**
Account Managers	Credible Source	Credible Source	-
Sales Managers	Vendor	Problem Solver	**2 Levels**
CRM Admin	Vendor	Credible Source	**1 Level**

As you know, being a Trusted Advisor takes time and effort, so you need to be selective in deciding:

- Which accounts your company wants to have Trusted Advisor status with (as an aggregate measure of the relationships between all of the people on your account team with all of the pertinent people in the account), and
- Who in the customer's organization merit the effort that it takes to develop a Trusted Advisor relationship.

Whenever you are deciding the Level of Relationship that you need, you always need to ask yourself: "Why is that the right level?" The higher you go up the Business Relationship Pyramid, the more resources you must apply to sustain that level. The lower you are, the fewer opportunities you have to shape requirements. Use the Customer Decision Cycle to assess whether you think that the person / role in the customer organization can establish initiatives, or if they are solely involved in negotiating contracts.

In **Figure 61** above the current Level of Relationship with the VP Sales is Problem Solver. That's not a bad place from which to start, but if the VP Sales is the person who sets the business strategy to respond to the business drivers impacting his company and establishes initiatives to drive growth in his organization, then you will need to be part of those early conversations.

In this example, the current Level of Relationship for Sales Operations is Trusted Advisor. If that is true, it means that you must be spending a lot of time there discussing potential initiatives. Perhaps on reflection you might determine that in fact the Level of Relationship needed for you to be successful here is only Problem Solver, so your investment of time and effort should reflect that.

For any account that you have selected to target (based on an Ideal Customer Profile) you should aim to at least be a Credible Source with each of the people who matter.

Perhaps the most significant discovery from doing the relationship gap analysis in this hypothetical situation is the gap for the Sales Managers. The current Level of Relationship is two levels away from where you need it to be. It may be that you need the Sales Managers to be advocates for you and you have identified that you have some work to do to be viewed as a Problem Solver.

Now let's look at the gap for Preference.

Figure 62: THE PREFERENCE GAP

PREFERENCE	Current State	Desired State	Gap
VP Sales	Supporter	Supporter / Mentor	-
Sales Operations	Mentor	Mentor	-
IT	Non-Supporter	Supporter	**2 Levels**
CMO	Neutral	Supporter	**1 Level**
Customer Success	Neutral	Supporter	**1 Level**
L&D	Neutral	Supporter	**1 Level**
Account Managers	Supporter	Supporter	-
Sales Managers	Neutral	Supporter	**1 Level**
CRM Admin	Neutral	Supporter	**1 Level**

Let me start by saying this: I never believe that someone is truly Neutral. It's rare that, if you said to someone that they had to pick between two vendors for a solution, they would be so paralyzed by indecision that they could not make a decision. So if you think a Key Player is Neutral, then you should put on your paranoid hat and assume he is a Non-Supporter. What's the worst that can happen? You might waste a little time. By assuming that Neutral means Non-Supporter you can then look to bridge to Supporter. Then you might indeed find that there were issues that needed to be resolved that you would have missed if you had not given the relationship gap some attention.

You might be surprised to see that I did not go straight to Mentor as the Desired State for my VP Sales role. Remember a Mentor is a Key Player who is selling on my behalf. If, in this example, the VP Sales is the 'main man' – not a technical term – then if he is a Mentor the deal would already be done. Also, if I am successful in elevating my Level of Relationship for him to Trusted Advisor he will by definition be a Mentor anyway.

This leads to a related topic that can help you to determine Desired State as it pertains to Preference, and that is Buying Role. I have listed and defined Buying Roles in **Figure 63** below.

Figure 63: BUYING ROLES – DEFINITIONS

BUYING ROLE	Definition
Approver	The person at a senior level who has the ultimate accountability for success of the project. They review the decision, bless it and typically release the funds. In large organizations, there may be multiple levels of approvers with dollar thresholds used to delineate their approval responsibility but they may not be the ultimate approver.
Decision Maker	Has the ability to commit the company to a vendor or to a certain strategic direction. They have accountability for the selection of the solution and / or vendor.
Evaluator	Has the ability to say "No," but they can't say "Yes." The best an Evaluator can do for you is to recommend your solution. Evaluators can block the competition or block you. Evaluators are formally assigned to the evaluation of a project (or an opportunity). They evaluate and accept based on defined standards.
User	Someone who will directly use your product or service or solution.

You really need to have positive preference – Supporter or Mentor status – with Approvers and Decision Makers. For example if the IT role in **Figure 62** above (Current State: Non-Supporter, Desired State: Supporter) turns out to be the Decision Maker in an opportunity, you will be less likely to be successful than if that Buying Role was occupied by Sales Operations (Current State: Mentor, Desired State: Mentor). It is also extremely unlikely that you can be successful in a deal if you don't have a Mentor. Others will refer to this a Champion or Coach, but whatever sobriquet you choose to use as a label for this role, you definitely need a Mentor, Champion or Coach to win.

Once you can put everyone in the right Buying Role for an opportunity you can use that information to inform the Desired State for Preference.

How Do You Bridge the Relationship Gap?

Wouldn't it be wonderful if, just like Google Maps, when you put in your desired destination, because it knows where you are, it can just map out how you get to your journey's end? Well, as you probably know, there are some intelligent software applications – for example, Altify (author's bias acknowledged – I was involved in designing a lot of the reasoning underpinning Altify's AI engine) that will take you a long way down the road. Even if you don't have an AI powered solution to help guide your journey, there are a few key principles that provide signposts to ease your path to bridging a relationship gap.

In essence, the key to elevating and expanding your relationships comes down to one key principle. You must create, measure and communicate value to the customer. Once again, context matters. If you have an existing relationship with a customer, you will already have had the opportunity to make a promise on which you could deliver, and then deliver on that promise. Often though, even when that they have previously delivered, sellers frequently do a poor job of communicating that value. If, for example, you deployed a HR Management solution to your customer that reduced the time to process job applicants by half, be sure not to keep it a secret. Make sure that you have captured the baseline data so that, when relevant, you can remind the customer of how hard it used to be to process job applicants. Their success is your success – just as when they have a problem with your solution, it is your problem. Don't forget to document customer successes. Your marketing team will love you if they can share them in the marketplace, but even if the customer does not want to share their success outside the four walls of the corporate HQ, make sure that everyone inside the walls of HQ knows that you delivered on your promise.

Buyers reward sellers who understand their business. You can't create or communicate value unless you can feel their pain. That takes work and research and all of the strategies described in *Chapter 9: Know Your Customer First*. Once you understand the customer's business you have the opportunity to leverage your own expertise and that of your company to expand their understanding of their business problem. Some methodologies refer to this as deepening the pain for the customer while another uses the more esoteric term of Rational Drowning, making the customer feel as if they are gasping for air. I am not a fan of either of these monikers. They both feel terribly vendor centric and a contrived way to position your value. I think a preferred approach is to consider what you would do, based on your knowledge, experience and expertise, if you were in their shoes. That forces you to 'get in their shoes' and walk with them. It forces you to consider the impact on their business if they make the right or wrong buying decisions and it illuminates dark spots in the buyer's mind where they have not yet seen what is possible. Your job is to shine a light, provide valuable insights into the business and into the market and guide them to see what is possible. Then they can connect their business priorities to potential solutions. That's one sure way to elevate your relationship.

The obvious behavioral factors apply. Always give more than you get to demonstrate that you want to add value. Don't wait until you need something from your customer or prospect before you send them that valuable research, the independent whitepaper (that is not selling your company), the story in the news about their competitor, examples of how others in similar situations have addressed the problems that they have, or the book review that you think might interest them. Always do what you say. Be respectful. Show up on time. Consider their interests first. And if they are selecting the wrong product from you, even if it means a bigger deal for you, advise them against it. If you want to become a Trusted Advisor, or if you want them to support you in a deal, you have to earn their trust. Trust starts with the first promise you make and ends with the first promise you break.

A Word About Trust in a Digital Age

Unfortunately, there is an increasing trust deficit in the world. The 2017 Edelman Trust Barometer reveals that trust is in crisis around the world:

> The general population's trust in all four key institutions — business, government, NGOs, and media — has declined broadly, a phenomenon not reported since Edelman began tracking trust among this segment in 2012.

Figure 64: THE DECLINE IN TRUST IN INSTITUTIONS

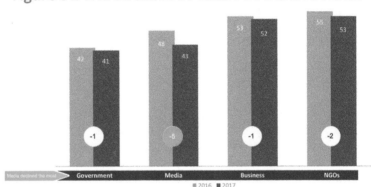

In many cases, companies and governments have defaulted on their obligations to customers and citizens, who feel ignored, poorly treated, and perceive that their concerns are rarely heard. In *Account Planning in Salesforce*, I examined the factors at the crux of sustained customer relationships and referred to this deficit in trust as the 'Trust Default.'

You have to counter the Trust Default. If you want to build a long term customer relationship you need to develop a deep level of trust with that customer. Customer acquisition is easier when you are starting from a foundation of trust. Once you have a customer, converting that customer to a loyal customer will happen only if the customer feels that she can depend on you. Unless you achieve that level of trust your customer will quickly become a former customer. Trust is the fulcrum upon which every customer relationship pivots. Trust is a valuable currency that must be earned, but never spent. Trust is built one step at a time, and unless protected, can be blown away in a moment.

There is cause for considerable concern that people's use of the Internet is a major contributor to the Trust Default. When the Internet was designed, it was not with an eye to the trolls and the abusers. As Vinton Cerf, one of the creators of Internet protocols, put it: "We didn't focus on how you could wreck this system intentionally."

According to Pew Research, when looking at trust in the Digital Age, the future of trust is uncertain. Six themes emerged from their extensive research:

1. Trust will strengthen because systems will improve and people will adapt to them and more broadly embrace them.
2. The nature of trust will become more fluid as technology embeds itself into human and organizational relationships
3. Trust will not grow, but technology usage will continue to rise as a 'new normal' sets in.
4. Some say blockchain[25] will help; some expect its value to be limited.
5. The less-than-satisfying current situation will not change much in the next decade.
6. Trust will diminish because the Internet is not secure and powerful forces threaten individual's rights.

The Internet has allowed for entirely new kinds of relationships and clusters of communities in which trust must

---

[25] Blockchain: a digital ledger in which transactions made in bitcoin or other cryptocurrencies are recorded chronologically and publicly.

be negotiated and developed in unfamiliar ways with unknown entities potentially doing nefarious things with our private information. In a world exploding with information of uncertain provenance, the Internet acts as a conduit for data compromise, scams and bad behavior. None of this causes our potential partners in business to default to a trusting relationship – hence the Trust Default.

The opportunity is for those who promise, exhibit, and exemplify good behavior to rise to the very top in a world where increasingly the winner takes all. That's another reason to pursue Trusted Advisor status with your customers.

Conclusion

Gaining access to the Key Players is critical. But walking through their doorway will be fruitful only when you have the support of the people around them and when your sense of the personal and company culture is well-developed. Then you can reflect that in how you shape the conversation.

When executed well, a strategy that blends people and their problems is far more likely to succeed. It will provide you with the ability to develop lasting relationships, and uncover and develop many new opportunities while delivering optimum value for your customer.

It is surprising to many people that customers are willing to work with you this way – but being a customer isn't as easy as you might think. When the customer makes that buying decision, we know that the risk shifts from the supplier to the customer, and the impact on the customer of a poor buying decision is usually greater than the impact on the salesperson of a lost sale.

For a customer to be comfortable, she must be sure that the supplier has a deep comprehension of her (sometimes unstated) needs. She has to believe in the relationship. In a corporate context, personal and company motives sometimes collide, or at least bring with them varying nuances of aspiration, and a panoply of potential wants and needs explodes. Customers and suppliers, sometimes unknowingly, share the consequent anxiety when they meet in the un-choreographed buy-sell dance. The only safe path though that mélange is one paved with value added relationships and a common shared vision of success.

Each customer will be different. Some will want to lead the buy-sell interaction; others are prepared to follow the direction of a trusted supplier. More are at their most comfortable when working in collaboration with their trusted supplier – and it's this last category that is most common, and certainly most productive, for both buyer and seller alike. That's the seat that you can choose to take.

CHAPTER 8:
THE EXECUTIVE SPONSOR: THEIR ROLE IN LARGE ACCOUNTS

The Case for the Executive Sponsor

In many sales organizations one of the most under-utilized assets is the Executive Management Team. When deployed effectively and with precision through a well-designed and consistently applied Executive Sponsor Program, companies can achieve deeper strategic relationships and an uncommon level of value alignment with their key customers. This results in accelerated value creation for you and your customer. An executive swooping in to help close a deal is not an Executive Sponsor Program – it goes much deeper than that. It's about the long game.

The most senior people in your company should be most conversant with the market in which you operate. They should be intimately familiar with your company's unique strengths (and weaknesses), its long term vision and the value you deliver to customers. Because they are at the nucleus of the organization, they are the recipients of distilled insights from the rest of the company, thereby gaining a richly textured and broad appreciation of what makes the company work. Their role is to guide the company's direction and often learn about the future trends in the market in which you operate in briefings from industry analysts, consultants and other experts.

The executives in the business, more so than other operating roles, consider the bigger issues: the competitive landscape, the economic, political and societal developments that inform future company strategy. They are most likely to be 'in the know' with respect to technological or other innovations that are in the melting pot. By function of their title and seniority they network with their peers in other organizations who operate in the market ecosystem, gaining water-cooler context and expanding their knowledge of customer trends and behaviors.

In most cases senior executives have extensive tenure in the business. On their journey to the senior role they have gathered tribal knowledge, experience of executive level customer engagements, stories of success and failure, and experiential best practices. They likely started in a more junior role in a specific functional area in the business. As they honed their craft, earning their stripes as a frontline contributor, they progressed to a management role, broadening their experience of how your business works and how you deliver value to your customers. It is increasingly common in modern organizations for successful executives to have assumed different roles and diverse areas of responsibility during their time with the business. On each step of their journey they learn more and gain a deeper understanding of what makes your company successful. As they progress to the senior ranks, building on their foundation of knowledge and competence, each experience they gain increases their proficiency and adds different flavors to their deepening appreciation of what tastes and smells good.

For executives who have traveled this path, gaining insights from executive quarterly business reviews and internal company reports, accumulating a treasure of industry perspective and learning first-hand the recipe for success, this rich tapestry woven from these disconnected but interrelated threads drives a conscious competence in all things company related. It serves as a compass by which they can guide and direct customer interaction, representing your company from a basis of informed perspective. Combined with the strength of the title – executives in your customer's company are more receptive to meeting executives from your company than someone from your company with a less senior title; that's just how it is – the senior executive is an asset that should be leveraged with your most important customers and prospects. They are one more important ingredient to add to your recipe for success. Think about it like this: it's as if you are adding garnish to an already flavorsome dish.

The Executive Sponsor Program Challenge

For an Executive Sponsor Program to work, it must first of all be a program: a series of strategically crafted objectives, activities and measures, understood by your internal team – the executives in your organization, the account manager who is responsible for the account, and all of the other customer facing employees in the business who interact with the customer – and the customer team, their executives and operational employees. Executives who participate in the program must also be held accountable, to the account team and to a broader group of executives.

An executive swooping in to help close a deal, save a customer, or just thank them for their business is not an Executive Sponsor Program. Fundamentally an Executive Sponsor Program is about elevating trusted relationships between your company and the customer. Like any interaction that is based on trust, it takes time to nurture and develop. A trusted relationship cannot be created if the primary focus is just to close a deal. That is not the time to initiate the relationship. An Executive Sponsor Program is a long game initiative, not reactive but proactive, and it requires a strategic plan and committed resources. For it to be successful it also requires commitment and accountability from the customer's executives.

But here's the reality. Executives are busy. They have a day job. Unless they are directly involved in the sales function of their business, they don't wake up every day wondering how to progress a relationship with your key customers. If you are a software company, for example, your CTO is fully consumed with product quality, the pressure of shipping deadlines, the constant battle to hire and retain engineering talent, and when he or she has time to stop and think strategically, the CTO is developing strategies to refine or redesign the technical architecture of the product to accommodate future development plans.

Unless the executive – CTO, CFO or CEO – is a fervent customer evangelist type of leader by their personal nature, they will not naturally gravitate to the behaviors that proactively build long term customer relationship *before* they are needed. You may need to enable executives who normally are not customer facing with further skills to optimize their contribution to the Executive Sponsor Program. (see *Enabling the Executive* below)

Executives in the customer organization have a similar profile. They too are busy, and will not necessarily be prepared to engage with you in an Executive Sponsor Program. It is likely that you are not the only vendor making the same ask of the same customer executive, so how do you get them to choose you? The challenge is to create a program that is truly valuable to the customer executive and articulate it in a manner that gets them excited. The bar is high.

Unfortunately sellers generally have not created an expectation of value creation in the mind of the buyer. According to Altify's research study *Inside the Buyer's Mind* most buyers don't believe that sellers add value. Executives, more than any others, dislike being sold to – they are looking for valuable business conversations. The Forrester report *Are Salespeople Prepared for Executive Conversations?* states that only 36 percent of executives believe that their meetings with a salesperson are valuable. So why will the engagement with the executive from your company, as opposed to the salesperson, be any different?

Many companies assume that customers appreciate increased attention, especially attention from senior executives. But that is possibly a somewhat arrogant view, assuming that, because your executives are willing to spend time with the customer's executives, the customer executives will prioritize that engagement over other priorities. You can't possibly know what else the customer executive has on his or her plate, so unless your company has earned that priority position, you are better off to expect that you have an uphill climb ahead to gain that slice of time. An executive's most valuable currency is their time, and unless you can clearly explain the value in their participation in your Executive Sponsor Program – justified in terms of return for effort and leading to a net positive impact on their project, their personal advancement, their team's goals and the benefit to their company, they will likely spend the time elsewhere.

At the start of this section I said that, for an Executive Sponsor Program to work, it must first of all be a program: a series of strategically crafted objectives, activities and measures. Measurement is critical but not always easy. Activity measurement can be useful, and in some cases companies who run an Executive Sponsor Program will set a goal for the number of meetings between the executives. I'd suggest however that it is better to focus on the meetings that count rather than focus on the count of the meetings. The goal of your Executive Sponsor Program should be to elevate trusted relationships, improve customer satisfaction and loyalty, increase strategic alignment and drive incremental pipeline and revenue.

Revenue is easy to measure but is a lagging indicator and one that is hard to attribute to the Executive Sponsor Program. Incremental revenue happens when you have better executive relationships, strategic alignment and improved customer satisfaction. Designing your program with evidential measures of these metrics will serve you well. I will show you later how to do this using a very simple model.

Beginning with the end in mind – incremental pipeline revenue through trusted relationships, strategic alignment and customer satisfaction – will help to define the leading indicators that will guide you to monitor progress and course correct as necessary. It requires some disciplined thought and honest introspection to arrive at the right metrics, but it is definitely worth the effort. Without this framework you are likely to stray off the path.

Designing the Program

Executive customer visits are often clumsy attempts to close a deal that the account manager has not been able to close on their own. These types of meetings often do more harm than good; the account manager is undermined, the executive is relegated to the position of salesperson (or sales manager) and the customers can rightly feel offended if the only time they get attention from the executive is when the executive is focused on selling them something. We know by now that this is not the path to success.

There are five foundational elements of an effective Executive Sponsor Program:

1. Program ownership
2. Selecting the accounts
3. Matching executive sponsors to accounts
4. Role definition
5. Measurement.

Program ownership: The position of the Executive Sponsor Program owner varies across different organizations. In some cases it reports to Sales, in others to Marketing or Customer Success, and it can in many cases report directly to the CEO. The last makes most sense in my opinion as the customers who are selected to be part of the program typically represent a disproportionately high percentage of the company's total revenue and the relationships are likely to be strategic in nature.

This further implies that the CEO must have direct input into or oversight of the Executive Sponsor Program design and execution, thereby communicating the strategic nature of the program to the rest of the organization.

Selecting the accounts: Your Executive Sponsor Program should be reserved for the accounts that are most valuable –

today and into the future – to your business. Strategic value, current revenue, account retention, and growth potential are factors that you should consider. Strategic value can go beyond direct financial measures. The account may be a lighthouse customer in a new industry, a well-known brand that other companies follow, or a very competitive account that you are looking to maintain to keep competitors at bay.

You should identify the accounts to whom you can add the most value in the medium term and long term. There are some customers for whom you will deliver disproportionate value. These are the accounts for whom you will most easily gain strategic alignment and thereby achieve accelerated revenue growth.

There is also the customer's perspective to consider. How important are you to them? Buyers re-evaluate their supplier relationships continuously to assess the value they receive or their organization's dependency on different vendors. Using something like the Kraljic Matrix (see **Figure 65** below), developed by Peter Kraljic to segment suppliers, your customer will place you in one of the quadrants in the matrix to reflect your profit (or revenue) impact on their business and the risk associated discontinuity of supply.

If you understand the customer's viewpoint it will help you to make the decision as to whether this customer should be in your Executive Sponsor Program, and whether they will be willing to participate. When you are placed in either the *Strategic* or *Bottleneck* quadrants, it is likely that to limit their risk the customer will want to be close to you and engage in your Executive Sponsor Program. Because you're not delivering high impact to them in the *Bottleneck* quadrant, you might not deem them to be a suitable candidate. Where you are delivering high impact, in the *Leverage* quadrant, but the customer views you as a commodity, you may want to engage the customer through the Executive Sponsor Program to better demonstrate your unique value and move towards the *Strategic* quadrant.

Figure 65: THE EXECUTIVE SPONSOR PROGRAM – RISK AND IMPACT

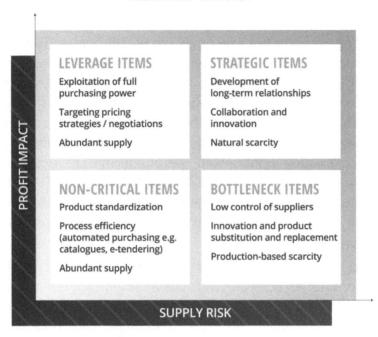

Not every account can or should be included in your Executive Sponsor Program. The value of an Executive Sponsor Program lies in large part in its exclusivity. So you need to ask whether the Executive Sponsor Program can add value to a particular account.

One final question that you should ask yourself before you put an account on the Executive Sponsor Program list: is the executive necessary to achieve the optimum value from the account? In a limited set of cases your account managers will have achieved all or most of the critical measures of success on their own. If that's the case you should reserve the executive for an account where the executive's presence will make a material difference. This may well be part of your strategic go-to-market approach, based on your Ideal Customer Profile, and effective market / account segmentation.

Matching executive sponsors to accounts: Selecting the right executives to participate is a critical first step in executing a successful Executive Sponsor Program. Typically the executive should be at Vice President level or above. The most important requirement however when selecting and matching executives for the program is that there is a good fit between the executive and the executives in the account. Consider cultural compatibility, executive style, proximity of location, existing relationship, pertinent market expertise, domain knowledge that will be considered valuable by the target customer executive, experience with similar customers, and any other common linkage between the customer executive and your executive.

The account manager should have greatest insight to the needs of their account and thus has an important role to play in selecting the executive sponsor for their customers. The relationship between the account manager and their own executive will be a key success driver of the program in that particular account. It is critical that there is a level of mutual trust and respect between the account manager who is in effect the quarterback in the account and the executive sponsor who is the coach.

Each executive sponsor should have responsibility for no more than three accounts. Because each engagement requires significant time and effort, and the executive has a separate full-time role, it is unwise to expect the executive to be able to commit the time and resources to more than three executive sponsor engagements. Exceptions to this rule may occur where the executive is directly involved in sales as their primary function.

Role definition: The executive sponsor's role is to position and represent the company to the customer. The executive sponsor should focus on the customer's industry, market dynamics and business strategy and how the customer's strategy can be advanced with help from your company. They should take a holistic company perspective and not focus on a specific product or a service. The customer needs to not only believe in your solution, which is the account manager's responsibility, but also in the company, which is part of the executive's role. The executive must not take the place of the account manager but seek to build the currency and credibility of the account manager. (See *The Role of The Executive Sponsor*, *The Role of The Account Manager*, *The Role of The Customer*, and *The Role of the Program* below).

Measurement: The purpose of the Executive Sponsor Program is:

- To establish your company as a trusted advisor to the senior executives in the customer organization
- To achieve strategic alignment between the two companies as it pertains to the business problems that you solve
- To increase customer satisfaction
- To enable business growth for the customer through the broader application of your solutions.

This results in more sales opportunities and will ultimately increase your revenue.

Figure 66 provides a suggested list, by category, of the KPIs to measure and to assess the progress of an Executive Sponsor Program.

Figure 66: THE EXECUTIVE SPONSOR PROGRAM – KEY PERFORMANCE INDICATORS

Category	Key Performance Indicators (Measure Improvement)
Trusted Advisor Status	Customer asks your advice on general industry matters, not just about the solution you are selling. You have continuous access to the most senior executives in the customer organization. Customers seeks your advice on projects to initiate. Customer invites you to collaborate with them in writing an RFP. Customer proactively calls you if there are developments in their organization that might impact your company. The executives have a personal relationship that transcends the business relationship.
Strategic Alignment	You have a deep understanding of the customer's business needs. Customer's executives actively engage in business reviews, discussing the relationship between the two companies. Customer engages in your Customer Advisory Board or otherwise contributes to your strategic direction. You help the customer measure the Return on Investment for your solutions and you consider yourself responsible for the outcome. You have an agreed multi-year strategic direction that aligns your solutions with the customer's strategic goals. The customer invests appropriate resources to ensure the successful deployment of your solution. The customer is willing to try new solutions from your company to help you improve them before you launch to the market.

Category	Key Performance Indicators (Measure Improvement)
Customer Satisfaction	Customer is willing to act as a reference for your company. Customer will actively provide you with referrals. Your Net Promoter Score (from the customer) is improving. Your solution is being fully utilized as intended. Customer expands their usage of your solution. Customer relationship health or risk score.
Pipeline and Revenue Growth	Your pipeline of business for new business is increasing. The renewals opportunities in your pipeline are healthy. With the customer you have identified opportunities in new areas of the customer's company. With the customer you have identified opportunities for new solutions that the customer has not bought from you before. The revenue from the customer is increasing.

As mentioned previously, the Revenue component is a lagging indicator. Revenue should be measured and you should definitely have revenue goals in the account plan – but the most impactful KPIs for the Executive Sponsor Program should focus on the other areas. In many cases there will already be progress against some of these KPIs in certain managed accounts, but with the Executive Sponsor Program you should be able to achieve performance improvement.

The Role of the Executive Sponsor

There can be no confusion about account ownership. Even though the executive might be the most senior person involved with the customer account, they are not the most important person on the team. That badge belongs to the account manager, who is the person responsible for the success of the account. The executive sponsor is just a tool, albeit a powerful and strategic one, for the account manager to use. Assuming that your organization has account plans in place for your key accounts, whoever owns the account plan and is responsible for keeping the plan up-to-date owns the account. If the account manager does not develop and maintain the account plan, then the executive might question whether the account should be assigned to someone else.

Before I get into what the executive sponsor should do – there are a few common pitfalls to avoid:

- The executive sponsor may feel ownership for the success of your company's engagement with the account. That's a good thing. A passionately engaged sponsor can be energizing for the account team. But the role of the account manager needs to be respected. The executive sponsor should never try to take over leadership of the account or the account team. Similarly the line-management of the account manager lies with his or her direct manager and not with the sponsor.

- One of the benefits of having an executive sponsor in an account is the potential to elevate trusted relationships and have higher-order business conversations. However, if the executive sponsor meets all of the same people, gets involved in the operational details of the relationship and talks about all of the same issues as the rest of the account team – then the power of the sponsor is lost. The executive sponsor should never get involved in operational issues like detailed pricing terms, product feature requests, or project planning except where the executive from the customer organization has escalated a problem to the executive sponsor.

- The executive should never visit a customer without the account manager's knowledge and should certainly not make unilateral decisions. Not only does it send the wrong message to the customer, it misses an opportunity to build the account manager's value in the account. Undermining or sidelining the account manager also places an extra burden on the executive sponsor to take personal responsibility for any follow-up actions.

- For companies who are just beginning an Executive Sponsor Program there is often a surge of great excitement and interest from executives to get involved. But remember the Executive Sponsor Program is a long game initiative. An executive must never start as executive sponsor and then lose interest in the account. That behavior will do more damage than good.

Having got the 'Do Not Do These Things' list out of the way, let's look at what we *do* want to see from the executive sponsor.

The executive sponsor's activities should be defined in the context of the categories of Key Performance Indicators:

- Trusted Advisor status
- Strategic alignment
- Customer satisfaction
- Pipeline and revenue growth.

Consider *Internal* responsibilities – inside your organization, and *External* responsibilities – those that involve the customer.

Figure 67: THE INTERNAL RESPONSIBILITIES OF THE EXECUTIVE SPONSOR

Commitment	Commit to the role for the account for a minimum of one year and ideally for two to three years. Execute the role solely in line with the Objectives, Strategies and Actions recorded in the account plan.
Strategic Input	Actively participate in the account strategy and review progress with the team on a regular (monthly or quarterly) basis. Ensure that the strategy being deployed to serve the customer is aligned with the company strategy. Always check that the account activities align with your company's overall business strategy, making sure key accounts contribute to rather than deflect from corporate goals.
Communication	Have regular communication with the account manager. Feedback to the account manager after each customer engagement. Strategic accounts should be visible to the executive leadership of the company. The executive sponsor should be able to explain what is happening in an account to internal executives. Evangelize the value of the program on a regular basis, taking advantage of opportunities to share successes. Doing so serves the dual purpose of best practice sharing and reinforces the program's importance across the broader organization.
Customer Advocate	Advocate internally on behalf of the customer to ensure the customer receives preferential treatment commensurate with their status as a key account.
Mentor	Act as a mentor to the account manager both in terms of the strategy of customer engagement and how to marshal internal resources to serve the customer. (This should not be confused with acting as a line manager for the account manager – that is the responsibility of their direct manager).

The natural inclination when first contemplating an Executive Sponsor Program is to immediately start thinking about how to engage with the customer. However, unless the executive sponsor has a solid understanding of the Internal responsibilities per **Figure 67** above, he or she will not be equipped to assume the External responsibilities as set out in **Figure 68** below.

Figure 68: THE EXTERNAL RESPONSIBILITIES OF THE EXECUTIVE SPONSOR

Elevate Relationships	In line with the account plan strategy develop relationships with senior executives in the customer account.
Joint Business Planning	Participate in any QBRs that the account team would have with their customer where the customer executive is present. Chair the annual review with the customer.
Strategic Input	In partnership with the account manager, work with the customer to develop a long term strategic plan for the customer partnership. With the support of the account manager, remain current in the customer's industry and business issues.
Communication	Engage with customer executive at least four times annually, including at least two face-to-face meetings which might include QBRs.
Customer Advocate	Be a point of escalation for the customer in circumstances where the customer is unhappy or is not receiving what they perceive as appropriate service levels from the account team.

The Role of the Account Manager

When account managers are responsible for the results from key accounts they will usually see value in having their account participate in the Executive Sponsor Program. The account manager's buy-in is critical and having a clear set of responsibilities will help ensure effective use of the executive sponsor's time.

The account manager should wake up every day thinking about how to make progress in the account – this is their role. On the other hand the executive sponsor has many other things occupying her mind. To make the most of the Executive Sponsor Program the account manager should take responsibility for helping the executive sponsor to be effective in their role.

The account manager therefore should manage the involvement of the executive sponsor proactively rather than the other way around. The account manager needs to manage the executive sponsor's engagement to the benefit of the account and in line with the strategies set out in the account plan.

Figure 69: THE RESPONSIBILITIES OF THE ACCOUNT MANAGER

Account Plan	Create the account plan that sets out the current situation in the account, the goals for the current and future years, and Objective, Strategies and Actions to achieve the goals. Add the executive sponsor to the account plan. Engage the team to deliver on tasks and keep the plan up-to-date. Solicit input from the executive sponsor on account strategy. Coordinate quarterly plan reviews with the executive sponsor. Identify potential risks in the plan and highlight issues to address.
Communication	Brief the executive sponsor on material activity in the account. Apprise the executive on market changes that impact the customer. Update the team on changes in the customer's business or organization. Provide feedback to the program owner on the efficacy (or otherwise) of the program.
Call Plan	In advance of every customer meeting, the account manager should present a call plan / executive briefing to the executive sponsor. The call plan should describe current status, meeting objectives, top-of-mind issues for the customer, and the roles in the meeting for the account manager and the executive sponsor. Debrief after the call, record the actions and update the account plan with the outcome of the meeting.

Manage & Coach	Coach the executive sponsor on how she can be most impactful. Remind the sponsor of responsibilities per the account plan. Create a cadence for executive visits, QBRs, and account reviews. Hold the executive sponsor accountable to her commitments to the customer. (When the executive sponsor is not delivering on her commitment, leverage the program owner).
Ask for Help	When conflicting priorities get in the way of access to internal resources or support the account manager should leverage the executive sponsor to facilitate action.

The Role of the Customer

The Executive Sponsor Program cannot be successful without customer collaboration. It is imperative that you are able to articulate the value of the program to the customer so that they see the value of applying extra resources of their own to their engagement with you.

In the first instance you may need to validate that you have earned the right to make that request. Just because you have identified an account as a potentially large source of revenue for your company does not mean that you can credibly invite the customer to participate in your Executive Sponsor Program. Unless there is some substantive history between your company and the account you should question whether, from the customer's perspective, the relationship with your company is sufficiently strategic for them to allocate executive time. You may have some preparatory work to do in the account before it is a valid Executive Sponsor Program candidate.

Assuming that the customer you have identified is a valid candidate for the Executive Sponsor Program you should then invite the customer to participate. The invitation should clearly describe the exclusive nature and value of the program, why they have been selected, the benefits to their company and team, and your expectations of their participation.

Figure 70: THE CUSTOMER'S COMMITMENT TO THE EXECUTIVE SPONSOR

Executive Access	The customer agrees to support you in gaining access to the executives in the customer organization who are impacted by your solution and who have responsibility for the business areas impacted by your solution.
Joint Business Planning	Make available the appropriate resources to participate in QBRs. Provide input on operational issues to determine improvements to the support that your company can provide to the customer. Provide honest feedback on the relationship between the two companies. Provide support to remove bottlenecks or logjams in their organization that are obstacles to progress.
Strategic Planning	Work with your company to develop a long term strategic plan for mutual benefit. Discuss long term business goals and changes in the customer's industry. Participate in your Customer Advisory Board meetings.
Communication	Engage with your company at least four times each year, including two face-to-face meetings.

In *Chapter 7: A Structure for Building Relationships*, I discuss when you might want to invest time and effort to become a Trusted Advisor to a customer. The same principles apply here. You might feel that the customer is strategic to you, but you can't assume that the customer feels the same way, and that gap needs to be explored.

The Role of the Program Owner

It is important to recognize that the Executive Sponsor Program must be a 'program' in all senses of the word. Common to other change initiatives it must have goals, a clear communication strategy and a framework to measure success. The program owner is responsible for the successful delivery of the whole of the proposed change so that you will realize the anticipated benefits as measured by the KPIs described earlier. That involves co-ordination of the program's components and people, the management of their interdependencies, and the mitigation of the risks and issues that will inevitably arise from time to time.

Program owners, while responsible for the whole program, cannot do all the tasks themselves. Apart from the account manager and the executive sponsor they might need the support of Sales Operations for measurement and system support, the CEO to encourage engagement where necessary, sales leadership to champion the program, and Marketing to help with some of the internal and external messaging of the program. As the Executive Sponsor Program is only one part of the overall account plan and strategy, the program owner will also have access to other members of the account team, including most importantly the Customer Success team.

The program owner has a central role to play in:

- **Program set-up:** Getting the program off the ground
- **Program execution:** Ensuring it is running well
- **Program measurement:** Reviewing progress and outcomes.

If the Executive Sponsor Program is not meeting its goals for a specific account, the program owner should highlight this at one of the regularly scheduled account review meetings. These meetings should happen on a regular cadence, monthly or at least quarterly, to provide an opportunity for the account team and the executive sponsor to identify problem areas and come up with remediation strategies.

See *Your Executive Sponsor Program Plan* for details of the program owner's responsibilities.

Enabling the Executive Sponsor

Just because an executive from your company has been selected to participate in the program doesn't mean that they are fully equipped to play the role. This can be particularly true in the case of executives who do not normally engage in customer facing roles. While the Executive Sponsor Program is not a sales call or a customer success call, the end result that you are looking for is elevated trusted relationships, strategic alignment and increased customer satisfaction, all leading to revenue growth. The program owner should ensure that the executive is armed with both the knowledge and the ability to represent the company's values to the customer and also provide value to the account.

It is generally true that the most senior people in your company should be most conversant with the market in which you operate. They should be intimately familiar with your company's unique strengths (and weaknesses), its long term vision and the value you deliver to customers. But that is not always the case. Although they are likely to consider the bigger issues in your business that inform future company strategy, they may not have experience of how to translate that knowledge into a meaningful engagement with a customer that progresses the relationship between the two companies.

For those executives who are not normally engaged in sales it would be helpful for the head of sales to bring the executive through the **life cycle of a deal**. A senior marketing or product management could lead a session on **industry and market trends**. You need to validate that the executive sponsor is well-versed in the **corporate story**, the **long term strategy**, and the **differentiated value** of the products and solutions of relevance to the customer. Equipping these executives with detailed reference **case studies** will help

231

build their font of knowledge. These general knowledge areas can be effectively supplemented for a specific account through the information in the **account plan**.

Those that occupy that rarified space of 'best-in-class' sales transformation programs deliver exceptional value to their companies. Without exception, the leader driving the change is passionate, charismatic, dedicated to the cause, and the guiding light for the rest of the participants in the program. One such leader is Glenn Davis, a senior executive in the healthcare industry. Glenn cares deeply about improving healthcare. He has his own personal reasons that underpin his passion to improve quality for all stakeholders: those who need healthcare, those who provide the service and those who support the healthcare system. That's the perspective that Glenn brought to his global sales transformation program.

Glenn understands better than most how Executive Sponsor Programs work, and how by looking ahead you can plan a program that makes a difference to your company's revenue, your clients' revenue and the success of your client's clients. As I was writing this chapter on the role of the executive sponsor, I asked Glenn to share his wisdom on the key principles that he followed to deliver a successful program.

I have packaged Glenn's insight into what I call 'Glenn Davis' 7 Key Principles of Enduring Executive Sponsor Programs.' In his words these principles are:

A Practitioner's Perspective
Glenn Davis' 7 Key Principles of Enduring Executive Sponsor Programs

1. **Understand the why and the what of the program:** Why do you need an Executive Sponsor Program in the first place? Save clients? Help clients? Grow clients? Then what are the metrics of success for the program? Revenue gained? LCV? NPS? Write a Program Charter to serve as the true north of the program and include *the why and the what* of the program.

2. **Identify targeted clients for the program using data:** Use data with your Charter to guide your senior executives to identify the right clients to engage in the program. A deep understanding of the goal of the program and the data elements required to find clients who can help achieve the goal are critical to the success of the program.

3. **Clearly define the roles and responsibilities of the executive sponsor and the client executive who owns the relationship:** The executive sponsor must not be viewed by the client as a substitute for the client executive who owns the relationship, but should be seen by the client as also reliant on the client executive for the day-to-day functioning of the relationship. The executive sponsor functions to align the firm's strategic direction to aid the client's best interest.

4. **Develop a training, development and onboarding program for executive sponsors:** "We are always calling on the same people." "We don't gain consistent results." These are two of the biggest complaints I have heard. The myth exists that executives know how to be executive sponsors. That's simply untrue. They may not know the specific program metrics, may not know much about a given client, or may not know the client team. Closing these knowledge gaps is a key step in any successful program.

233

5. **Executive Sponsor Programs must exist in a larger context of a client engagement program:** Other programs associated with the engagement model might include: a client planning process; quarterly executive reviews of client progress to plan; a Net Promoter Score focused on not only NPS but driving activities to improve NPS. This approach to executive sponsorship and client engagement more broadly drives deeper, more lasting, more prosperous client relationships.

6. **Executive sponsors should be incentivized to create stated metrics for clients assigned to them:** These roles can be the proverbial 'off the side of the desk assignment.' This may indicate that complete organizational alignment has not been achieved for the Executive Sponsor Program. Executives are extremely busy; if their compensation is not at stake it may be hard for them to dedicate their time and efforts to a single or a few client relationships.

7. **The CEO must be briefed at least quarterly on the success of the overall program:** There is an underlying assumption that the Executive Sponsor Program is extremely important – after all we are investing the precious time of executives in the engagement. Thus a routine, metrics based review of the program with the CEO is a critical lever in ensuring the success of the program.

Your Executive Sponsor Program Plan

Like any new initiative involving many interrelated components and multiple stakeholders it is best to start small and think big. The CEO's sponsorship of the ESP is critical – as is the role of the program owner. Work through as many of the core elements of the program as possible before kicking it off. Focus most specifically on the value to the customer and seek general support from your own executive team. Then select your initial Executive Sponsor Program customers and pay a lot of attention to how to match the executive sponsor to those accounts. Ensure that the account manager is on board and that everyone is clear as to their roles and responsibilities and the KPIs that will be measured. Then as you learn from these first few Executive Sponsor Program engagements, make sure that you communicate any refinements to future participants.

There are three components to the plan for the Executive Sponsor Program:

1. **Program set-up:** Getting the program off the ground
2. **Program execution:** Ensuring it is running well, and
3. **Program measurement:** Reviewing progress and outcomes

The detail of each component is listed in the Figures that follow.

Your Executive Sponsor Program will be transformative for both you and your customer, but the worst thing to do is to start and not follow through. Do the upfront work and then commit to it – it will definitely be worth the effort.

Figure 71: THE EXECUTIVE SPONSOR PROGRAM ACTION PLAN – PROGRAM SET-UP

Topic	Description	Owner
Vision and Goals	Set out the vision for the Executive Sponsor Program and outline your aspirational goals. Quantify your goals around relationships, strategic alignment, customer satisfaction, and pipeline and revenue growth.	PO, CEO
Value Proposition	There are two distinct value propositions to consider: (1) Why is the ESP good for your company and (2) Why is the ESP good for the customer?	PO
General KPIs	This should be a description of how you measure Trusted Advisor status, strategic alignment, customer satisfaction and pipeline and revenue growth.	PO
Internal Communication	Introduce the ESP to the company to explain its purpose, how it works, the process to get involved, and the critical program milestones. Include the value proposition and an overview of the general KPIs.	PO
Roles and Responsibilities	Agree, document, and communicate to internal stakeholders the roles of the program owner, account manager, the executive sponsor, customer executive as well as other supporting roles within your company.	PO
Rules for Account and Sponsor Nomination	In conjunction with sales leadership, Marketing, and the CEO, agree and document the rules you want to follow to select accounts for the program, and guidelines for nomination of executive sponsors. This should then be communicated to the account managers and potential executive sponsors.	PO

Topic	Description	Owner
Account Nomination	Each account manager nominates accounts for inclusion in the program according to the rules.	AM
Internal Sponsor Nomination	Each account manager suggests an executive sponsor for each of the nominated accounts following the rules for executive sponsor nomination.	AM
Account Selection	It is always better to start with just a few accounts, certainly fewer than 10 to begin with. Then as you learn more and refine the program you can add more accounts in line with the resources you can apply. Use the guidelines in *Selecting the Accounts* section above to choose the 10 accounts that best fit your criteria.	PO, AM
Internal Sponsor Selection	Use the guidelines in *Matching Executive Sponsors to Accounts* to assign executive sponsors to each account.	PO, ES
Update Communication	Update the account managers, executive sponsors and other internal stakeholders on the selected accounts and the assigned executive sponsors.	PO
Enable Internal Executive Sponsors	Executive sponsors who are not traditionally in a customer facing role may need to be coached on the customer interaction, life cycle of a deal, industry and market trends, the corporate story and long term strategy, and your differentiated value.	PO

Figure 72: THE EXECUTIVE SPONSOR PROGRAM ACTION PLAN – PROGRAM EXECUTION

Topic	Description	Owner
Account Plan Review	The account manager should take the executive sponsor through the account plan to familiarize the sponsor with the account history and the current goals for the account.	AM, ES
Identify Customer Executive(s)	Following the review of the Relationship Maps in the account plan, the account manager and executive sponsor can identify the right customer executive to invite to participate in the Executive Sponsor Program.	AM, ES
Customer Specific Value Proposition	Description of the value to the specific customer of their participation in the ESP. This should be in context of the current relationship between the two companies.	AM
Invite Customer Participation	Using the value proposition defined for this account, the account manager invites the customer executive to participate in the program. It is likely that the account manager will need to leverage his counterpart in the account to gain access to the executive.	AM
Define Account KPI Baseline	To measure progress in the account, you must first record the starting position for each of the KPIs. For example, if increasing customer satisfaction is an area for improvement you might record your current Net Promoter Score. Similarly, record current pipeline for the account so you can track growth. Each of your baseline elements should be recorded in the account plan.	AM, ES
Executive Introductory Call	This is the first time the executives from the two companies will meet / talk. The account manager should prepare a call plan for the executive sponsor to review to get ready for this important call.	ES, Customer

Topic	Description	Owner
Account Plan Review / Update	Now that the sponsor has some knowledge and interaction with the account it is time to review and update the account plan and potential set new Objectives in the account.	AM, ES
Define Sponsor Objectives	Aligned with the account plan review and the updated account strategy the Sponsor and the account manager can agree on what the sponsor's role is in furthering the objectives that map to the strategy.	ES, AM
Agree Meetings Cadence	The need for a cadence of interactions between the executives should have been communicated to the customer executive in the introductory call. To begin the program in earnest, the two companies should now set the first series of meetings.	ES, AM, Customer

Figure 73: THE EXECUTIVE SPONSOR PROGRAM ACTION PLAN – PROGRAM MEASUREMENT

Topic	Description	Owner
Program Accounts	The number of customer accounts in the Executive Sponsor Program, by account manager and executive sponsor.	PO
Enabled Executives	The number of executives who are certified to be part of the Executive Sponsor Program.	PO
Active Accounts	The number of selected accounts that have engaged in the Executive Sponsor Program. This should be measured by first executive engagement after the introductory call. It will be a subset of the Program accounts.	PO
Engagement	Per account, the measure of the engagement between the sponsors – measured against the agreed engagement cadence.	PO
Account Plan	Per account: Account plan completeness, and account plan scorecard.	PO
KPI Measures	Per account: Measurement of progress against relationship, strategic alignment, customer satisfaction, and pipeline and revenue growth goals. This detail should come from the account plans.	PO
Feedback	The program owner should solicit feedback directly from the account managers and executive sponsors on the program. With the account manager or executive sponsor, the program owner should solicit feedback from the customers to ascertain whether the customer is getting value from the program. Acting on this dual feedback will help the program owner to adjust as necessary to optimize the business outcomes.	PO

Conclusion

I have been struck by how many early reviewers of this book have a deep passion for the role of executives in customer engagements. I have learned a lot from their insight, particularly from people like Thanhia Sanchez, a Vice President at Deltek, and Jon Ireland at SDL. I will leave the last words in this chapter to Thanhia and Jon.

Prior to her current role at Deltek, Thanhia served as executive sponsor for a number of clients while at Cognos and IBM where she observed at first-hand how an Executive Sponsor Program helped to cultivate lasting business partnerships with key clients in industries as diverse as banking, oil & gas, US federal government and hospitality.

I asked Thanhia to share in her own words the top five benefits she has personally witnessed from an Executive Sponsor Program.

Jon Ireland, an executive at SDL – one of the world's leading localization companies – has been a practitioner of successful Executive Sponsor Program initiatives for many years. At SDL, he is responsible for ensuring all company strategic objectives, tactical projects and major transformation programs that align with the strategy are executed to budget and on time. He knows how to get things done. Jon was kind enough to contribute his experience.

A Practitioner's Perspective
5 Benefits of Executive Sponsor Programs
Thanhia Sanchez, Vice President Solutions Engineers and Sales Enablement, Deltek

1. **Overcoming challenging obstacles:** Having strong relationships in place allowed us to maintain a calm and professional atmosphere by leaning on the strength of the trust we'd built. The client knew we were going to get them through the hurdles; they knew our commitment to their success. We could focus on solving problems and using straight talk *versus* escalating into contentious dialog.

2. **Supporting the sales team:** In closing transactions with new clients or expanding footprints with existing clients.

3. **Cultivating references through project success:** With marquee clients who often aren't willing to speak on behalf of vendors.

4. **Shaping future product direction:** By giving voice to client needs with product development.

5. **Fostering a network of collaboration:** By linking clients to clients – at executive-to-executive levels.

A Practitioner's Perspective
Jon Ireland, Business Change Executive, SDL plc

The Executive Sponsor Program is a missed opportunity in most companies. We all know that the best account managers use and abuse the 'best customer influencing' executives to their advantage. They know who is good and will be respected by the customer and who is not. They understand the value that the influence of a credible and experienced executive will add to a deal. But customers see through and usually dislike this 'fly, close, commit' option. What's not always talked about is that internally the 'executive team' wants to be seen to 'help sales and close deals' for the greater good (or their careers) and be 'proud' when it pays off. This is just arrogant internal chest beating! Having executives being 'forced to help' is a disaster waiting to happen for the account success and the customer.

A far more successful approach is to launch a robust Executive Sponsor Program to secure executive engagement with a limited number of strategic accounts to drive to the genuine premier league in customer and supplier relationship as the trusted advisor. I really enjoyed reading Glenn Davis' 7 Key Principles. They are absolutely spot on so I won't duplicate that very sound approach. They highlight the challenges in terms of implementation, buy-in, change management, communication, expectations, funding (mainly travel), follow up, KPIs, skills, training and dedication of the executives' time. All these points are addressed in this book.

What I tried to do differently (in Sun Microsystems) may sound weird but it worked. Many of us travel around the world collecting premium hotel, airline, hire-cars cards and points that 'get us more benefits' and a better customer experience. So why not do this at a commercial level?

It occurred to me several times that I felt better with that experience and guess what – I spent more with the ones that were the most rewarding to me and provided me the best service. So to put this in context I created alongside the Executive Sponsor Program, the 'ELITE customer program.' We selected the accounts in the ways that have already been written about but basically on revenue and margin-spend and not as strategically as we might have done – but you can't be perfect! We actually gave the customer 10 'Elite credit-type' cards to distribute across their company (of course they could have more), a welcome pack and a list of benefits that they got 'free' for being in the 'ELITE club.' The actual card had the CEO's and the Executive's personal mobile number, plus the customer's single 'help-line' number and email – with the key benefits. I went to many of the 30 accounts (contributing to ~40 percent of our revenue) around the world to introduce this and it blew them away. The blunt question I got was: "Why us?" The blunt response was: "You are our best customer and spend the most! We want to look after you." The privileges of the club were not small and made a difference – escalated build time, preferential shipping, emergency call out, parts distribution, access to early release products, access to online ordering, shipping information. (In 2007 this was ground breaking).

We measured various KPIs: revenue, pipeline, customer satisfaction but most importantly two or three individually agreed account objectives around strategic products, specific up-sell or cross-sell, or joint trials of new releases. Another critical point was to make this a transparent objective for each executive. This was shared across the company and updated regularly, which helped with executive peer pressure. Each executive sponsor performed an annual '360 degree' assessment on his / her own with the 'main contact' to get a real feel of the account (Sales, Support, Product, Services, Administration, etc.). They presented this back to the executive team and developed an action plan to improve areas of concern.

Key technologies to support the plan revolved around making our internal systems reflect the importance of these 30 accounts. We communicated this across the company and in every interaction, we could give them a superior experience. The Altify account management software system is the central 'über' place to manage the whole experience, actions and results. Having this open and transparent to the customer reinforces trust and brings the Customer First spirit to reality.

The results of this investment showed that these accounts on average grew double digit above the non-Elite accounts and always above plan and satisfaction was significantly greater. We have already started the program for the top 36 accounts in SDL and just agreed that an Elite Customer approach will be implemented for a small subsection <10 in 2018. I am really looking forward to driving the results. An unexpected outcome from this Customer First approach was that what we learned from being real trusted advisors to our key accounts made us better with the next level of customers and actually enabled us to sell these benefits and provide a better level of experience.

CHAPTER 9:
KNOW YOUR
CUSTOMER FIRST

Introduction

In today's world of more informed buyers, it is clear that you need to do more than just communicate the capabilities of your product if you are to truly partner with the customer for a long term valuable relationship. But a long term relationship is not arrived at easily or in a single event. Nor is there a common path to follow for all customers. Different customers buy different products or services. Frequency, complexity, urgency of purchase and organizational impact vary. The role of the supplier and salesperson as guide, confidante, and counsel has both a temporal aspect – many things need to happen along the journey – and a texture that must be aware of the buyer's context.

It's a truism that most customers don't care how much you know, until they know how much you care. The best way to convince customers that you care is to demonstrate you understand their business, their business issues, the cost of resolution, and the full implications of inaction. Buyers reward sellers who:

- Understand where they are starting from
- Expand their understanding of their business problem
- Provide valuable insights into the business and the market
- Connect the buyer's priorities to specific solutions.

Delivering value to the customer is not just a Sales function. It's not just a Marketing function. Against the canvas of the more informed buyer, the always on, always available, completely connected, information source that is the Internet, an organizational approach to being Customer First is a strategic imperative for the whole go-to-market function of the company. Sellers, equipped merely with off-the-shelf elements of marketing collateral, without specific reference to the issues facing the customer, bereft of insights that in and of themselves add value, will lose to more insightful competitors.

The following story paints an all-too-familiar picture:

A SALES STORY

Laura was angry. Her biggest customer just told her that she had placed a big order with a new supplier.

"You know it's not you. I like working with you, Laura. How long are we working together? It's been a long time," said Joanne, the EVP Operations at DeepEarth Oil, "but Matt Adamson at Innopartners – he blew us away. I know they are a little more expensive than you, but Matt agreed to share his vision with the whole executive team as well at our next exec QBR. He helped me think about this company – this industry really – in a whole new way. I find this very exciting."

Laura knew Innopartners. She beat them in most competitive situations – even with brand new customers. Her solution was superior to theirs, and she certainly did not expect them to unseat her. This was deeply aggravating. Matt Adamson? Laura thought she knew most of the sales team there, but she had not come across the name Matt Adamson before.

And yes, she was angry too; angry with herself for listening to Jack, the Chief Marketing Officer at her employer, JKHiggs Global. "Just present Dynamix14 this way and focus on the energy saving. That's our key differentiator," he had said, "and be sure the customer knows that we've been in this market longer than anyone else." Laura was going to have a reality check conversation with Jack as soon as she got back to the office.

When Laura checked her phone, she was glad to see a message from her friend Tom. Before Tom left to start his own business, he and Laura had been in the trenches together for seven years and had become good friends. Now that Tom was building his new business he had little time to socialize.

Turning the corner as she walked towards her car, the sky darkened and Laura was buffeted by a chill wind. Under grey skies, she looked for something to brighten the day. Dialing Tom, hoping he'd be free for lunch or a coffee, she wondered what Tom would think about what she planned to say to Jack.

"Has your chandelier popped a bulb? Is your brain past its 'Best Before' date?" Tom's colorful speech always amused Laura, and she usually enjoyed spending time with him, but this time, sitting in the Starbucks across from his 'starter-upper-sorry-we-don't-have-a-coffee-maker' office, she was disappointed in Tom's reaction to her suggestion.

"Look, Jack has been following the same path now for far too long. But the world has changed. Customers know more about our business than we do about theirs and introducing a new product with just a datasheet and a Features & Benefits list isn't working. This approach is costing us business, and Jack is costing me money. Someone needs to put his lack of market understanding in front of the Executive Management team meeting."

Tom took off his glasses, and rubbed his eyes slowly. This was getting tense, and Laura had that I-don't-care-what-anyone-says look. Time to defuse things a little. "OK, so what you're saying is that Jack is about as useful as an ashtray on a motorbike. But even if that is true, is this the best way to solve things? Do you really want to lead a witch-hunt against Jack? This is not a Jack issue. It is a strategic company issue."

"Tom, I thought you'd understand," Laura responded. "Jack and the rest of the marketing team think that, just because they've spoken to the analysts and done some market research, they can tell us how it works in the field. But they rarely get in front of customers, and meeting with customers every day is what we do. I've been successful selling ever since I came to JKHiggs, but now I am losing to competition when I should win."

"OK", Tom interrupted, "let's look at this calmly. From what I heard, the marketing team is delivering more sales collateral than ever before, and built a really cool micro-site for Dynamix14. You can't criticize their work-rate. What exactly are you saying?"

Laura took a long sip from her latte, and sat back in the soft leather chair. "OK, I admit I'm getting some leads – that's not my problem – and I know marketing is investing heavily in brand awareness. There are more marketing materials than we have ever had in the past – but even if I could find the piece I need, I am still going to get my butt kicked if the competition is helping the customer to ... how did Joanne at DeepEarth put it? – 'help me think about my business in a whole new way.' We don't know how to do that. We have spent all this time on our 'Sales and Marketing Alignment Project,' when in fact we should have been thinking about the customer first. Henry in Engineering gets this stuff. Customers love him – he knows more about the impact we can have than anyone on the planet. If we can get him in front of more customers, then maybe that will help. That's what I need. That's the answer."

"Look, Laura, you've nailed the problem – but not the solution. Henry doesn't scale across 400 reps. And if you think the marketing department at JKHiggs is going to help you solve this, then I'd like some of what you're smoking. Your job is to sell. Do the research yourself. Use Google. Buy Henry lunch. If Jack is filling the top of the funnel, that's just as much as you can expect. I wish I had someone hand me leads. Now, my dear friend, don't be a whiner. Accept that your meeting today wasn't great, but dust yourself off. Learn more about your customer's industry and get back in the saddle."

"I don't know, Tom," Laura sighed, "I hear what you're saying and I know you have my interests at heart, but customers are getting smarter and more knowledgeable all of the time. They are using the Internet to educate themselves on everything that's going on; not just with us, but with our competitors, their industry and other companies like them. It's not my pipeline volume I'm worried about; it's my sales conversion rate and the pipeline velocity. If JKHiggs doesn't sort this out, we will lose our position in the market and that will make my job harder. Marketing is investing in the wrong place, and something needs to be done about it. I think Jack needs a good dose of reality."

Tom stood up and dropped his empty coffee cup in the trash. "Listen, I've got to get back to the day job. But ask some of the other people on the sales team what they think before you take on Jack, or maybe call the guys over at Innopartners and see if they have any openings. They seem to have figured it out."

Know Your Customer's Business

It is clear from this story, and I'm sure from your personal engagements with customers, that most deals are not lost because you don't have the best solution. It is also true that a good personal relationship doesn't suffice to secure the account. It comes down to knowing the customer's business. Whether you are pursuing a single strategic opportunity or building a strategy to maximize revenue from a large customer we know that this matters. In fact, knowing the customer's business, and showing how you can add value, is the cornerstone to maintaining long term business relationships and delivering value to your customer.

The following seven steps provide a repeatable method to know the customer's business and help them make progress:

1. Who is the customer?
2. What goals matter to the customer and who cares?
3. Why do these goals matter to the customer?
4. What related projects or initiatives are in place?
5. What is broken that is stopping them being successful?
6. How can you help?
7. What is your gap in knowledge or solution?

Who is the customer?

If you have used the ICP framework in *Chapter 4: The Ideal Customer Profile* to select this customer you should have a good match of customer to product. With the other functions in the business, there should be a common understanding of the customer target and you should already have a base level of knowledge about the 'typical' customer's business. Now you need to get specific.

The first step along the *Know Your Customer's Business* journey is to complete the Firmographics section of the ICP framework in the context of your specific customer, adding a high level description of the customer.

Figure 74: FIRMOGRAPHICS – A HIGH LEVEL CUSTOMER DESCRIPTION

JKHiggs is an American technology company based in Seattle. It produces software and services that assist businesses in moving to digital operations. Its software serves functions including IT service management, data center automation, performance management, virtualization lifecycle management and cloud computing management. The company identifies its strategy as 'digital enterprise management,' and focuses on platforms including mainframe computers, mobile devices, and cloud computing.

Attribute	Description	ICP Fit
Industry	High Tech	Ideal
Size	1,200 sellers	Ideal
Geography	US, EMEA, ANZ (APAC)	Ideal
Job Titles	Both VP Sales, VP Sales Ops	Ideal
Business Maturity	Maturity	Ideal

Once you know that the company fits the Ideal Customer Profile, and you can describe the company at a high level, you next need to understand what they see as important.

What goals matter to the customer and who cares?

Most modern companies have a goal and metrics oriented management model. There may be some differences at a detail level and there will sometimes be a debate about the relative hierarchy of Vision, Goals, Objectives, Mission, Strategies, etc. In the end, most organizations use a multi-layered performance model to describe what a company, business unit or individual is trying to achieve, and how success is measured. I have four layers in the model that I like to use called the Customer Insight Map:

- Goals
- Pressures
- Initiatives
- Obstacles.

Goals is the descriptor of what they want to achieve as a business. As goals are established and communicated within the company, strategies for achieving these goals are developed, and ultimately, specific initiatives or projects are put in motion to execute on the strategies.

Figure 75: THE CUSTOMER INSIGHT MAP – 2

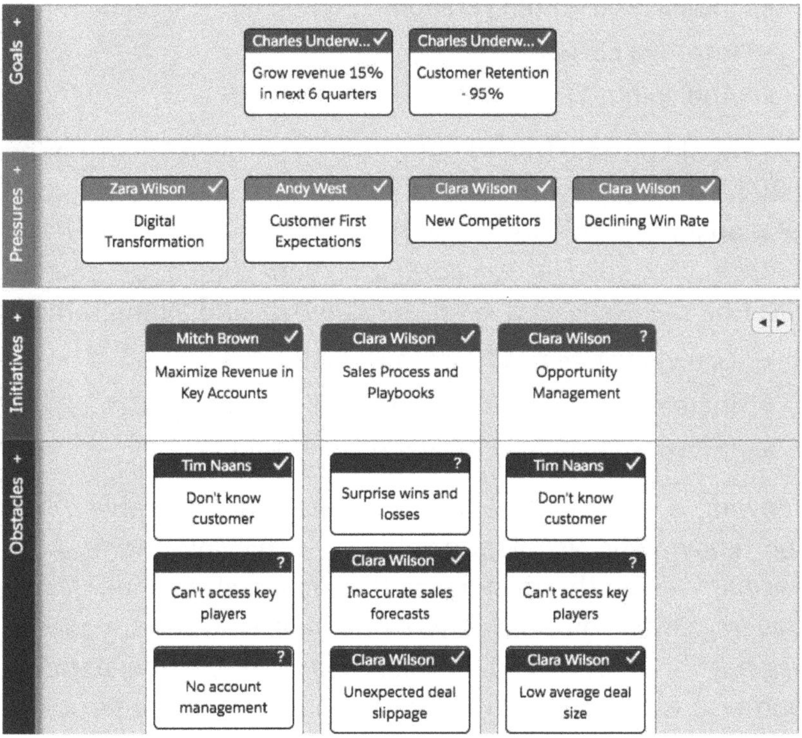

You will see the other layers emerge as we get to know our customer better.

In *Chapter 5: The Ideal Customer Profile*, I listed and described a number of information sources that you might use to get the information for who they are and what matters to them. These include corporate reports, earnings calls, investor relations, analysts' coverage and press releases. See *Chapter 5* for the details.

Goals are generally easy to understand and usually easy to uncover. In truth though the Goals by themselves don't give you a lot of insight. Most companies' Goals are going to go something like this:

- Grow revenue
- Increase customer retention
- Improve EBITDA
- And so on ...

You should be able to find out a little more useful information either through your research or if you have good relationships with the people that matter (see *Chapter 7: A Structure for Building Relationships*). You should be able to describe the Goals with associated metrics and a timeframe:

- Grow revenue to $700m in FY2019
- Increase customer retention by 6 percent by 2019
- Improve EBITDA by 7 percent in current FY.

Knowing a company's Goals becomes really valuable when you know who is responsible for achieving them. At a company level, the owners of the Goal will be Inner Circle players. Once you know the owners of the Goals, you can begin your relationship development work, understanding who else is on their team, and who in the Political Structure you can look to for further insight and influence. At this point in getting to know your customer at the account level, you should be aiming to describe the goals as follows:

- Grow revenue to $700m in FY2019 [Julie Davis, EVP Sales]
- Increase customer retention by 6 percent by 2019 [Frank Delardo, CCO]
- Improve EBITDA by 7 percent in current FY [Harris Witherspoon, CFO].

Within most companies, the goals are established at the C-level and then, as they cascade down through the organization, they become more granular as they reach other executives and management.

If, for example, you take Julie Davis, our EVP Sales; her goal is to hit a $700m revenue number. She likely has regional VPs who together need to deliver their regional results so that Julie achieves her overall revenue goal. She may allocate $400m to George, her VP Sales North America, $150m to Francine, her VP Sales EMEA, $50m to Carol in APAC, and then Julie will look to Harry, her head of Indirect Sales and Strategic Partnerships, to come up with the remaining $100m.

As each of the executives develop their strategies for how they will achieve the goals, they will delegate different goals to others on their teams. Understanding how this works is important to know the context in which your customer is operating. If you're selling a solution to Carol in APAC to help make her sales team more productive, she is going to care a lot more about her own revenue goal than about Julie's $700m, and she is likely to sponsor projects or initiatives that help her achieve the $50m number. Context matters.

But why does Julie (or Julie's company) need to achieve $700m? That's the real question.

Why do these goals matter to the customer?

Obviously is it better to know the goals and initiatives of your customer than not know. But Goals are just the WHAT. As Simon Sinek will tell you: *"You should always start with WHY."* Knowing the WHAT sheds little light on the thinking that led to defining the goals and is never enough to understand the corporate business drivers or personal motivations at play.

When customers decide to pursue a goal or sponsor an initiative, they are doing so to remove a problem in their business, or to gain advantage by pursuing an opportunity to improve a key metric. When you understand the reason – the WHY behind the goals or initiatives – then you can fully understand the buyer's perspective, and gain alignment with the real personal or business motivations. Great sellers understand and expand the customer's WHY.

In our Customer Insight Map model WHY is represented by Pressures, the second item on the list.

- Goals
- **Pressures**
- Initiatives
- Obstacles.

Pressures are internal and / or external forces that impact the business and serve as the catalyst for solidifying goals and initiatives. While Goals are usually positively stated, pressures are always expressed in the negative form. If everything were positive there would be nothing to fix or improve. If a company has a Goal to Increase Market Share, the pressure might be articulated as Missing Market Opportunity.

Pressures at a company level are typically situational – like Increasing Market Competition, or Decreasing Customer Retention Rates – as opposed to task or process focused –

like Sales Win Rate is Declining, or Customer Response Time is Too Slow.

Internal pressures are usually a consequence of a group of broken tasks or processes. You can be sure that, if Customer Retention Rate is declining, then having an inadequate Customer Response Time doesn't help. I call these broken tasks **Obstacles**, the fourth item in the model. I will get to Obstacles later.

For now, let's get back to Julie. She needs to achieve $700m in revenue. At the same time, her colleague Frank, the Chief Customer Officer, has been tasked with increasing customer retention by 6 percent and Harris, the CFO, is looking to improve EBITDA by 7 percent. The big question is why.

Think about it for a minute.

Does it feel to you like there are some external forces at play? Is there something rotten in the state of Denmark? Or put another way, are there internal pressures that are causing these goals to be the goals that are set for FY2019?

The easy answer is that it is just a case of an ambitious company looking to improve a number of core metrics at the same time. Feels fishy to me – and it's never that simple.

We can speculate that perhaps customers are defecting from JKHiggs. After all we don't know the current retention rate. It might be the case that their share price has stalled and Harris needs to improve the EPS numbers to get it back on track. Maybe JKHiggs just acquired a competitor and the CEO is putting pressure on Julie to get some revenue synergies from the acquisition by cross-selling each company's products to the other company's customer base. Understanding the pressures or the WHY points to problems or opportunities and gives you a focus for how you can help.

So, how do you know?

Here's a conversation I might have with Julie:

Me: So, Julie, you have a big revenue target to hit! I know you're awesome, but let's just say for a minute that for the first time in your career you miss your number. I've seen that only 53 percent of sellers in your industry are making quota, and according to Forrester, only half of new product introductions are successful. With your new Dynamix14 product, you must be feeling some of that pain. Now, apart from potentially losing your job, or not getting to go to Hawaii on your amazing Sales Winners Club trip again, what are the really bad things that would happen to JKHiggs if you don't achieve your quota? What problem doesn't get fixed?

Julie: Well, that's not going to happen. I always make my number.

Me: OK, just suspend reality for a minute and assume you're a normal mortal like the rest of us. Tell me one bad thing, apart from the actual number miss.

Julie: OK, I'll play your game – but I'm not going to miss my number.

Me: Just one bad thing ...

Julie: Well, in APAC, Carol will miss her number if she can't sell our new products into the installed base – and she has sucked at that so far. Our competitor Innopartners is starting to eat our lunch there.

Me: OK, but that just means that Carol misses her number, and it's the smallest number on the board anyway. You could probably make that up somewhere else. So why was that the first thing that came into your mind? Why do you care about Innopartners?

Julie: Look, it's like this. We have invested heavily in our new Dynamix14 product. It's where we see the future of the company. Laura, one of Carol's top performers, was hoping to get a seven-figure deal for Dynamix14 with DeepEarth, one of her biggest accounts. But she lost that deal to Innopartners.

Me: But that's just one account, one salesperson and one competitor. Is anyone else on the sales team having success with Dynamix14?

Julie: Nope. Nada. And it's not just in APAC. The product seems to be pretty good, should fit well with our target market, but we are just not getting traction. It's as if the sales team don't yet understand the problem that Dynamix14 was designed to solve. It's our first Cloud offering, and maybe that's part of the problem. I'm carrying $140m in quota for this product and we are still on the starting blocks.

Me: What happens if you miss that number, but make up for it with other products? Who cares if you still make the number?

Julie: Not sure if you heard me. We are betting the company on Dynamix14. It's not just me. If Jack, our CMO, can't use some of his enormous marketing budget to equip the team to succeed with it, he's going to feel the heat. We won't make our customer retention numbers either if the customers don't buy into our future direction. According to Harris, if that happens, we will need to start making headcount cuts to hit our EBITDA target. Welcome to my world!

Me: Got it. Here's what this sounds like. You've got a decent product that you think is a good match for your customer base, but the sellers are struggling to connect the product to the customer's business problem. The net impact of that is your number is at risk, but it seems more importantly this is a strategic imperative, or put another way 'an existential crisis' for JKHiggs. Have I got that right?

Julie: Yep. That about sums it up.

Me: Well, I've good news and bad news. Which do you want first?

Julie: Start with the bad, and let's get that over with, but the good news better be good.

Me: From what I've heard from others, you're not really sure that the data security issues associated with the Cloud are something the customers are ready to sign up for. You've not changed the sales compensation model for the sales team to account for the Dynamix14 recurring license model. So, this is not just about a sales enablement issue. You've got to address your services capability for cloud security and you need to rethink how you pay the team in a different way for recurring license revenue. Does that seem like the whole picture?

Julie: I bet no one ever accused you of being a bundle of joy, but yes, that's probably pretty accurate. Where is the good news?

Me: Here's the good news. You're not alone, and this is a pretty tractable problem. I've seen the same story play out many times. Let me set up a call with Ken over at LightAI – you know Ken, right? He can tell you about how we helped him solve a similar problem.

Julie: OK. Not sure it's fixable, but let's give it a shot. I'm under pressure, so sooner is better than later.

Me: In the meantime, let me chat with Jack, your CMO, and the product people, and we can get a quick start on getting things moving. Will Jack be willing to invest something to solve this, or is he putting it all on your shoulders?

Julie: Oh, Jack will find the money to fund it. He doesn't quite understand the pain the sales team is going through here, but he just got an earful from Laura when she lost DeepEarth, and in fairness to him, he's ready to step up.

Me: Gotcha. I'm on it.

The Problem Discovery Model

The conversation above is an example of the exchanges that can happen when you can get the customer focused on the problems that they have to address because of the pressures they are under. In this case JKHiggs need to establish a new product in the market ahead of their competition.

The conversation, of course, is a little artificial. It would not usually all happen in one interaction, or with just one person, but the principles of the Problem Discovery Model behind it work well every time.

Because it is a repeatable model it's pretty straightforward to use and it lends itself nicely to the application of technology. It can be a very useful way to help you to uncover your customer's business problems.

Figure 76: THE PROBLEM DISCOVERY MODEL

	PROBLEM	IMPACT	CAUSE
	1	4	7
DISCOVER	What's really the Problem? Is there anything else?	What's the impact of the Problem? Who else is impacted?	What's the root Cause of the problem? Is there anything else?
	2	5	8
DEVELOP	Is the Problem also this?	Is the Impact also this? Is [Name] also impacted?	Is the Cause also this?
	3	6	9
CONFIRM	So here's what I heard about the Problem. Do I have that right?	So, here's what I heard about the Impact. Do I have that right?	So, here's what I heard about the Cause. Do I have that right?

The Problem Discovery Model uses three different question types, each applied against the three stages of questioning. It is important to follow the questions in the order shown in the model:

- **Discover** questions should be open and inviting, giving the customer an opportunity to talk, prompting the customer to tell you about areas that are of concern to her. It is important that you open these questions with some insight based on your knowledge of her business, and other trends you are seeing in the market. The next chapter (*Chapter 10: Create and Communicate Value*) describes in detail how you might do that. You need avoid the 'What's keeping you up at night?' type of question and lead with insight to build your credibility. You should know what to listen for. You're looking for cues to problems that you know how to solve. The more you listen, the more you learn.

- Once the customer has explained the areas of concern that are top-of-mind, you can progress to the **Develop** questions to expand your understanding. Because of your knowledge of similar customers you should have a list of potential problem areas that they should care about. When you have targeted this account using the Ideal Customer Profile (*Chapter 5: The Ideal Customer Profile*) you should be aware of the typical customer problems. Using something like the Customer Insight Map described below (see *Pulling It All Together* and *Making It Scale*), you can be equipped to have a knowledgeable business conversation. Product Management and Marketing both have a role to play in help you fill out content for boxes 2, 5 and 8 in the model. Furnished with this knowledge, you can expand the customer's understanding of the problem and, if it is in the interests of the customer, guide them to areas where your particular solution is strong.

- You close your questioning for each stage with **Confirm** questions to show the customer that you have been listening to what she says and that your understanding of the problem is correct.

You might have noticed the question in box 5 in the Problem Discovery Model: "Is [Name] also impacted?" This is where you can expand your access in the account to:

- Triangulate the information that you have received
- Broaden your relationships
- Extend the potential impact area for your solution.

Of course you won't always have a compliant customer who just answers all of the questions you ask. If the buying process is controlled tightly by Procurement, or you are in a 'restricted access' RFP process where you are not supposed to talk to business stakeholders, it can be more difficult. When providing a value-add solution, I am not a fan of participating in a 'restricted access' RFP process. If you can't talk to the business stakeholders it can be really hard to propose the right solution, particularly if what you are selling will have a material impact on the business. At some point in this situation you need to decide whether in fact you and the customer can be successful if you don't have the requisite access and information.

Before you make that 'qualify out' decision you should learn as much as you possibly can about the customer's business, so that when you do get to that stage in the RFP process you know as much as possible.

In general I'm not a fan of RFPs. Unless you're involved in writing the RFP you should assume that your competitor had a part to play in its creation. Following the RFP rules rarely works, particularly in a 'restricted access' RFP process. You need to assume you are losing from the outset and rigorous and continuous qualification is the order of the day before you decide to invest time and resources. If you do decide to play you will need to apply tremendous ingenuity to get to know the customer's business if you're going to have any chance of success.

My friend Graham told me this story:

> It was just as you describe, Donal. Procurement wouldn't let us in. Really, how did they expect us to recommend the right solution if they wouldn't let us talk to the business? It was crazy.
>
> However, the RFP wasn't totally blind. We had some early engagement before the RFP came out but, to be frank, we expected to see more of our capabilities described in the document. We thought we had influenced it quite a bit.
>
> It turned out of course that Procurement had created the RFP without getting any input from the business. Sometimes you just wonder, don't you?
>
> Anyway, we decided that we were still going to pursue. This customer passed the Truth Test, as you call it, Donal: "If I were the prospect, I would buy our solution."
>
> Because Marketing had done a good job of targeting the customer, we knew the general issues they would have. But we wanted to get more specific.
>
> So, we called their competition saying that we were looking at providing a solution into their market and wanted 15 minutes of their time to explain what they saw happening in the market. We called their customers with a similar story. We called their sales team and their customer service. Surprisingly perhaps, we learned most from the competition and the customers.
>
> To cut a long story short, when we got our time in the sun with the business stakeholders they were amazed at how

much we knew about their business and the pressures they faced. That's why we won the business, even though we were nearly twice as expensive as the competition.

Pressure is not just for tires and inflatable toys. True story! So let's dig a little deeper into Pressures and Problems.

Different Types of Pressures and Problems

Not all Problems are created equal. It is worth taking a few moments to contemplate the factors that shape a customer's decision to create a Goal. This might guide you to recognize more quickly where opportunities to help might exist.

Over the years I have participated in many sales pursuits, interacted with many buyers, and worked with a large number of sales professionals. It is clear that the awareness a buyer has of a need to act correlates with his propensity to buy something from somebody. That is really no surprise.

However, the parallel pattern is that his level of awareness is inversely proportional to your opportunity to create value. If the buyer does not know that he has a problem or if he cannot identify an opportunity before you point it out to him, you have a strong platform from which you can create value for him.

In my experience there are three types of customer need:

1. Active
2. Known
3. Unknown.

Customers who have an **Unknown** need are a blank canvas and therefore more receptive to value creation. Those in the **Active** camp are most likely to act soon and will have a higher propensity to buy. Each of these customer types needs to be dealt with differently.

Figure 77: THE PROPENSITY TO BUY CURVE

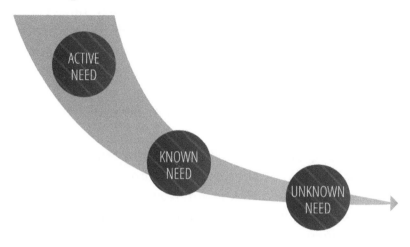

Figure 78: THE VALUE CREATION CURVE

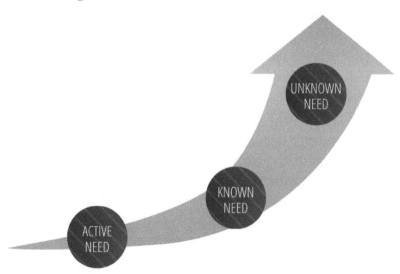

Active Need – Solution Vision: When senior executives move from one organization to another they often will be charged with using the experience gained in their previous company to accelerate the deployment of new systems at their new location. This is just one example of an Active Need. As a buyer, or a prospective customer, this executive will be typical of a customer with an Active Need; he will actively want to work with a supplier to determine quickly the actions to be taken to implement a solution to solve the known problem. He undoubtedly has a vision of the possible solution and understands that it's his responsibility to get the job done.

Without doubt, this is a qualified sales opportunity, and the buying cycle should be shorter than in either of the other two scenarios (Known and Unknown). However, the bar is set a little higher and it will be somewhat more difficult for you to add value in the application of your product to establish creative solutions, as the customer is already quite proficient, and might well achieve the solution unaided.

You need to focus not just on the 'what,' but also on the 'how.' The customer knows what he wants. You need to be able to identify for him how to best apply the product, how you can help better than anyone else, and how you have insight that will add extra value.

Known Need – Unknown Solution: Opportunities abound when a customer knows he has a problem but doesn't know what to do about it. Customers in that situation will place high value on consultative support to aid in the development of a strategic buying vision. They will take comfort from your experience of similar situations with their counterparts in other companies and will value your experience. They will place great value on your ability to identify for them opportunities for applications of your product or service that add value to their business. Going beyond obvious product features, or obvious applications, the customer will want you to help them to uncover business process improvements that you can help them achieve.

Anxiety levels are high and the customer feels at risk because he can't necessarily visualize the solution. If you can transcend the Vendor perspective and become at least a Problem Solver the customer will go the extra mile for you. He also will be less focused on squeezing your margins, if you join with him in establishing a long term joint supplier / customer vision.

Unknown Need – Unknown Problem: Even though your product might be flush with competitive features, each designed meticulously to deliver real business value, the customer might not care, and may not know that there is a better way. That's his prerogative! If the customer does not feel business pain, or does not believe that his problem can be solved, or considers that the attendant risks in addressing the problem are too high, then he won't see why he should take it on. He simply can't visualize a reason to change.

Assuming that your product or service offering in fact would deliver quantifiable benefit to this customer, then something is amiss. This is an Unknown Need. The need is there, but the customer has not yet realized it and, from your salesperson's perspective, this is a situation that must be developed by deeply examining the Goals and Pressures that are shaping the customer's business decisions, and finding where your solution might be applied to help solve a problem or exploit an opportunity. Here is where you act as a Trusted Advisor, helping to create and shape initiatives to achieve or exceed the goal – but most importantly to relieve the Pressures for the customer.

You might find it easier to think about pressures by looking for stress in the following categories: the first two categories are internal pressures, those customers can control; and the remaining six are most often external, those that they don't control:

- **Financial:** Declining or flat revenue or profitability
- **Operational:** Unpredictable forecasts, low productivity, escalating turnover, poor product quality
- **Customer:** Customer defection, customer demands
- **Competitive:** Declining win rate, superior solutions, growing competitive market share
- **Market:** Unfavorable economic conditions, regulatory requirements, new emerging markets
- **Partner:** Channel conflict, partner requirements (demands), partner performance
- **Suppliers:** Supplier dependencies, supplier performance
- **Technology:** Cloud growth, AI or mobile expectations.

When you understand the typical pressures that the key influencers encounter, you can have real executive level business conversations. The customer feels the empathy and your relationship status is improved.

What related projects or initiatives are in place?

That's the hard work out of the way. You now know the WHAT – the Goals, with metrics and owners – and you've uncovered the WHY – the Pressures. Next up is Initiatives, the third layer of the Customer Insight Map (see **Figure 75** earlier):

- Goals
- Pressures
- **Initiatives**
- Obstacles.

Initiatives (or Projects or Assignments) might be described as WHAT ARE YOU DOING ABOUT IT? They are the set of activities that are sponsored and funded to drive an outcome that will relieve the Pressures to achieve the Goals.

As you get to know your customer, there are four things that you need to know about Initiatives:

1. Are there any Initiatives already identified?
2. What is the priority of identified initiatives?
3. What approach, if any, has the customer tried to solve this problem before?
4. What problems exist for which there are no Initiatives?

When you know the answer to the first two questions you can assess, in priority order where there might be an opportunity for your solution. These Initiatives probably fall into the Active Need category, where the customer knows there is a problem and has at least an outline vision of what the solution might look like.

In Julie's case, now that she understands the problems that she has, she may sponsor two initiatives like these:

- Connect Dynamix14 to customer problems
- Implement a redesigned sales compensation plan.

The third point in the list of things you need to know about Initiatives helps you to understand what did not work in that past – if it did they would not be doing it again – so that you get a better sense of what was broken in that approach.

If there is an identified problem or pressure with a related sponsored Initiative, the customer has a Known Need, and you have a great opportunity to help design the solution.

Staying with JKHiggs, we know that they have a potential Cloud Services problem, so I might suggest that they need an Initiative to address that:

- Cloud Services upgrade.

In every case though, Initiatives are instigated to solve a problem that is caused by processes that either don't exist or are broken.

I refer to these broken processes as Obstacles.

What is broken that is stopping them being successful?

It is much more advantageous to fix something that is broken, than just make something better. Let me say that again. *Broken is better than better.*

People react much more emotionally to the risk of loss than to the possibility of gain. I consider these broken items in the fourth layer of the Customer Insight Map: **Obstacles**.

- Goals
- Pressures
- Initiatives
- **Obstacles**.

Staying with Julie, our EVP Sales. Within Initiatives, if you can identify a set of specific Obstacles that are causing recurring problems – such as the underlying reasons why her team cannot connect Dynamix14 to her customers' business problems – it will help you understand the obstacles, the specific processes that need to be fixed. Then connecting a specific capability that you can provide to fix one or more of those obstacles charts a path to a business focused conversation.

Consider this: when your engineers, product managers or product designers first built the product you are selling, they usually started with a customer problem that they were looking to solve in a unique way. The solution they developed was designed to fix something that was broken in the customer's organization, or to provide a capability that didn't exist but was needed. Assuming that the product concept was well-informed, the essence of those product design decisions should provide you with a list of common

Obstacles. They should be the inverse of the product's capabilities.

Of course customers are not all cookie-cutter replicas of each other. Each will have its own peculiarities. But for a company like JKHiggs, that we know is in High Tech, operating in the US, EMEA, and APAC, at the Maturity business stage, we know that it will look at a lot like other companies of the same profile. Pressures and Obstacles will look remarkably similar, so as you build your list of Obstacles you should not be starting from scratch.

Bringing it all together

Now that you know about Goals, Pressures, Initiatives and Obstacles, you should be getting a clear picture of the customer's business (see **Figure 79** below).

If we brought this to Julie, how do you think she would feel?

Hopefully Julie would appreciate the fact that you understand her business, that you have helped to her to understand better the problems she has, and she should be excited that you have identified a potential way to help remove the Obstacles. This helps JKHiggs deliver on the Initiatives, to relieve the Pressures, so that Julie can make her Goal of achieving $700m in revenue.

Job well done!

Figure 79: THE CUSTOMER INSIGHT MAP – ANNOTATED FOR THE SALES LEADER

Component	Description	Examples for Sales Leader
GOALS	The results to be achieved by senior key players with a measurable outcome within a specified timeframe (the what).	Grow revenue to $700m in FY 2019.
PRESSURES	The internal or external pressures on senior key players driving them to work to achieve the Goals (the why).	New competitors in the market. Failing new product launch. Poorly designed compensation plan.
INITIATIVES	The plans or programs created to relieve the Pressures and achieve the Goals (the how).	Connect Dynamix14 to Customer Problems. Redesigned compensation plan.
OBSTACLES	Something that is not working well and is needed so that an Initiative is successful.	Relating to first initiative ... Product focused sales enablement. Sellers only sell what they know. Can't have business conversations. No business focused marketing content. ...
SOLUTION	A set of capabilities, services or products that help to remove the Obstacles to deliver a successful Initiative to relieve the Pressures and achieve the Goals.	Customer Insight Engine.

How can you help?

OK, you got me. You caught me out. You see that I slipped in Solution into my Customer Insight Map in **Figure 79**. The solution is of course the fifth layer – but I wanted to leave it out until we got a deep understanding of the customer's business – because that's what you do when you have a Customer First perspective!

- Goals
- Pressures
- Initiatives
- Obstacles
- **Solution**.

As you can see from the description in **Figure 79** above, a Solution is a set of capabilities, services or products that help to remove the Obstacles to deliver a successful Initiative, to relieve the Pressures and achieve the Goals.

The Customer Insight Map tells a story. It's a narrative of the customer's business. But it also points to episodes where you can help by mapping the specific capabilities of your product to the customer's specific obstacles so that you have a happy ending to the story.

Don't you think that Julie, having looked at the Customer Insight Map that you have created, will feel that you have earned the right to have a conversation about your solution? I think so. That's what happens when you put the customer first.

What is your gap in knowledge or solution?

As you work through the Customer Insight Map with your customer, you won't learn everything at once. The customer will not necessarily be comfortable in sharing their innermost secrets. You need to understand the gap in knowledge. The best way to do that is to have the customer validate that the map is an accurate report on their world. Until your stories align, you've not completed your work here.

You may need to broaden your access (see question 5 in the Problem Discovery Model, **Figure 76** above). To get to the end of the journey you will probably need to create value in the sales process and then communicate that value to more people in the customer's organization. I will show you how to do that in the next chapter, *Chapter 10: Create and Communicate Value.*

Even when you have all the information about Goals, Pressures, Initiatives, and Obstacles, there may be gaps in your Solution. It's OK not to have all of the answers. It is better to acknowledge a deficit in your solution rather than try to shoehorn what you have into the customer's organization. You may need to find partners or complementary solutions to fulfill the customer's need. Remember, it is a Customer First world and taking care of the customer should be your guiding star.

Making It Scale – The Role of Technology

Winning sales teams are using technology to transform how they uncover customer business problems, and then connect their solutions to those problems. They are leveraging all the raw information available from product experts, from Marketing and from their customers, to deconstruct, process and repackage it so that everyone – Sales, Marketing and all customer facing personnel in your company – can apply it to facilitate good business conversations with customers that lead to the right solutions. Typically mobile as well as cloud-enabled, this approach can help to connect your solutions to the customer's business problem, create more value and generate more revenue, every day, whether the seller is operating from his desk, or meeting with his customer in the field.

Experienced sellers have learned through multiple engagements with similar customers the issues that those customers typically face, and those who are successful understand how to connect their solutions to the customer's business problems. With less tenured sellers, there needs to be a mechanism to help them gain that familiarity in a compressed timeframe. The world is moving too quickly to wait for each new salesperson to come up to speed on their own. Even with more experienced contributors, the struggle to adapt to new market entrants, introduction of new products, or changing macro-economic factors means that it is incumbent on their supporting organization to help accelerate their contextual experience such that they can engage effectively with today's customer.

Too many times sales onboarding or product launch initiatives are focused on what the company does, or the capabilities of its products or solutions. Not enough time is spent equipping the sales team to first understand the customer's business issues, so they can then collaborate on how to apply the solutions to address the customer's problems.

This is an opportunity to provide value both to new sellers who are coming to grips with a company's offering and to experienced sellers learning about how to apply the capabilities of new products to their customer's problems. When you can accelerate their expertise in the pertinent business issues, and provide them with a path to real customer engagement you will see more impactful sales enablement, shorter onboarding and time to revenue for new hires, and more successful introduction of new products to enable account teams to sell wider and deeper in existing accounts.

Smart solutions can equip sellers with a representation of the Customer Insight Map to accelerate the seller's experience in the customer's business. With that foundation, the seller can engage in a real business conversation, because only when he has demonstrated that he comprehends the buyer's world, their Goals and Pressures, Initiatives (known or potential) and Obstacles, has the seller earned the right to talk about his Solutions.

CHAPTER 10:
CREATE AND
COMMUNICATE VALUE

Humans can be irksome creatures. When asked, they say they want to make rational decisions based on evidence and science. In practice that's never the fully story. Emotion plays a critical role. If math was the single arbiter of customer decisions then the role of the salesperson would be greatly diminished.

Anyone can present the facts, and as long as those facts are correct and independently verifiable, the messenger is less important than the message. But math without magic is just math: a cold guardian of rational decisions, but a poor custodian of personal connections. Insights – honed from deep knowledge of the account, the buyer's persona, their typical personal goals – are the key to unlocking a connection that is both rational and emotional.

Cast your mind back to a time when you had irrefutable facts, reason, and logic on your side. You knew that there was no way the other person could not agree to your perfectly constructed argument. Surely that would be impossible? Your evidence was deep, your reasoning was considered, and your rationale beyond reproach. But yet, you failed to sway the other person's opinion. She just refused to budge and your argument came to nothing.

Many buyer / seller interactions work out like this. The seller expends a lot of effort in crafting his proposal confident in the knowledge that the facts are on his side, but the buyer, immune to his argument, remains seemingly indifferent.

Modern salespeople are expected to use their experience to deliver industry knowledge and proven best practices from similar customers to the customer at hand – to create value for the buyer. But if they don't understand how the customer's business works, the typical business pressures that exist, or obstacles that must be overcome, then facing the more educated buyer is going to be a daunting prospect (pun intended). They're doomed to fail, however, because decision making isn't only logical, it's also emotional, according to the latest findings in neuroscience.

If prospective customers are discontented or feel thwarted by salespeople who are trying to win their business as a new account, this frustration is exacerbated if they have similar disheartening experiences when meeting with 'their account manager' as an existing customer. The account manager is the person who is supposed to know their business issues; who they expect to corral the necessary resources of the supplier to help them chart a path towards a more informed strategy to solve their most pressing business challenges.

Customers take similar but different paths and are on different points of their journeys at each engagement stage. Their frame of reference varies. The complexity of purchase, from the buyer's perspective, is one of the key arbiters of whether insights can be used well. Where complexity exists in the mind of the buyer, the seller can use insights to bring clarity to the situation. If the buyer knows everything they need to know already, then they don't need your help. In most cases in enterprise B2B sales this is not the case. So it is important from the outset to understand whether the buyer needs assistance in navigating their buying journey.

Figure 80: ORGANIZATIONAL IMPACT FACTORS

Consider two aspects of any offering: *Cost* and the offering's *Intellectual Property*. As you can see from **Figure 80**, as *Cost* and *IP Value* increase, they have greater potential net impact on an organization and affect how soon a buyer is willing to engage with potential vendors.

Two other important factors are *Risk* and *Frequency of Purchase*. As *Frequency of Purchase* increases, *Organizational Impact* tends to decrease.

As *Risk* increases with *Cost* and *IP Value* – for example, in the case of business infrastructure projects or a CRM system – *Organizational Impact* increases, along with the buyer's need to engage earlier and more intensively with sellers for guidance and input. This is a great place to apply Customer Insights.

Figure 81: ORGANIZATIONAL IMPACT OF PRODUCTS
AND SERVICES

Figure 81 then shows what types of products and services have more or less organizational impact. With *Business Process Infrastructure* at the top right, Risk and *IP Value* are greatest, and a buyer is more likely to engage a supplier early. Buyers need assistance with these complex purchases and so they require the vendor to provide insight earlier in their buying cycle.

Office equipment is a straightforward commodity, with lower risk, greater frequency and less cost. It therefore requires less seller assistance. I suggest that there is little cause to offer insight when selling items in the bottom-left quadrant, where unit *Cost* is typically low, purchase *Frequency* is high and *Risk* is low.

A critical factor that influences the degree of a buyer's independence and decision-making ability is the organizational impact. **Figure 82** presents a visual representation that helps identify when the seller can use insights to educate the buyer on value considerations that might not have been identified.

283

Figure 82: VALUE CREATION

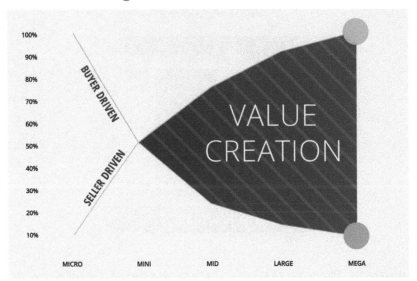

Moving left to right on the bottom axis you progress to engagements with greater impact on the buyer's organization. Micro impact (for example, copier paper) has little business impact. There is little opportunity for the seller to engage beyond price discounts. As impact progresses from mini through mega, the level of purely buyer-driven decisions decreases.

Conversely, as organizational impact increases, sellers have a greater opportunity to create value for their customers. At some critical point, crossover will occur where the seller can create more value than the unguided buyer can accrue single-handedly.

Beyond that point, the widening gap between the buyer's ability to make an unassisted decision and the seller's ability to shape needs and help the buyer to visualize the best solution presents a key opportunity: *Value Creation*. That is the point at which Customer Insights should be applied and is their very purpose for being. Driving value creation is the mission of the professional salesperson. Buyers already have a wealth of sources from which to learn about cost, capabilities and benefits. A simple Internet search produces a vast amount of information from company websites, analysts and case studies. Buyers don't need sellers to communicate that type of value. The Internet does that.

The seller's job is not just to communicate value – but to create value for the customer.

The Scale of The Problem

According to the *Executive Buyer Insight Study* from Forrester Research, most salespeople (71 percent) are knowledgeable about their own products and services, but only just over a third (36 percent) of the business leaders involved in the study think that salespeople are knowledgeable about the customer's business.

In a sense though it has always been this way – at least from the customer's perspective. Customers have always wanted a knowledgeable salesperson with ideas and insight to help them on their journey. Dissatisfaction occurred either when the customer's expectations were unreasonable or the salesperson's delivery was substandard. The difference today, in this digitally transformed world, is that buyers have more choices than ever before and, with the availability of technology solutions to help sellers overcome this insight deficit problem, there really is no excuse. In many cases, sellers, or their marketing colleagues, self-profess as carriers of wisdom and insight and set expectations too high. In a world of choice, where attention spans are getting shorter and tolerance for imperfection is getting lower, knowledgeable Customer First engagements represent the new survival threshold for sellers. Sellers need to both create and communicate value as part of the sales engagement. The unfortunate truth is that, as buyer's expectations have expanded, sellers, in many cases, have been unequipped to respond.

Confirming the results of the Forrester Study, according to *Inside the Buyer's Mind*, the value received by customers when meeting with a salesperson falls short of their expectations. Just less than half (49 percent) feel that the meetings are valuable. On the other hand 70 percent of salespeople are confident that, in fact, they deliver value. This misalignment is one of the reasons why most (68 percent) of buyer / seller meetings do not result in a positive outcome. That's right, only 32 percent of new engagements between customers and their suppliers progress to a subsequent meeting. If the seller brought valuable insights to the customer the numbers would surely paint a different picture.

Figure 83: WHAT PERCENTAGE OF MEETINGS ARE VALUABLE TO THE CUSTOMER?

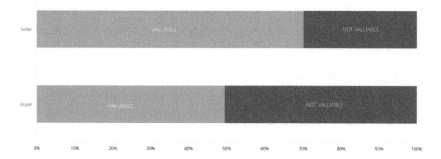

This gap between sellers' and buyers' perspectives causes friction. The buyer's role is not unimportant, of course: if the buyer is not a willing collaborative partner, the salesperson cannot succeed alone. However, I will deal here with the issues that are most commonly the causes of sellers' struggles.

At its core the gap from the seller's point of view is a combination of two things. Firstly, sellers, by their very nature and the demands of their role, are more optimistic than buyers. In many cases this optimism blinds them to the objective reality. Sellers sometimes see an opportunity where there is none or, even when there is an opportunity, they mistake engagement with advancement in a deal. Just because the buyer was friendly to the seller, the seller arrived at the erroneous conclusion that real progress had been made – where in fact the buyer was being no more than polite. If there is no measurable evidence of progress and specific actions taken, or agreed to, by the customer, then no matter how pleasant the meeting, either there is not an opportunity to be pursued or the customer is going down the path with another supplier.

The challenge for sales organizations therefore is to ensure that each of their sellers is equipped with the requisite knowledge, at each stage of the sales cycle, so that they can demonstrate to the buyer that it is in the buyer's interest to engage further with them. The buyer will only do that if she feels she can gain competitive advantage from the seller's expertise.

The responsibility to uncover the knowledge of the account lies clearly with the sales team – they should know enough about the account to be clear on the evidence they seek to confirm that the customer perceives them as more than just another vendor – but there is also an obligation on the supporting functions (Sales Operations and Marketing) to provide the sales organization with a framework so they are clear on what knowledge needs to be captured.

The second, and possibly more systemic, problem is that even when the seller has the requisite knowledge of the account and does more than just present product features, the connection to issues that the individual buyer cares about sometimes still falls short. It is often the case that the seller, genuinely excited about the potential value of their product, forgets that they first need to take the customer on a journey, signposted by insights, so that when the seller explains the benefits of the destination – how the application of the product will solve the specific business problem of their prospective customer – the customer will already have arrived at the destination.

Assuming the seller has a real understanding of the buyer's goals or business problems, jumping to presenting a solution too early can be damaging. This is where well-crafted insights can help the buyer discover a 'solution destination' that they have not previously considered.

If a salesperson does not bring new ideas that connect emotionally with the customer, they have lost a pivotal opportunity to differentiate their offering and to close the door on the competition. When a seller limits his proposal to responding to the customer's stated needs, the unique opportunity to create a first impression has passed, the sales cycle is lengthened and there is more time for the buyer to consider alternative solutions or different projects.

Customer Insights

Much has been said about the need to bring insights to your customers. In some circles bringing insights to the customer is presented as the singular solution to the challenge of the more informed buyer. *"Place a few insights in the hands of your sales team and Shazam! all of a sudden those salespeople who heretofore were product centric, 'features-and-benefits' practitioners have become consultative solution oriented artisans."* Of course this is not how the world works. Insights are valuable and powerful but only when crafted well, and applied selectively and assiduously in the context of the buyer's journey.

Not much has been written about the real purpose of Customer Insights, how to create insights, or how to operationalize what I call the *Insight Machine* that ensures that all sellers are equipped with appropriate guidance when engaging with the different buying personas in an account.

A Customer Insight is an opportunity for the supplier to:

- Teach something they want the customer to know (when they want them to know it)
- Bring value to the customer
- Demonstrate pertinent business expertise
- Reset the buyer's frame of reference
- Make an emotional connection, and
- Point to the supplier's solution.

Sellers understand the need to bring value to help shape the buyer's buying criteria, but many are struggling to know where to start. Even many of the buyers are struggling. The buyers often cannot communicate buying criteria or the outcomes they desire. Often a buyer's stated needs are a smorgasbord of different wants from multiple stakeholders. Most Marketing or Sales Operations teams flounder when trying to build an Insight Machine that reflects this complexity and scales across the sales and marketing organization.

The brutal truth is that buyers have been conditioned to expect insights – and that sales and marketing organizations are failing to deliver. The result is that buyers are often frustrated with the meetings they have with salespeople. In too many cases, the salespeople they meet do not add any value to the conversation.

How to Create Customer Insights

How can you ensure that your Insight Machine:

- Delivers insights that teach customers something you want them to know to reset the buyer's frame of reference?
- Connects with them both emotionally and logically?
- Demonstrates expertise?
- Guides them to your solutions?

A seller who adopts the buyer's perspective in his approach to a customer meeting will engage a buyer more effectively. This is because he sees things as the buyer does. He inhabits their world, and speaks to their pains, challenges, and fears. Using insights as a core part of the sales engagement strategy forces this perspective and results in more successful sales calls. Recent research from SiriusDecisions indicates that providing industry and business expertise is four times more valuable than having product knowledge and developing good relationships. That's the value of a well-designed insight.

Insights are different from traditional marketing messages: Insights help your customers discover problems (or opportunities) that they didn't know they had. Traditional marketing approaches sell to a buyer's identified need. But, as Daniel Pink said in his book *To Sell is Human*:

> Your products and services are far more valuable when your prospect is mistaken, confused, or completely clueless about their true problem.

The purpose of an insight is not to confuse, but to illuminate. Unlike traditional marketing materials, the insights themselves provide something of intrinsic value to the customer. Insights teach the customer something that you want them to learn, but have inherent worth such that, in an extreme case, a customer should be not be averse to paying for the insight itself. Traditional marketing messages tend to address just the need that the buyer has identified. Remember, that is what all your competitors are doing, so it is hard to differentiate by doing the same.

Companies sometimes struggle to identify the recipe for a great insight, wondering whether they have the core ingredients. In my experience, every company that has created a valuable product or solution has the knowledge and the critical components to present the capabilities of their offering in an insightful manner to the market. But many don't think of it that way.

Consider this: when your engineers, product managers or product designers first built the product you are selling, they usually started with a customer problem that they were looking to solve in a unique way. The solution they developed was designed to fix something that was broken in the customer's organization, or to provide a capability that didn't exist but was needed. Assuming that the product concept was well-informed, the essence of those product design decisions should be the foundation on which you build your insights.

Unfortunately, in many cases, some of the ingredients for that great sales insight are lost on the journey from product designer to salesperson. Good insights lead a customer to the unique value that you can provide with your solution. This is important. If your sales team is bringing insights to your customer that are not leading to your unique value, then your sales efforts become an expensive educational exercise, and you may end up educating the customer right into the arms of your competitor.

Insights are tremendously powerful when well-crafted and used in the right context. However, this is one of those cases where if you can't do it exceptionally well, you should not do it at all. You can fall on your face really easily.

1. **Start with the 'typical' customer problems:** All customers are different, but few have truly unique problems – just problems that are not sufficiently well-understood at a detail level in the context of that customer. Companies of a similar size, at the same stage of company maturity, in the same region, and serving the same markets tend to have similar business challenges. There are other attributes that apply, and while the issues vary by role and the ability to meet those challenges might diverge, the context generally remains the same (or at least similar). This is just how business works.

2. **All businesses have Goals (or Key Business Requirements) and Business Pressures to which they must respond:** This is why they undertake Initiatives (or projects): to relieve those pressures so that they can achieve the goals. In essence, these Initiatives fix things that are broken or add things that don't exist but are necessary for a successful initiative. I refer to these as Obstacles. Remember, the reason the product was built in the first place was to help fix something that was broken, or to fill a gap in the market.

3. **Consider the Buying Personas:** Companies don't buy – people do. In a typical B2B scenario there will be multiple personas involved in the buying decision. Each of these will have different concerns and issues that they care about. If, for example, you are selling a Cloud based CRM system, the VP Sales in the buyer's organization may care about how the CRM will help with sales productivity, while the CIO is more likely to be concerned about the deployment effort and data

security concerns. Insights must be designed with the buying persona in mind. In this example, it may be valuable to provide the CIO with insights around the relative cost-of-ownership of SaaS *versus* on-premise software. The VP Sales might care about that, but probably not too much. He is much more likely to be interested in the ease of use for his sales team and access over mobile devices, and might see value in a whitepaper that discuss trends in mobility.

4. **Make it interesting – add intrigue:** While it is important to address the buyer's stated needs, and demonstrate your understanding of how the buyer might deploy your solution to meet those needs, it is a lot more valuable if you can create that *"Aha"* moment when the buyer says: "That's interesting, I never thought about it that way before. I can see how we might benefit from that approach." You want to teach the customer something that you want them to learn. You have to bring something new to the table and make it interesting.

5. **Lead to your solution:** You can create an insight that leads to your solution if you have a deep understanding as to why the product was developed in the first place. This is where sales enablement and product marketing / management can deliver dramatic value to the sales team by synthesizing those specific capabilities that your product uniquely delivers that the customer should value, based on your understanding of their business. You want to use the insight to lead to your product's capabilities mapped to the customer's known or unknown needs, rather than use traditional marketing approaches to lead with the product.

6. **Do not (overtly) self-promote:** As I said above, the insight you provide should have intrinsic value. 'Here

are 12 steps to building a great sales playbook,' 'Check out your sales velocity equation' and '64 percent of sales calls are ineffective' are all examples of Insights that all have intrinsic value – independently of whether the customer chooses to do business with the insight provider. They each cause the buyer to think in a potentially different way about the challenges or opportunities in front of them. Good examples of insights are things like third party studies, survey results, or industry analysis. Anything that is overtly self-promotional, and presented as an insight, does more harm than good. Datasheets, customer testimonials, or demo videos are not insights. Insights should be vendor agnostic. Bear in mind that you are asking the buyer to spend their time consuming whatever you provide. Does the insight add value to their job? You should be using the insight to build credibility.

Leveraging Digital Sales Transformation to Scale

Crafting effective insights is designing for a crucial component of the buyer / seller interaction: the point at which credibility grows or dies. It is not reasonable (or responsible) to ask all your salespeople to figure this out themselves. They just don't have the time and are not as close to the problem as your product people were when they were building the product, or where your sales enablement or product management / marketing people should be. In many cases you will end up with marketing collateral masquerading as insights; or insights that are only lightly-informed and can't flex when faced with any level of analysis; or, at worst, insights that have not been thought through well enough and in fact lead to a capability that you cannot provide.

There are too few sales and marketing organizations that package insights in a manner that can be consumed easily by an individual salesperson and then shared with the customer. Even fewer have put the infrastructure in place to scale such a solution consistently across a sales team. This is where things typically fall down. I've seen marketing portals brimming with collateral, sales portals littered with data sheets and case studies, and CRM systems grinding to a halt under the weighty burden of content, content and more content. There is lots of content, but very little customer context. We need less content and more context.

In recent years I have seen dramatic benefit accrue when sales and marketing take this approach to align around their customers. Many are good – but some are really excellent, when the visionary for the project is passionate and driven to drive value for the customer through the sales engagement. Janice Rapoza, Sr. Director, Global Sales Enablement and

Programs at Brocade, is one such visionary, and kindly agreed to tell her story for this book.

A Practitioner's Perspective
Janice Rapoza, Sr. Director, Global Sales Enablement and Programs, Brocade

What customers want and need are solutions to their problems; solutions that advance their position in the industry, give them a competitive advantage, and save them money. Selling with a focus on customer issues – what matters to them – provokes disruptive thinking and requires behavior change for both sales and product marketers.

To achieve this, we needed to arm the sales force with collateral, content assets, and quality insights that would enable them to engage customers in a tailored conversation about what matters to the customer, so that they could identify how our solutions meet their needs. Addressing this shift in content creation through the alignment of sales and marketing was critical in enabling a sophisticated sales force to be disruptive and achieve a trusted advisor status.

Making this shift is a significant change. It impacts how and what our highly skilled product and marketing professionals do in their roles. It requires training and coaching about working collaboratively, communicating, and developing relevant customer insights.

We could not have succeeded if we had not leveraged technology. It operationalized this process for both sales and marketing. Using technology to facilitate the change, ease the transition, and lessen the apprehension of the content creators is vital. This shift to an insight sales approach will become the norm for our business going forward.

In the previous chapter (*Chapter 9: Know Your Customer First*) you were introduced to the Customer Insight Map. As you know, the Customer Insight Map tells a story: it's a narrative of the customer's business. But it also points to episodes where you can help by mapping the specific capabilities of your product to the customer's specific obstacles so that you have a happy ending to the story.

We know that when the salesperson has demonstrated that he comprehends the buyer's world, their Goals and Pressures, Initiatives (known or potential) and Obstacles, only then has the seller earned the right to talk about his Solutions.

But the question is: What does he say?

Behind every solution you need a critical set of assets that combine the wisdom of the company: the tenured sellers, the product management and marketing people, and the customer success and support team. Pouring all that knowledge into a single receptacle – I call it the Solution Sales Kit – equips all sellers, old and new, to extend their business conversations with their customers.

The Solution Sales Kit describes the personas the sellers engage with, the messages to be conveyed, how to handle the competition, insights they can deliver, questions they should use and how to address objections that they might encounter. Each component of the Solution Sales Kit is designed so that the salesperson has something valuable to say to each of the personas at each point of the customer engagement.

There are six components to a Solution Sales Kit, as shown in **Figure 84** below.

Figure 84: SOLUTION SALES KIT COMPONENTS

Key Messages	Statements that describe your solution's unique business value, capabilities and benefits for your key buyer personas.
Insights	Insights help the customer better understand their business problem, and set the context for your conversation, by helping them learn something that you want them to know.
Sales Tools	Documents and other media to be used by the sales team to describe solutions and provide proof of value.
High Yield Questions	Questions that demonstrate your business expertise and reveal the most information to uncover motivations to buy.
Competitive Positioning	Statements to position unique capabilities (that the buyer considers valuable) compared to alternatives, allowing the buyer to arrive at their own conclusion.
Objections	The most difficult questions that customers typically have about your solution, and suggested responses to address them.

Key Messages: If there is one thing (or just a few things) that you want the seller to convey to the prospective customer, to position your solution, then this is it. Key Messages should relate to your Unique Business Value – that 'special sauce' that only you can provide that the customer deems highly valuable – and should be considered in the context of each of the key buying personas. It's your short value proposition.

EXAMPLES: KEY MESSAGES *(from Altify)*

We wrote the book on Account Planning in Salesforce, Because we are focused on Salesforce (and count Salesforce as one of our key account planning customers) we have a greater insight into what Salesforce customers need to do to maximize revenue from their key accounts by deploying an Account Planning solution. In fact we wrote

Account Planning in Salesforce as the 'go-to text' for anyone who uses Salesforce and wants to grow revenue from key accounts.

Automation & Intelligence: Native on the Salesforce platform, Altify Account Manager applies automation and intelligence so it is easy to adopt account planning and management as part of your company's processes. Using Altify analysis and advice, the account team can work together to execute the account strategy.

Insights: I have covered Customer Insights in detail earlier in this chapter. You will remember that a Customer Insight is an opportunity for the supplier to teach the customer something they want him to know, bring value, demonstrate expertise and make an emotional connection to reset the buyer's frame of reference to point to the supplier's solution.

EXAMPLES: INSIGHTS

68 percent of all sales calls are ineffective: According to *Inside the Buyer's Mind*, most sales calls are not effective because the seller does not have a plan for what they want to achieve.

Selling to existing accounts is 6 times easier: Research shows that you can add new business to existing accounts 6 times more easily than acquiring a new customer. The key is to understand where your whitespace exists, by exploring the customer's business, their people and their challenges. Only 54 percent of sellers know how to access key players and only 61 percent can uncover customer challenges.

Sales Tools: These are the materials that Marketing creates as part of the normal course of business and usually include datasheets, product videos, customer case studies, product specific whitepapers, ROI calculators etc.

High Yield Questions: Customers do not want to be peppered with lots of traditional 'discovery' questions. High Yield questions demonstrate your business expertise and reveal the most information to uncover motivations to buy. Buyers do not have an unlimited amount of time and, unless you are proving your value with the questions you ask, the buyers will quickly run out of patience. A well-crafted High Yield Question should result in a long informative answer from the prospective customer. The customer should be doing most of the talking.

Instead of asking a customer when they want to start a project, much more valuable questions might be: *"When do you want to see impact of change from this project?," "Would it matter if the project was delayed by six months?"* or perhaps: *"According to the latest industry report, 72 percent of companies underestimate the upfront work necessary to get a return from this type of project, resulting in delays in getting the requisite returns. Have you considered when you need to see impact from the project and what resources you will need to deploy to make sure you are part of the 28 percent who get there on time?"*

Creating a High Yield Question takes time and preparation. Often, these types of questions don't come naturally. People are generally more comfortable with factual types of questions, not perception or impact type questions.

First you need to identify what information you need to advance the sale or gain momentum. This is the purpose of the specific question. Next, determine who would know the information you need. Be prepared to ask different questions to different people to confirm or uncover the necessary information. The trick is to think about the response you want before you formulate the question. When you write down the possible answers you can construct the question to ensure you'll get the desired result and you know what to listen for. Begin with the end in mind.

Then you need to build credibility by demonstrating your business expertise. This is easier than it sounds and is achieved by thinking about the structure of the question, as well as the question itself.

For example, when you state an inarguable fact in front of the question, you have the opportunity to present your business expertise. For example you might say:

- *"According to Forrester, only 36 percent of salespeople are adequately prepared for sales calls, and as a result only 25 percent of sales calls result in a follow up meeting. What processes has your sales leadership implemented to ensure that you don't suffer the same outcome?"*

- *"Many of our customers begin looking at solutions for Business Intelligence Standardization, but once their planning needs are considered, they realize they need Corporate Performance Management. What are your initiatives around Corporate Performance Management?"*

- *"Many organizations are challenged with information in disparate systems. What impact does information have on your Compensation Planning initiatives?"*

- *"The latest Gartner report suggests that that while 82 percent of companies are looking for ways to improve customer service, of these 76 percent are also under pressure to reduce operational costs. What initiatives is your organization considering to improve service while reducing costs?"*

The optimum structure of a High Yield Question is one that starts with a statement or presentation of information that teaches something to the customer and demonstrates that you have some expertise (an Insight), and then follows with an open question inviting the customer's answer and opinion.

EXAMPLE: HIGH YIELD QUESTION

Question: According to Bain Consulting, the likelihood of winning additional business from an existing customer is 6 times greater than winning a new account. What is your win rate variance between existing and current customers?

Purpose: Highlight what is possible with Account Planning as it relates to win rate.

What to listen for: Win rate 30 percent or less from existing accounts; they had not thought of that. They need to improve the win rate. We have hunters and farmers. We are not proactively creating opportunities; we are responding to requests.

Competitive Positioning: According to *Inside the Buyer's Mind,* most buying organizations invite more than three potential suppliers to bid for business. The last thing you want to do is to have to react when a buyer has become enamored with a specific feature of one of your competitor's solutions, ignoring a unique capability you have that you know is really much more valuable to the customer. If you have to react, it is much harder to position the value of your capability without being seen as just trying to sell something. The key is to position that capability early in the cycle in such a way that it shapes the framework of the conversation.

According to *Inside the Buyer's Mind*, more than 67 percent of buyers actually want suppliers to engage early in the buying cycle. Unsurprisingly, from the same study, sellers who are 'early engagers' have a 30 percent higher win rate than those who don't.

Effective competitive positioning follows a similar structure to High Yield Questions. It starts with a statement of fact and then follows with a question that leads to your competitive advantage or exposes a competitor's weakness. In my opinion, you should never overtly criticize a competitor but instead highlight your strengths or lead the customer to discover the competitor's shortcomings.

In the case of customers who buy applications from Salesforce's AppExchange, the fact that many of these solutions are built natively on the Salesforce Platform is critical to large enterprises who care about security, reliability and performance. If a competitive alternative solution is 'off platform,' then the customer should be concerned about data security, the reliability of the third party hosting infrastructure and their ability to manage it. This should be compared with the fact that they are evidently already happy with these factors on Salesforce. As shown in the example below the best approach here is not to point out that the competitor's solution is on a separate cloud infrastructure, but to point out the benefits of being native in Salesforce and suggest that, if these benefits are important, the customer should satisfy themselves that the same capabilities are available from all offerings under consideration.

EXAMPLE: COMPETITIVE POSITIONING

Native on Salesforce Platform: Many of our customers are concerned with response time and security of third party apps, but their concern went away as soon as they discovered we are native on the salesforce.com platform. How does your IT department feel about the security and reliability of third party applications with a separate cloud and hosting infrastructure *versus* an application that is native on the same Salesforce platform as Salesforce itself?

Objections: Handling objections should mean answering your customer's questions in a way that will help them better understand how your solution addresses their goals, pressures, initiative and / or obstacles. It is also your opportunity to clarify the difference between what the customer thinks is true and what is actually true.

Objections are not necessarily negative. The very fact that the objection was raised shows that the customer is sufficiently interested to engage in the conversation. When well-handled, it is an opportunity to get the focus back on the business challenges and value that you provide. The buyer's mindset is predisposed to challenge the supplier – particularly when you are dealing with an experienced buyer. So it is natural for buyers to raise objections – in reality, in many cases, they are only asking questions to better understand your proposition.

First you should pause to ensure that you understand the objection correctly, and where necessary probe for deeper understanding. Then it is useful to confirm what you heard. You want to be sure that you are addressing the right issue for the customer and not responding to an objection that has not been raised.

If your solution is not a good fit you should not press the point as that will not add value for either party. If the objection relates to the commercials, then the only avenue is to restate your value and make sure that you have articulated it well. Where possible, as with all objection handling situations you should limit your response to the topic that is being raised, be confident in the value that you provide, and where possible use other customer stories as proof points.

EXAMPLES: OBJECTIONS

Account Planning is hard: Account Management is more than we need; it's too hard and too involved for our sales teams.

Response: That used to be true perhaps – but much less so now. Our R&D team has done a great job in making Altify Account Manager easy to use, easy to share, and easy to work with every day. More importantly, the benefits of planning are dramatic. 3x to 4x pipeline growth is not uncommon. Now, with the easier to use tools, Account Planning is definitely worthwhile. When Salesforce deployed Account Manager the average new pipeline uncovered in each account planning session was $15m.

Need is for Opportunity Management: We really focus and need Opportunity Management. We need to win the deals we are working. I don't see how Account Planning will help us win more deals this quarter.

Response: Altify Opportunity Manager might well be the best place to start so we should consider that. As you know, Account Management will help you to find new deals to work. You know that you are 7 times more likely to win a deal from an existing customer than find a new one. Account Manager also has big influence on average deal size – so in fact you may need to win fewer deals.

Pulling It All Together

Customer First engagement is not just a sales issue. It is an organizational issue, combining the expertise and experience of sales, marketing, and product management all aligned around the customer. There is a question that I believe lies at the heart of all buyer / seller interactions:

> What business problems does your customer have that you solve better than anyone else?

I call this the **Customer Value Question**, and at the core of the answer is the essence of why a company exists. Usually a company starts with a product idea that addresses a gap in the market. There is a problem to be solved, and either the available solutions are inadequate, or there are no effective solutions available. Winning salespeople need to know the answer to that Customer Value Question and understand how to tell the story in conversation with the customer. In doing so, they will achieve win / win outcomes by putting the customer at the center.

Too many times sales onboarding or product launch initiatives are focused on what the company does, or the capabilities of its products or solutions. Not enough time is spent equipping the sales team to first understand the customer's business issues, so they can then collaborate on how to apply the solutions to address the customer's problems. Think about what would happen if you wrapped up all the expertise in your organization into an easily consumable package for your customer facing employees to use anywhere, anytime, from their smartphones. It would accelerate your employees' experience in your customers' business, help them adopt the customer's perspective and answer the Customer Value Question much more easily.

Marketing portals are brimming with collateral, sales portals are littered with data sheets and case studies, and CRM systems are grinding to a halt under the weighty burden of content, content and more content. There is plenty of content, but little customer context. To be successful, the requisite software infrastructure should be implemented to scale this Customer First approach across a sales team, and other revenue team members. Everyone should understand the typical problems that your typical buyer faces. Creating and organizing marketing and sales materials with a Customer First focus will facilitate business conversations with customers that lead to the right solutions.

I believe that's how sellers gain an unfair advantage and outpace the competition.

CHAPTER 11:

COMMUNICATE VALUE AT SCALE: ACCOUNT BASED MARKETING

Introduction

ACCOUNT BASED MARKETING IN A NUTSHELL

Definition: Account Based Marketing is one component of a strategic approach to targeted accounts. ABM aligns Sales and Marketing and other customer facing team members around a focused set of accounts to deepen relationships and build trust to make it easy for the customer to choose your company as their business partner.

1. Target Accounts: You start with a limited set of targeted accounts that fit your Ideal Customer Profile. These accounts are then segmented into tiers: Key Accounts, Portfolio Accounts and Market Accounts.

2. Define Personas: The next step is to define Personas – the multiple buying roles in the account who care about the problem areas that your solution solves.

3. Design ABM Plays: An ABM play is a number of coordinated and interconnected actions that follow a strategy for an account (or set of accounts) to achieve a business development objective. It is dependent on Sales, Marketing, and other customer facing functions using multiple channels of engagement to achieve a measurable outcome with one or more buying personas in the account.

4. Execute ABM Plays: Depending on your current status with each of these accounts, deploy ABM plays to some or all of the personas to achieve a specific business objective.

5. Measure Outcomes: Gauge effectiveness by measuring Contacts and Coverage, Awareness and Interest, and Preference and Impact for each of your Target Accounts.

All of a sudden, the world is awash with marketing pronouncements about Account Based Everything: Account Based *Marketing*, Account Based Selling, Account Based *Targeting*, and even Account Based *Profitability*. It is as if the need to develop long term relationships with customers has crept up on us, unforeseen and unanticipated. We know that is not so. Account planning and management has been around for decades – particularly among the winning sales organizations that repeatedly outpace their competitors.

The principle of integrating sales and marketing in a connected way to serve the customer is not new. In my first book on sales – *Select Selling* (2003) – I wrote that the future of selling and customer engagement:

> ... combines high-level, strategic marketing principles to draw the map, with focused sales execution to complete each journey, addressing the practical stops along the way.

Customer engagement is a continuum with a constant focus: consistent delivery of value to the customer.

Account Based Marketing on its own is dangerous – automated ABM even more so. Customers are more colorful than black and white data, more textured than market segments, and the relationship you develop with them is deeper than a series of touch-points designed to get their attention. Relationships are based on a trust equation that starts with the first promise you make and ends with the first promise you break.

While the arrival of account focused marketing tools is very welcome, thinking that these tools alone enhance customer engagement is foolhardy. To accept the premise that an account based focus is new or innovative would also just be plain wrong. We would miss the opportunity to learn lessons from those who have been delivering mutual value with their customers, as part of an integrated go-to-market, territory planning, account planning, and or account management strategy – the essence of which is connected and comprehensive. Your customer engagement strategy needs to be coordinated and collaborative. It is both strategic and tactical. The account team, like an orchestra, is playing 'in tune' and 'on tempo,' maintaining rhythm and cohesion between sales, marketing, customer service and yes, most importantly, the customer too.

Account based anything is an organizational discipline and Account Based Marketing has a critical role to play. Your ABM program must be designed in the context of your account planning approach, and consequently all ABM related marketing activity must align with the Sales strategy for the account. It is really important to consciously manage the hand-off from marketing to sales, to customer service, and back to marketing. We need to recognize that augmenting sales strategy with supporting marketing strategy is a good idea. It can influence the strategy to engage effectively before, during, and after the sale. It is essential that you apply ABM, not as a separate disconnected program, but as an integrated program in your account-focused Go To Market engine.

Figure 85: THE SALES AND MARKETING CONTINUUM

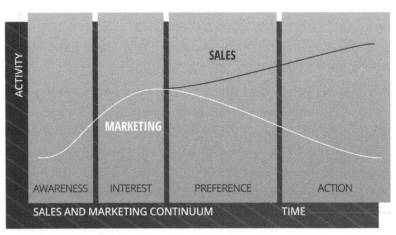

For any purchase, the customer goes through a number of phases, beginning with *Awareness* on the Sales and Marketing Continuum (**Figure 85**). At the *Awareness* point, they learn that you and your product exist. This is followed by *Interest* where they care about what you (and others) have. The next phase is the critical one. This is where they establish *Preference* for a given solution or supplier.

We have seen ABM work very well, but unfortunately there are many situations where ABM fails, causes headaches for the account team, and becomes a nuisance to the customer.

Five common ABM pitfalls

These are the most common reasons why ABM fails:

1. **No Insights:** If you don't know anything about the account, the people in the account, or their business needs, it is hard to develop an effective marketing strategy for the account.
2. **No Sales Alignment:** Marketing needs to know what Sales needs to accomplish in order to construct the strategies and activities to deliver on those goals.
3. **Lack of Skilled Resources:** ABM managers must have the necessary skills and bandwidth to act as an integrated part of the account team.
4. **Poor Customer Alignment:** Account planning, and ABM, must be all about the customer: authentic, informed and grounded in the customer's success. Know the customer's world.
5. **Undifferentiated Execution:** Using generic messages to too many 'specific' accounts does not work. The customers must perceive that they, individually, are at the center of your thinking.

ABM – Getting Back to Basics

The determination of what specific value you can provide to a customer better than anyone else is the fulcrum upon which successful customer engagement is balanced. In ABM, once you have targeted the right accounts using the framework described in *Chapter 5: The Ideal Customer Profile,* and identified the personas, your vehicle to communicate this value is your ABM play.

> **Definition:** An ABM play is a number of coordinated and interconnected actions that follow a strategy for an account (or set of accounts) to achieve a business development objective. It is dependent on Sales, Marketing, and other customer facing functions using multiple channels of engagement to achieve a measurable outcome with one or more buying personas in the account.

As companies experience the pressure of more knowledgeable buyers – a pressure felt most pointedly by Sales and Marketing – there is a need to get ahead of price dominated sales conversations.

Value must be expressed, and value expression implies that you understand the position you want to occupy in the mind of the buyer. Positioning is not about you, your product or your company, but about the place in the customer's mind that you want to inhabit.

As each of us as consumers become more attuned to the 'X-as-a-service' mindset, our expectations change. We expect our business partners to earn our trust every day with consistency and transparency. ABM, as part of your approach to your selected accounts, is often the first point of contact. It's where you make your first promise – so it must be part of the continuum that delivers on that promise.

For ABM to be effective, Sales and Marketing need to align around the customer. According to the Altify *Business Performance Benchmark Study*, organizations that manage to crack that sales and marketing alignment nut experience a win rate that is 26 percent greater and a sales cycle that is 18 percent shorter than companies where the relationship is less harmonious.

Figure 86: THE IMPACT OF SALES AND MARKETING ALIGNMENT

On today's playing field, successful customer engagement – resulting in long term customer relationships and revenue growth – encapsulates the best of strategic marketing, but at an individual customer level, where Sales and Marketing are focused not just on aligning with each other but on aligning around the customer. Paraphrasing my assertion in *Select Selling*, it combines high-level, strategic marketing principles to draw the map, with focused sales execution to complete each journey, addressing each customer need along the way.

Where ABM is adopted effectively as part of an integrated account focused program, concentrated activity becomes the norm. The customers that you select are those who gain most from your unique differentiated capabilities, the value that you deliver to the customer increases and, as a consequence, you build sustainable relationships that drive revenue growth. When adopted throughout the symbiotic functions of Sales, Marketing, Service and Operations, uncommon organizational alignment is achieved, driving profits as well as revenue.

Defining your ABM Scope: Create Tiers and Assign Owners and Roles

Sometimes we struggle to choose the companies we should pursue for business. In many cases, the irrational fear of potential missed opportunities drives otherwise rational sales and marketing professionals to adopt a scattergun approach to target customer selection. But we need to *select* carefully. *Select* means many things. According to Merriam Webster, it means "chosen from a number or group by fitness or preference;" "of special value or excellence: exclusively or fastidiously chosen often with regard to social, economic, or cultural characteristics;" and "judicious or restrictive in choice." In the context of ABM it should mean all of these things.

Select is about both efficiency and effectiveness, spending time only where it's worthwhile, choosing the customers that are more likely to buy, those for whom you can deliver most value, and controlling your destiny as a business or as a seller. It's where all the forces align. The benefit of selecting well is that the value you deliver to your customer is extreme and it doesn't cost you too much to acquire new business. As a consequence, you are not wasting time or resources with accounts that will not deliver a return. Profitability increases. Customer satisfaction is high, and the conversion rate of prospect to customer is greater than the norm.

Few companies have products that truly appeal equally to broad horizontal markets – and very few companies ever went bankrupt for being too focused. Concentrating exclusively on customers whose needs mirror the advantages and benefits you offer is the most effective way to build your business. Making choices means that you must exclude some opportunities. What you're left with is your 'sweet spot' – that group of accounts who map to your Ideal Customer Profile (ICP) – see *Chapter 5*.

Figure 87: ACCOUNT TIERS

Create account tiers

Not all accounts are equal – even if you restrict your view to those that fit your ICP – so you must create layers of focus and effort, depending on your current relationship with the account, future revenue potential and the amount and type of resource you can apply.

Most companies stratify their accounts into three or more layers reflecting their actual or potential strategic importance, and that's a good model to adopt when defining the tiers of an ABM program.

At the top of the pyramid are your **Key Accounts**: the companies that can have a material impact on your company as a function of the current level of business or their future potential. Each seller will likely only have one, or at a maximum three companies that fit this profile and will have a detailed account plan for each company. It is likely that your Key Account will be that 15 percent to 20 percent of existing customers who represent 80 percent of your company's revenue.

There may be exceptional cases where you identify a New Logo or new account that you deem to be sufficiently strategic, either in potential revenue or other strategic terms, to justify giving it the 'Key Account treatment.'

Next up is the **Portfolio** of named accounts where you have already done some preliminary research using your ICP framework to determine that each is a viable target. Sellers might each have 20 of these named accounts in their portfolio.

The third tier comprises the companies in the **Market** that Marketing or Sales Operations has identified as fitting your ICP who are not already included in the Key Account or Portfolio Accounts.

Finally, beneath the pyramid, there will be other companies who have not yet been tracked down but who should be nurtured by Marketing into Market, and then Portfolio, when they come on your company's radar.

Deciding on how many accounts fit in each tier is really a function of the complexity of the sales engagement. This can be determined by considering:

- The average deal size
- Sales cycle
- Dimensions of the typical buying group
- The sales effort required to pursue an account
- The resources you have available to apply to the program.

In short, how many can you handle effectively?

If, for example, your company is typically engaged in six- or seven-figure sales, with a complex product, involving many participants from your company in the sale, and you're selling to a committee of multiple buyers on the customer's side, then it is likely that the right number of accounts is:

- **Key Accounts:** 1 to 3 per salesperson
- **Portfolio Accounts:** 20 per salesperson

- **Market Accounts:** 1,000 per salesperson (in reality, this tier is owned by Marketing).

You can turn the numbers up or down to map to your business. For example, if your average deal size is $40,000, you might have 50 accounts in your portfolio instead of 20 mentioned above. If on the other hand your average deal size is $1,000,000, it's unlikely that you should have more than 10.

As with all components of account focused activity, account selection for your ABM program is a long game activity. Switching accounts in and out of the program is not a good idea. This is usually less of an issue with Key Accounts, as by virtue of their already having been identified as companies that can have a material impact on your business, volatility is less common. Tenacity and discipline are particularly needed in the middle tier – the portfolio. It can be natural for impatience to raise its head.

When you are a few months into your ABM program and you are not seeing immediate return or engagement from one of the accounts on your list, you may be inclined to want to drop that account from the program and substitute it with another. This is most likely the wrong move. You will waste much of your investment in the program unless your ABM metrics clearly point to poor selection and a need to change.

Assign owners and roles

When the account lives in that small triangle at the top of the pyramid, the account manager is the owner of the account, the account plan and the ABM plays. Marketing is involved in a supporting role. At the bottom of pyramid, ownership clearly lies with Marketing. In the middle it is a blend: Marketing owns the execution but collaborates extensively with Sales on which ABM play to apply to each account so that it is integrated into the rest of the account planning activities.

Figure 88: ABM – OWNERSHIP AND ROLES

	Qty	Owner	Play	Where	Focus
Key Account	1	Sales	Account-specific ABM plays defined by Sales supported by Marketing	Sales Defined	Revenue & Pipeline
Portfolio	20	Marketing & Sales	Strategy by sales; Customized template play from Marketing	Multi-channel	Pipeline & Revenue
Market	1000+	Marketing	Persona & Industry led play by Marketing	Multi-channel	Awareness & Interest

Success with ABM is highly dependent on alignment between Sales and Marketing. The last thing you want is Marketing running an ABM play to a Key Account without the knowledge or insight of the account manager. The account will get confused. Messaging from Sales and Marketing might conflict with each other, and bad things will happen. Similarly, if Marketing invests in a set of ABM plays to an account in a seller's portfolio, but the seller is not involved or engaged in the exercise, the investment is wasted and your company will appear unprofessional to the target account.

The mandate for a symbiotic relationship between Sales and Marketing, and the need for an integrated approach that combines ABM with account planning, become crystal clear when you consider the activities that must occur for an effective ABM program. ABM is not a standalone exercise –

but just one component of your strategic account planning and management investments – one act in a play where the customer is in the starring role and the director, the account manager, is choreographing the roles of the sales and marketing actors.

Figure 89: ABM ACTIVITY, MAPPED TO OWNER AND APPLICABILITY FOR ABM TIERS

	Primary Owner		Tier Applicability		
	Marketing	Sales	Key	Portfolio	Market
Market Intelligence	◆		✔	✔	✔
Account Intelligence	◆		✔	✔	✔
Account Selection	◆		✔	✔	✔
Marketing Campaigns	◆				✔
Account Plan		◆	✔		
Portfolio Plan		◆		✔	
Business Drivers / Account Needs		◆	✔	✔	
Stakeholder Identification	◆		✔	✔	
Stakeholder Analysis		◆	✔	✔	
Account Strategy		◆	✔		
Relationship Development		◆	✔		
Executive Sponsor		◆	✔		
Competitive Landscape	◆		✔	✔	✔
Targeted Value Proposition	◆		✔		
Custom Content Development	◆		✔		
Tailored Content	◆			✔	
ABM Play	◆		✔	✔	✔

ABM Personas and ABM Plays

To express value, you must understand the position you want to occupy in the mind of the buyer. Positioning is about the place in the customer's mind that you want to inhabit. If, from the broad expanse of the world's companies, you have selected your customer targets well, accounts chosen to meet the inherent value of your product, and pruned by profile to meet the competitive advantage you bring, then your positioning should self-suggest and come to life in your ABM plays. It will encompass an expression of value that sets you apart as the preferred supplier or customer partner.

Defining the personas

Before you can influence what the buying roles in the customer organization are thinking, you have to get inside their mind – and that is what persona development is about. Companies don't buy, people buy. In ABM parlance, buyer profiles or buying roles are described as personas. (And yes, to the Latin scholars out there, I know it should be personae – 1st declension / feminine / plural, and all that – but that would just make it awkward, so let's leave it for now.)

> **DEFINITION:** The personas you should care about are those who care about the problem or opportunity areas in their business that solutions like yours address or impact.

The primary persona is the owner of the business problem. Typically this role has the ability to commit the company to a strategic direction and has accountability for selecting the solution. In addition to the primary persona, there will likely also be secondary personas for whom you will need to craft separate and distinct messages.

For example, if you are targeting a company with an ABM play designed to encourage a company to invest in an account planning software solution, the primary persona is the Vice President of Sales. The Director of Sales Operations will usually be involved and someone in IT will frequently be an influencer. If the company is strategic about how it approaches strategic accounts then Marketing, Customer Success and Learning and Development will be part of the decision cycle also. It is also important to remember that, in addition to those involved in the decision cycle as part of the buying group, the end users – the salespeople, sales managers, and CRM administrator – are other people *who care about the problem or opportunity areas in their business that solutions like yours address.* So in this example, you can have as many as nine personas:

- **Primary Persona:** VP Sales
- **Secondary Personas:** Director of Sales Operations, Head of IT, CMO, Director of Customer Success, Senior Director of L&D (and Account Manager, Sales Manager, and CRM Admin.).

In consumer industries, persona definitions tend to describe their target buyers in terms of their personal attributes and desires.

Vogue magazine targets *"women in their late twenties or thirties who work in fashion or have a desire to work in fashion or simply enjoy reading about it."*

An extract from the marketing plan of golf club manufacturer TaylorMade for the TaylorMade R9 Driver describes its primary persona as *"a male who has been playing golf at a high level at the amateur or professional level. The club is geared toward the individual who seeks to make adjustments mid game ... consumers with a household income over $100,000 ... fluent in usage of the internet ... drives a luxury vehicle and belongs to a local country club."*

For individuals involved in B2B enterprise sales – the broad persona to whom this book is targeted – persona development should focus first on the factors that the personas care about with respect to the business problem that your solution addresses. You might secondarily consider the personal or company cultural aspects that influence their behavior and determine their propensity to be attracted to your solution.

THE PERSONAL FACTOR

When you think about why a businessperson cares about something, remember that there is usually a personal aspect to consider.

It may be financial – will I achieve my bonus or commission? Or perhaps recognition is most important – what will it take for my sales region to be the top performer? Future career progression, or positioning for my next role in my next company could be a factor.

As you reflect on the profile of each persona, and particularly as you get to know the individuals in your key accounts, don't forget to take these personal aspirations into account.

What does your persona care about?

To get inside the mind of the personas, you first need to figure out what they care about. In business that is usually governed by how they measure success. Typically their business goals will align to their success measures. For example, the VP of Sales may have a goal to grow revenue, increase revenue per head, or improve forecast accuracy. That's normal, and while it is good to know, it does not tell you much about what he cares about beyond achievement of the goals.

Going one level deeper you can assume that he cares about quarterly targets, maximizing the productivity of each member of his team, and having visibility into what deals are likely to close in any given period. As your VP Sales is busy running his business he will inevitably hit bumps in the road that cause him to stumble. He might miss the quarterly targets. It is likely that he will not have balanced performance across all his team, or that a forecasted deal might slip upsetting the forecast. The best sales VPs are constantly focused on the things that might go wrong so that they can proactively take action to mitigate the risks. These are the things that they care about in their business.

For example, you might consider the potential reasons why your primary persona, the VP Sales, might miss a quarterly target.

We know most companies achieve the majority of their revenue from their existing customers, so a miss in that area is likely to impact his ability to make his number. Effectiveness at maximizing revenue from his key accounts is one thing that he cares about. He is measured on revenue and one of the main sources of revenue is his current customers, so knowing how to grow revenue through cross-sell to a broader footprint in the account and up-sell other solutions are issues he should be concerned with.

To help the VP Sales mitigate risks in any area of his business you need to consider the potential tasks that he needs to perform, the business practices that need to be in place for him to be successful and the common problems that he might encounter. If you know your persona well, you can create messages, content, and thought leadership pieces that resonate. He should be able to see himself in the pictures you paint.

In the case of the account planning solution, the symptoms that the VP Sales will recognize as being areas that need to be improved might be: inability to access executives in the account; selling just one product to each customer when his company has a breadth of related solutions; difficulty in understanding how his solutions connect to his customers' business problems; no common approach across the sales team to collaborate on growing the account, etc.

Delivering content to the primary persona that he (or she) can relate to shows that you have taken the time to understand his world and the things that he cares about. Use the following model as a way to make sure you understand your persona well so that you can list the things that he cares about and then develop a content map as part of your ABM play.

Figure 90: UNDERSTANDING PERSONAS

Category	Description
Goals	An end result to be achieved by the persona with a measurable outcome.
Pressures	The internal and / or external pressures that significantly impact the persona and serve as the catalyst for initiatives or action.
Initiatives	Typical projects initiated and owned by the persona created to address the pressures and achieve the goals.
Obstacles	Something that isn't working; a task, situation or process that is broken and needs to be fixed or is required to deploy the initiative but does not exist.
Solution	How your capabilities or products help the persona to remove obstacles to relieve business pressures.

Building the ABM plays

You must be very clear on the differentiated value you can provide to a specific customer. This is the fulcrum upon which successful customer engagement is balanced. Get it right and you tip towards trusted relationships, mutual value and revenue growth. Get it wrong and you slip down the vendor slide, perceived by the customer as being consumed solely by self-interest – seeking only to sell something. The result of getting it wrong is that you are relegated to the last column in the RFP list, fulfilling the need for three quotes but never occupying the customer's side of the table, or finding your place inside the buyer's mind.

Successful companies employing ABM programs to drive revenue are not concerned about marketing activity to win marketing awards. They are not focused on the quantum of activity or demonstrating their ability to generate Marketing Qualified Leads (MQLs). They are focused on providing a compelling expression of value that helps them win sales by making it easy for the customer to choose you. The purpose of your ABM play is to help the customer begin that journey.

> **ABM PLAY DEFINITION:** An ABM Play is a number of coordinated and interconnected actions that follow a strategy for an account (or set of accounts) to achieve a business development objective. It is dependent on Sales, Marketing, and other customer facing functions, using multiple channels of engagement to achieve a measurable outcome with one or more buying personas in the account.

[Note: The definition uses *business development* in its broadest sense to encapsulate all Awareness, Interest, Preference and Action objectives that form part of the Sales and Marketing continuum.]

Personalization

How you design your ABM play depends on the tier to which you are delivering the play. The main distinction between plays designed for your Key Accounts, *versus* your Portfolio or Market tiers, is the level of customization. Your goal is for the recipient of the play to feel that the play has been designed specifically for them, but you need to balance effort with potential return as follows:

- **Key Accounts:** Hand-crafted for each account. You may already have content for a play to a key account but each message, deliverable, and engagement needs to map specifically to the account refined for the target persona.
- **Portfolio:** You will likely use some of your standard content as the core of the ABM play, but you should at least personalize the introduction, tailor the core content to speak to the issues of the target accounts, and personalize the end of each deliverable to tie to the profile of the targets.
- **Market:** The optimal approach for this segment is to use content that is customized for industry and persona and personalized just to *name* and *company*. It is likely that you do not know enough about the accounts to effectively personalize to any greater degree, and because the number of accounts is greater than in the other tiers you can't apply resources on an account-by-account basis.

Types of ABM plays (Your ABM playbook)

When most people comment on ABM today they usually position ABM as the evolution of Demand Gen. But it needs to be much more than that. Considering that most companies get more than 60 percent of their revenue from their existing customers, it is clear that ABM should have a role in existing customers as well as prospects. According to the Business Performance Benchmark Study, Customer Retention is the #1 Strategic Imperative for business in 2017. My expectation is that this will continue to hold the top spot for a number of years to come and that its dominance will only increase. You should consider how ABM could be used to aid Customer Retention. In general, the question to be asked should be:

"How can ABM be applied to one or more personas in an account (or set of accounts) when I have a specific business development objective in mind?"

If the customer is ready to act and has a known requirement for a solution such as yours, then, in the first instance, all you want to do is make sure that they know that you exist and have a favorable impression of you. Ideally, they perceive your company as a valuable resource to engage with early to help with their initiative. Of course it is unlikely that the majority of your prospective customers are in that 'ready to act' state at any specific time – so the purpose of your ABM play, for that profile of account, is to prepare them for that moment.

Each ABM play should be designed with a specific objective in mind.

Awareness and Interest Play: In some cases your play might comprise many elements to bring a new prospect account on the journey from *Awareness to Interest*. Multi-touch plays are necessary to gain interest. Various research studies show that it takes a minimum of six to 10 touches to gain someone's interest, and that is dependent on existing relationships and where the prospect is in the buying cycle.

Figures 91 and **92** are examples of an *Awareness and Interest* play – *Get Closer To Your Large Accounts* – that was executed very successfully by Altify to Portfolio Accounts to introduce them to Altify's capability and proven success with Account Planning deployments.

Figure 91: AWARENESS AND INTEREST ABM PLAY: GET CLOSER TO YOUR LARGE ACCOUNTS

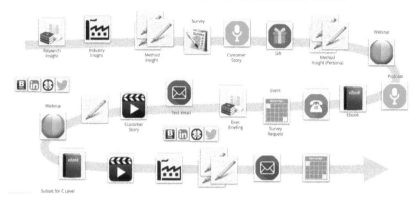

The purpose of this type of ABM play is to encourage accounts to investigate a project with you. If they are not ready to do that you want to be sure that your ABM play is sufficiently interesting and valuable so that when they are ready, they will consider you as a potential partner. In **Figure 92,** you can see that the play ran for six months for each target account delivered to up to nine different personas.

In addition to the items listed in the table below, there was ongoing, targeted social media activity through LinkedIn, Twitter, retargeting, and Google Ads.

Figure 92: AWARENESS AND INTEREST ABM PLAY: GET CLOSER TO YOUR LARGE ACCOUNTS – DETAILED STEPS

Day	Task Name	Persona	Industry	Call to Action
0	Research Insight: Impact of Account Planning: Research Study	All	All	None
7	Industry Insight: Inside the Buyer's Mind	All	Industry	Related Items
14	Method Insight: Account Planning – The Missed Opportunity	1, 2, 4, 5, 6, 7, 8	All	Related Items
21	Survey Invitation: Business Performance Benchmark Study	All	All	Contact Us
28	Podcast: Customer Story - Podcast	1, 2, 4, 5, 6, 7, 8	Industry	Related Items
35	Holiday Greeting: Email | Wishing you a prosperous 2017	All	All	None
42	Tech Ops Insight: Operationalizing Sales	2, 3, 9	All	Related Items
49	eBook: How Salesforce does Account Planning	1, 2, 4, 5, 6, 7, 8	All	Related Items
56	Webinar Invitation: Webinar: Results of Benchmark Study	All	All	Contact Us
63	Method Insight: It is Hard Being a Customer	1, 2, 4, 5, 6, 7, 8	All	Related Items
70	Thank You – Gift: *Account Planning in Salesforce* Book	1, 2, 4, 5, 6, 7, 8	All	Related Items
77	Infographic: Benchmark Study "Moving the Needle"	All	Industry	Related Items
84	Podcast: Account Planning Best Practices	1, 2, 4, 5, 6, 7, 8	Industry	Related Items

Day	Task Name	Persona	Industry	Call to Action
91	Tech Ops Insight: Native in Salesforce	2, 3, 9	All	None
98	Call: Follow up to Benchmark Study survey	1, 2	Industry	None
105	Video: Customer Case Study	All	All	Contact Us
112	Method Insight: What Customers Should You Pursue?	1, 2, 4, 5, 6, 7, 8	Industry	Related Items
119	Video: Customer Case Study	All	All	Contact Us
126	Text: Invitation to Executive Dinner	1,2	Industry	Contact Us
133	Research Insight: Account Planning	1, 2, 4, 5, 6, 7, 8	All	Related Items
140	Webinar Invitation: Account Planning	All	All	Contact Us
147	Industry Insight: Compilation of 3rd Party Industry Trends	All	Industry	Contact Us
154	Method Insight: 10 Measures of an Effective Account Plan	1,2,4,5,6,7,8	All	Related Items
161	Event: Account Planning Best Practices Exec Breakfast	1,2	All	Contact Us
168	Call: Follow up to Benchmark Study survey	1,2	Industry	None

I wouldn't recommend that every play is as complex as this, and most companies will only be able to concurrently run a maximum of maybe four to six of these types of plays at any one time.

Positioning Play: For Key Accounts it is critical that your ABM play is aligned with the strategy for the account and coordinated with the rest of the Objective, Strategies and Actions in the account plan. In this case the ABM play might be as simple as a four-part marketing activity.

Figure 93: A SIMPLE ABM ACCOUNT PLAY

Target Account	Organic Products		
Marketing Objective	By the end of next quarter create awareness of our position in the Security Server marketplace with at least two of the IT executives responsible for security at Organic Products.		
Persona	IT Buyer.		
Strategy	Leverage social media and thought leadership program.		
Validate contact information and get social contact profile for each exec. Follow each on Twitter, LinkedIn etc. Engage with their social media activity.	Social Marketing Unit	4/17	Jane Raitt
Invite James Brown, Vicki Estevez, Henry Johnson to our Security Leaders Summit	Eric King	3/18	Eric King
Deliver custom whitepaper to Organic	Jane Writer		Eric King
Ask Tom Harrison at Organic to ask the exec leaders to participate in Security Benchmark Study	David Matthews		David Matthews

Customer Trigger Plays: The most effective customer engagement usually happens when you can connect to a specific trigger event. Company mergers, organizational changes, developments in the market, new regulations, technological innovations, contract renewals, new competitive entrants, macro-economic changes, and demographic shifts are all events to which most businesses need to respond.

The response you are likely to evoke in a time of volatility or change for your prospective customer is much greater than when you are trying to unseat the inertia of *status quo*.

Similarly, there will be personal trigger events like meeting at a conference, a company press release, promotion to a new role, blog post (from a target persona or related individual in the company), website visit, speaking at a conference, etc.

Other types of ABM plays that might be applicable to your business are listed in **Figure 94**. Each play below is described at a high level. You can determine whether these should be triggered plays based on external events as described above, or whether they are manual plays launched at your discretion.

Then for each of the plays you will need to specify the personas in the account with whom you want to interact and the players from your team who will participate. Finally, you will need to find the right timing and spacing of communication to achieve maximum impact.

Figure 94: OTHER TYPES OF ABM PLAYS AND THEIR COMPONENTS

Play Type	Purpose	Potential Components of ABM Play
Awareness & Interest	Position your company as a valuable potential partner to your customer.	Per *Awareness and Interest* example above.
Executive Change	Develop relationships with new executives in the account.	Welcome and congratulations. Provide history of relationship. Restate value proposition. Provide testimonials from existing users. Send 'First 30 days' guide. Offer executive briefing.
Product Launch	Introduce a new product.	Thank you for current business. Explain reason for new product. Show value to customer. Offer presentation / demo / trial.

Play Type	Purpose	Potential Components of ABM Play
Renewal	Ensure the customer sees the value in your solution so they renew their subscription to your service. It should start 90 to180 days before the renewal date. Each step has conditional elements to it so you can take remedial action if needed.	Validate connections and relationship. Measure customer satisfaction. Share best practices. Document ROI. Share product update information. Advise of renewal date. Confirm process for renewal. Send renewal agreement.
Onboard New Customer	Welcome new customer and get them off to a good start with your solution and good relationship with your company.	Welcome from CEO. Introduction to Customer Success team. Share best practices. Monitor usage. 30 day check-in from CS team. 90 day check-in from CS team.

ABM Metrics

Even though ABM is partly a Marketing activity, executed in harmony with Sales, it is part of your strategic planning initiative and the measures that you apply will be very different than most other marketing activities. Traditional marketing measures activities and leads. With ABM you are developing the target accounts in your market and your metrics should focus on progress with these accounts.

There are three categories of ABM metrics:

1. Contacts and coverage
2. Awareness and interest
3. Preference and action.

Contacts and Coverage: In the first instance you need to connect with the personas in your target accounts. For each of your target accounts you enrich the contact information that you have for each of the personas. These are the people that matter. As David Ogilvy said:

> Don't count the people that you reach; reach the people that count.

Using the example referenced earlier, your contacts metrics might look like the table below where the numbers in each of the cells represents the number of contacts (contact information and profile) you have for each persona in each account.

Figure 95: CONTACT METRICS

Account	#1	#2	#3	#4	#5	#6	...	#15
Customer Personas								
VP Sales	1	1		1		1		1
Sales Operations		1	1		1	1		
IT	1	1			1			1
CMO	1		1			1		1
Customer Success	3	1	1			2		
L&D			4		3			1
Account Managers		4			3	12		3
Sales Managers	4	3	11					4
CRM Admin	1		1	1	1	1		1
Total Contacts	**11**	**11**	**19**	**5**	**6**	**18**		**12**

Account executives are an expensive commodity – so using them to update the database is not really the best use of their time. You should consider using your internal Business or Sales Development Reps if you have them, or an external vendor to enrich and append the data.

> According to TOPO, the sales and marketing consulting company, you should acquire or append records until 100 percent of the target accounts and at least 70 percent to 80 percent of buyer personas are represented in the database.

The combination of contacts and engagement with those contacts is a measure of the Coverage you have in the account. As with Contacts, your Coverage map is likely to be fluid. We have all heard the statistic that the average tenure of a sales leader is two years. That means that every month there is a one in 24 (or 4.2 percent) chance that the sales leader – the VP Sales persona in this example – will have changed jobs. Maintaining the currency of your contacts and coverage data is an on-going task and should be reviewed about once a quarter for each of your ABM accounts.

> ABM specialists Engagio suggest that, even if you start with perfect data and 100 percent coverage, the data will decay at a rate of between two and seven percent per month depending on the role and industry.

Your coverage plan should map to the Relationship Objectives that you have in your Account Plan for each target account. As you strive towards becoming a Trusted Advisor in the account it is likely that you will need the support of many different roles in your own organization.

Marketing can only take it so far, and the account manager cannot possibly have either the bandwidth or the breath of skills to engage effectively with each persona type in the account. For your Key Accounts (and possibly a limited set of your Portfolio Accounts) you should build a Coverage Map that highlights the engagement that you need from every role in your company – the Contact Role – with each of the personas in the target account.

In **Figure 96** below, the Contact Roles are those people in your organization who can best represent the value proposition of your company to their persona counterparts in the target account. (The shading in the cells indicates importance of coverage for the role.)

Figure 96: CONTACT ROLES

Contact Owners	Account Manager	Executive	Marketing	CIO	Sales Engineer	Consulting
Customer Personas						
VP Sales	✓	✓	✓			
Sales Operations	✓		✓		✓	
IT			✓		✓	
CMO			✓			
Customer Success						✓
L&D						✓
Account Managers	✓		✓			
Sales Managers	✓		✓			
CRM Admin					✓	

There will be many people from your company involved in the ABM program and each has a role to play. For example, in your team, the Contact Roles might include the Account Manager, Executive, Marketing, CIO, Sales Engineering and Consultants all as part of the account facing team. They may be further supported by Sales and Marketing Operations or your Business Development or Sales Development Representatives.

The account manager still owns the account and either Sales or Marketing owns the ABM plays for that account. Nevertheless, it is important to identify and measure the involvement of the supporting functions in the ABM program as a part of the overall strategic account plan.

Awareness and Interest: Remember, your ABM program is a component of your strategic account planning initiative. Its purpose is to deepen relationships and build trust with the account to make it easy and natural for them to choose your company as their business partner.

First, they have to be aware that you exist. Next you want them to become interested in what you have to offer and develop a positive emotional – how they feel – connection about your company and your solutions as they travel down the path to developing a preference for you as a preferred partner. Awareness and Interest is a measure of engagement.

Website traffic

You know that the people in your target account are aware of your existence if, for example, they visit your website. If the traffic from a specific account to your website is increasing, then that is a good indicator of growing awareness, and probably growing interest. The easiest way to track this measure is by using a reverse IP lookup service that can identify the domain names associated with the IP addresses of your website visitors. This provides you with simple stats like unique visitors, number of visits and page views per visit.

Correlating your ABM plays to a specific account with the website traffic is one way to measure the effectiveness of the ABM play. Remember though that this is just a correlation and your ABM play itself may not be the sole reason why you have increased traffic from that account.

Figure 97: WEBSITE TRAFFIC

Account	#1	#2	#3	#4	#5	#6	...	#15
Website Traffic (September 18, 2017 – September 24, 2017)								
Visits	28	12	1	45	9	27		32
Unique Visitors	16	6	1	28	2	17		12
Pages per Visit	2.4	1.7	3.0	2.2	4.6	3.4		1.9
Minutes on Site	84	26	4	124	52	115		76

Figure 98: WEBSITE MINUTES SPENT

Account	#1	#2	#3	#4	#5	#6	...	#15
Website Minutes (September 2017)								
Sep 4-Sep 10	26	9	0	38	19	31		0
Sep 11-Sep 17	43	18	0	86	21	71		43
Sep 18-Sep 24	84	26	4	92	52	115		76
Sep 25-Oct 01	64	32	0	124	34	164		139

As you review the website traffic measures for an account, it is useful to look at the numbers and the trends: in absolute terms for each account, relative to each of the other target accounts, and relative to those accounts that are not in the ABM program.

Raising hands – Tell me more

Depending on the nature and complexity of the ABM plays there are different points at which you want each person in the target account to hold up their hands and say: "Tell me more." In some cases, this can be as straightforward as someone completing a form on your website asking to be contacted. Not all interactions are equally valuable, of course. Some require the account to make a greater commitment or spend more time. It can be useful to classify these different engagements.

Clearly, when someone asks to be contacted they are demonstrating a high level of interest. This is your **Gold** tier of engagement. Other interactions that fall into this classification might include an arranged meeting at a trade show, attending a physical event that you are hosting or participating in an Executive Briefing or involvement in your Customer Advisory Board. Each of these is a strong indicator of interest. The account is opening the door for you to walk through to have a conversation.

Other noteworthy, but less valuable interactions, at the **Silver** level of engagement, include attendance at a webinar, participation in a survey, or downloading a whitepaper from your website. These are other good indicators of both awareness and interest.

At the **Bronze** level of engagement are actions like opening an email you sent and clicking through on your Call To Action. Until this latter activity converts to one of the stronger indications of interest at the Silver or Gold level you've not really started to win their hearts and minds. In fact you are only one step away from them clicking on the 'unsubscribe' link in the email. This is why it is very important to invest the time and effort to make sure that your outreach is as valuable to the recipient as your resources allow. Otherwise you will just burn through the database of Contacts that you worked hard to build.

For each of your accounts you should track the interactions from each of the people in the account and calculate their aggregate score for Awareness and Interest. Depending on how valuable you consider each interaction, assign points to each one and multiply by the number or quantity.

Figure 99: AN ABM PLAY – INTERACTION SUMMARY

Interaction	Points	Account #1		Account #2		...	Account #15	
		Qty	Score	Qty	Score		Qty	Score
Per minute on website	1	84	84	26	26		76	76
Open email	0	12	0	7	0		25	0
Click thru	5	3	15	5	25		15	75
Survey completion	12	2	24	4	48		3	36
Attend webinar	15	4	60	1	15		5	75
Download whitepaper	20	4	80	1	20		0	0
Request contact	60	1	60	2	120		1	60
Meeting at trade show	35	2	70	0	0		0	0
Attend physical event	65	1	65	1	65		3	195
Executive briefing	100	2	200	0	0		1	100
Customer Advisory Board	100	2	200	0	0		0	0
....								
Awareness / Interest Total			858		319			617

Depending on the objective of a specific ABM play there may be other interactions that you need to measure. For example, if you are applying ABM to existing customers to maximize retention rates for your SaaS software solution, you will need to keep an eye on your usage and adoption stats, percentage of users who complete the onboarding of your software in the target timeframe, the number of times an account consumes a best practices whitepaper related to your product, their engagement in your support community, participation in a user group, or agreement to engage in your customer reference program. These items might not naturally come to mind as being in the remit of your marketing program, but they are all part of the sales and marketing continuum, particularly as the world moves increasingly to a 'subscription economy' where you have to earn the customer's trust over and over again each and every month.

Preference and Action: When we created account tiers I specified different focus elements for each tier. In *Key Accounts* I identified *Revenue & Pipeline* as the focus area. For *Portfolio Accounts* I reversed the order to *Pipeline & Revenue*. For the last tier, *Market* at the bottom of the pyramid, *Awareness & interest* is the specific focus area. In each case you're looking to help the customer or prospect account to move along the path from *Awareness*, through *Interest*, on to *Preference* and finally to take an *Action* to engage with you as their business partner.

If your ABM plays are effective, the period from first contact to first opportunity creation should be shorter than it is for accounts that are not in your ABM program. Similarly in your Key Accounts, the *Number of Opportunities* – the growth in the pipeline in each of those accounts – should exceed those outside the ABM program. In both your Key Accounts and Portfolio Accounts, as you get to know the account better and market to the whitespace in the account, the growth in Potential Opportunities – opportunities that are not yet qualified but that you can create because of your understanding of how your solutions can potentially be applied to solve customer business problems, even if the customer does not yet have a defined project – should be measured against the Potential Opportunity goal in your account plan.

As your ABM program increases the account's perception of you as a Trusted Advisor your *Win Rate* will increase. You should track *Win Rate* for each account tier and correlate that to the *Awareness and Interest* scores and the specific interaction types that contribute to that score. For example, my empirical evidence suggests that *Win Rate* increases dramatically if the customer invests the time to participate in an Executive Briefing or engage in your Customer Advisory Board.

Similarly, as you track *Average Deal Value* and *Sales Cycle* you should monitor relative metrics and trends for each of the different account tiers. Attribution – linking the specific ABM activity to the outcome – will always be imprecise but after a while the data will begin to tell a story. You just need to be sure that you are tracking the data from the outset so that you can reverse engineer the outcome to get a better understanding of the contributing factors.

Integrated ABM

If you have only one take-away from this section it should be that ABM can be truly valuable, but only as part of an orchestrated strategic account planning program. ABM is a wonderful opportunity to align Sales and Marketing and other customer facing functions around the customer. In a world where the customer is increasingly empowered, crazy busy, and overstressed, the need for this alignment couldn't be greater. Customers want a single consistent message from their business partners: from the time they receive their first marketing communication to when they consummate the first deal, and onwards into a long term mutually beneficial relationship.

The evolution of commerce towards the subscription economy is not just happening in SaaS. It is evidenced in much of our daily lives. Companies like WeWork provide office accommodation as a service. Many of us subscribe monthly to iCloud for data back-up for our Apple devices. Amazon delivers computing capacity on-demand, and Dollar Shave Club provides razors as a service, while Trunk Club (*We help people build better wardrobes*) does the same with personalized high-end fashion.

Remember the (almost subconscious) transition or evolution that is happening to us all. While not all consumers are business people, all business people are consumers. Our expectations are changing as we adopt the 'X-as-a-service' mindset.

Earning trust is now a daily mandate to be delivered through consistent transparency in your interactions with your current or future customers. While ABM is often the first contact point – it's frequently where you make your first promise – it must be part of the continuum of the overall approach to the account that delivers on that promise.

Select your accounts carefully using your Ideal Customer Profile and get to know your personas. Coordinate your team to deliver value to the customer as part of the marketing process, part of the sales service, and part of the after-care service. Design your ABM plays with a Customer First mindset.

You are starting on the road to mutual value but you must give first without getting. Don't overload your plays with aggressive Calls to Action. Avoid the *get it before midnight tonight*' mentality. Allow the accounts space to reach out to you in their own time, before you poke them with the "*Can I have 15 minutes of your time? Does Monday or Tuesday suit you better?*" interruptions. Then engage with knowledge and empathy. Lead them on the journey through the sales and marketing continuum, making sure not to drop them along the way.

As I said at the start of this chapter, the future of selling and customer engagement combines high-level, strategic marketing principles to draw the map, with focused sales execution to complete each journey, addressing the practical stops along the way. Customer engagement is a continuum with a constant focus: consistent delivery of value to the customer. ABM is an important part of that continuum and when designed with strategic thought and a Customer First mentality, it can provide you with a tremendous foundation for pipeline and revenue growth.

ABM is a long game play. Stay the course and you will reap the rewards.

CHAPTER 12:

THE ROLE OF AI IN ENTERPRISE SALES

Salespeople operate in constantly shifting environments. Every day they contend with new situations and changing information. To remain in control, many companies deploy a CRM as their system of record, or 'single source of truth.' They ask their sellers to keep the system up-to-date – if it's not in Salesforce, it doesn't exist – and then, armed with bucket loads of data, they generate reports and dashboards to try to understand the business.

While easy to generate, reports and charts are often hard to interpret. Often the glut of data makes it hard to assess what is relevant and what is just noise.

An abundance of product offerings using artificial intelligence (AI) or predictive analytics have recently emerged as potential solutions to solve the problem for sales teams. However, in the context of enterprise sales, there are two key factors to be considered:

- First, enterprise sales is a *Small Data* problem, not a *Big Data* problem – there is not enough consistent data for an individual rep to draw accurate conclusions from patterns – and the individual seller is a key variable.
- Secondly, any functioning AI system must first be taught the intelligence. It can't learn it on its own. The system needs a base of knowledge from which it can make assertions based on data, and it needs to understand the context of the problem it is solving.

Even when AI is used to predict that a sale is likely or unlikely to close, the question remains: "So, what do I do now?" In the context of enterprise sales, AI should mean Augmented Intelligence, not Artificial Intelligence. 'Augmented' is the right tool for the job where vast quantities of homogenous data do not exist and where reasoning, judgment, creativity, emotional connections and imagination matter.

As I said in *Chapter 1: Introduction*, I wrote my first AI book, called *Expert Systems Introduced,* in 1988. 'Artificial Intelligence' and 'Expert Systems' were two sides of the same coin back then. My goal back then was to deliver AI or expert systems for the *rest of us*. In that book I described an expert system (AI) as follows:

> An expert system (AI) makes or saves money by codifying and encapsulating the knowledge of an expert in a system that makes it available to, and easily consumable by, a non-expert.

If I were to modify the definition today, in the context of enterprise sales, I would make two changes:

> An expert system (AI) makes or saves money <u>or time</u> by codifying and encapsulating the knowledge of an expert in a system that makes it available to, easily consumable <u>and actionable</u> by a non-expert.

Time is the most valuable currency for salespeople and accordingly I have added *'or time'* to the definition. The addition of *'and actionable'* is important to help drive business results. However, the part I have not changed in 30 years is that the encapsulation of knowledge is the foundation on which any true smart system is built.

Much of this chapter is informed by the research I did for my most recent AI book, published in 2016. (It is striking how much has already changed in the past 12 months.) In *Tomorrow|Today: How AI Impacts How We Work, Live, and Think*, I explored the developments over the past 30 years. Today, some of that knowledge on which today's smart systems are built comes from data or information. But in most cases, particularly in the world of knowledge workers – like sales, marketing and other customer facing functions – human knowledge plays a huge part. There is no deficit in data or information; there is a deficit in insight – and that insight is not solely the dominion of machines.

It is evident to me that the success of any knowledge-based business or human endeavor is dependent on the reasoning ability of the people involved. A growth mindset, curiosity, problem solving, deductive reasoning and an ability to cast aside the box, rather than just think outside it, are indicators of success. That's the world that sales professionals who engage at Customer Impact Levels 1, 2, and 3 (as described in *Chapter 2: Digital Sales Transformation | Part 1, Discover Impact 3*) inhabit. You have to feel it, let it touch you, and never forget that it touches others. Maybe that is a good thing. People are at the core.

When Does the Machine Win?

There are many things that machines are better suited to than humans. Machines don't get tired or emotional; they are not subjective or judgmental in their assessment; they don't spend a lot of time in meetings, on social media sites, or reading emails; they don't get bored with repeating the same task – in fact, they seem to enjoy it; they rarely get interrupted by their family or in-laws, need to take vacation, or leave a task unfinished. If you need the same thing done over and over again, without variation, consistently, following a prescribed set of instructions, then the machine is your man (or woman) for the job.

On the other hand, machines are not good yet at nuance, judgment, reading body language, imagining different scenarios, solving problems that they have not been programmed to solve, managing people, dealing with sudden change, applying expertise without guidance, undertaking unpredictable physical tasks, interpreting patterns they have not been taught to recognize, or interacting with people. In fact, without explicit programming, there's a lot that machines are not good at, and these are mostly things at which humans are pretty adept.

I think about this in the context of what I call the Knowledge Curve (**Figure 100**), mapping *Competitive Advantage* and *Scope of Impact* against the *Application of Knowledge* across the spectrum Simple to Complex tasks. The further you move to the right, the greater is the need for human intervention. As you move up the knowledge curve the role of Artificial Intelligence diminishes, but the role of the augmented variety becomes more powerful.

The opportunity for Augmented Intelligence is to maximize the potential of enterprise sellers – today.

Figure 100: THE KNOWLEDGE CURVE

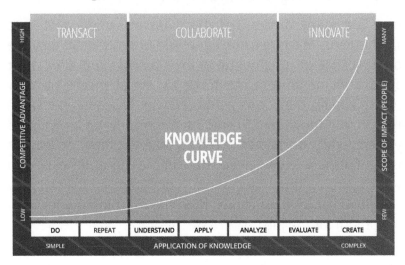

But What About Skynet?

We can put aside our concerns about robot overlords. The reality is that we have no idea yet how to explain human consciousness and we even struggle to define intelligence. We don't know what to build, much less how to build it. The latest estimates are that the human brain contains about 30 billion neurons in the cerebral cortex – the part of the brain associated with consciousness and intelligence. The 30 billion neurons of the cerebral cortex contain about 1,000 trillion synapses (connections between neurons). Without a detailed model of how synapses work on a neurochemical level, there's no hope of modeling how the brain works. Until we figure that out, the likelihood that we will see sentient computers is infinitesimally small. Certainly, this will not happen in the next three or four decades.

As David Autor points out in his article, *Why Are There Still So Many Jobs? The History and Future of Workplace Automation*:

> Tasks that cannot be substituted by automation are generally complemented by it ... improvements in one do not obviate the need for the other.

Brynjolfsson and McAfee said in *The Second Machine Age*, there's never been a better time to be a [knowledge] worker. The scope of occupations that automation can effectively address is bounded because there are many tasks that people understand inherently but are hard to represent in binary structures. Autor refers to this constraint as Polanyi's Paradox, named after the economist, philosopher, and chemist who observed in 1966:

> We know more than we can tell.

There is a story told of a conversation between Marvin Minsky, the mathematician who founded AI and who advocates downloading human intelligence, and Doug Englebart, the inventor of word processing, the computer mouse, and hypertext and a strong proponent of Augmented Intelligence.

> MINSKY: We're going to make machines intelligent. We are going to make them conscious!

> ENGELBART: You're going to do all that for the machines? What are you going to do for the people?

Englebart reasoned that, because the complexity of the world's problems was increasing, and any effort to improve the world would require the coordination of groups of people, the most effective way to solve problems was to augment human intelligence and develop ways of building collective intelligence.

The Augmented Journey

Taking the stage at Austin's SXSW festival in March 2016, Chris Urmson, who was at that time director of Google's self-driving car project, detailed what happened when Google's self-driving Lexus RX 450h crashed into a bus. It was the first accident caused by one of Google's self-driving cars, despite having already covered 1.4 million miles of real world testing.

Urmson explained that "the company had taught its cars to move next to the curb when planning a right turn, sidling by traffic stopped at a traffic light, much as human drivers do. As the car proceeded along the curb, it sensed a few sandbags on the road ahead of it, so decided to stop and wait for the lane next to it to clear. After the light turned green, the traffic began moving. The car detected a city bus coming up the lane, and made the assumption the bus driver would slow down." As Urmson told it, the bus driver assumed the car would stay put, and kept on going. The car pulled out, hitting the side of the bus at about 2 mph.

The key phrases here are *"the company had taught"* and *"much as human drivers do."* Before Google taught the cars what humans do, it could not even conceive of putting a driver-less or human-less car on the road.

About a billion people every month, who between them conduct about a billion searches every day, use Google Maps. The maps we used to keep folded in the glove compartments of our cars were a collection of lines and shapes that we overlaid with human intelligence. Now, as we've seen, a map is a collection of lines and shapes with embedded knowledge and intelligence.

Through a series of acquisitions and licensing agreements, with companies like TeleAtlas, Google built its maps on a host of knowledge sources. In 2007, Google initiated a project – called Ground Truth – to control its own map data. A team of

20 people across the world worked full-time on acquiring map data. Megan Quinn (now General Partner at Spark Capital), who led the data acquisition project, sent out an email to every Google employee asking them to find inaccuracies or bugs in the maps for their home towns, promising them she would bake them a cookie for every bug they found. Quinn ended up baking 7,000 chocolate-chip cookies. This was a critical wave of human input to Google Maps.

The sheer amount of human effort that goes into Google's maps is just mind-boggling. Google understands that the best way to figure out if you can make a left turn at a particular intersection is still to have a person look at a sign – whether that's a human driving or a human looking at an image generated by a Street View car. Humans are coding every bit of the logic of the road onto a representation of the world so that computers can simply duplicate (infinitely, instantly) the judgments that a person already made.

When I have American visitors to my home in Cork, I recommend taking a trip to Waterville Golf Club in the extreme South West of Ireland. Even if you are not a golfer, the trip to Waterville is stunningly beautiful and shows off the best of Ireland. When I can, I drive my guests to Waterville myself, but if I don't have the time, I just use my iPhone to show them how to find this gem of a destination for themselves. Using all the Augmented Intelligence capabilities in Google Maps my friends can confidently head off on their trip.

Figure 101: CORK TO WATERVILLE

It starts with Knowledge. Because Google has effectively mapped the world, it has a foundation of knowledge with which it can work to build the journey plan. Then we key in Data: our chosen destination 'Waterville Golf Links.' As Google Maps has geo-location services built in, it does not need to be told the starting location. It has the Context. Now it begins its Reasoning. Because I live in a neighborhood that has only one way out to the main road, it tells us to make a U-turn if the car is facing the wrong direction. As we are in Ireland, Google knows that we should drive on the left-hand side of the road and, when we encounter a roundabout (rotary), it knows that we should navigate it in a clockwise direction.

As you can see from the map, the trip takes a little over two and a half hours. Along the way, as the location or Context changes, the user is continuously receiving Notifications, pushing information to the driver in plenty of time for the driver to know the next action to take: *"In 500m, at the roundabout take the second exit and continue on the R641."*

How Google Maps works provides us with a blueprint for Augmented Intelligence applications in business. Knowledge,

Data, Context, and Reasoning are critical components of these or any Augmented Intelligence applications for knowledge workers. Where updates occur in any of Knowledge, Data, or Context, then Notifications are needed to keep the user in the loop on anything that might impact the situation.

Augmented Intelligence applications need to have knowledge of the core concepts of the specific domain to which the application is being applied. Experienced practitioners and domain experts know the 'How to,' the 'Best way' – the proven approaches to solving the problem and getting to a specific solution destination. Making that available to someone who is making that journey for the first time by providing signposts – effectively a map of the journey – means it is less likely that they will take a wrong turn. Knowledge on its own is not enough; Data and Context are necessary. Without Context, it is really hard to apply the knowledge and, without Data, you don't know the specific problem you are trying to solve.

Without Google Maps, or similar technology, we wouldn't have Uber, or Lyft, or any other service that depends on geo-location services, and we would still be struggling to fold up the paper map to fit it back into the glove compartment in our cars. Those days are better left behind. Our collective challenge is to provide the same augmented utility to enterprise sales professionals.

Augmented Intelligence for Sales Professionals

The enterprise salesperson represents one of the most knowledge dependent professions, where, while every journey is different, the map to success, though extremely complex, is still materially the same – from one journey to the next. Imagine if sales professionals had the muscle memory of a million sales engagements, represented as a multi-dimensional map, sitting on their phones, right beside Google Maps. They will surely be likely to get to their chosen destination – a closed sale or growing account – much more frequently.

The 800-pound gorilla in the sales productivity market today is undoubtedly Salesforce. Through the extraordinary vision of its founder, Marc Benioff, the cloud computing industry in business has evolved to be one of the core future trends that we all should care about. Could Salesforce be the Google of knowledge workers, providing the Augmented Intelligence equivalent of Google Maps? Is there an app for that?

With the August 2016 announcement of Salesforce Einstein, launched at the company's Dreamforce event in that year, we got a peek into the potential of an Augmented Intelligence platform that Salesforce and its partners (with specific domain expertise) could bring AI, in its many forms, to the broader business world.

When you look at the profile of Salesforce's customers, you see knowledge workers. You see people whose mental acuity, experience and knowledge are the ingredients that, when fresh and invigorated, deliver a recipe for success. These are the knowledge workers who drive successful businesses forwards, who think for a living. The anatomy of the Salesforce ecosystem suggests that it is from here that the democratization of Augmented Intelligence might emerge.

While it is a minnow in comparison with the Internet giants – Amazon, Alphabet (formerly Google), Facebook, and the other technology titans Apple and Microsoft – Salesforce is the company best positioned to deliver Augmented Intelligence solutions for knowledge workers. It has the reach, the breadth of applications, a scale of daily transactions – at more than 4 billion transactions per day – data traffic, and signal inputs to be able to begin to emulate Google Maps' behavior in the context of business.

The difference between Salesforce and the aforementioned Internet giants is that, for today at least, Salesforce is focused solely on business, not consumer, applications. Over its 18 years in business it has developed a deep understanding of the breadth of application needs of its customers. With its own offerings for Sales, Marketing, Service, Analytics, Platform and Apps, and IoT (Internet of Things), Salesforce can solve a lot of problems for its customers.

Now with Salesforce Einstein, this is where it gets very exciting in the context of AI, particularly the Augmented Intelligence variety. I see a future where the Salesforce AppExchange is augmented to become the Salesforce Knowledge Exchange, where its partners – who specialize in business areas that Salesforce itself does not serve – can bring domain specific knowledge to the market that leverages the Salesforce Einstein platform.

Altify Max – Augmented Intelligence on Salesforce

One of Salesforce's partners is Altify.[26] Its primary purpose in life is to improve performance and productivity for sales professionals, sales managers, and executive sales leadership in companies that sell complex business applications to business enterprises. Founded by a team with heritage in AI, sales methodology and enterprise cloud applications, the company provides a range of intelligent software applications on the Salesforce platform that guide salespeople to win sales opportunities, increase revenue from large customers, and maximize the effectiveness of a sales organization. In April 2016, through its research and knowledge arm, the company announced Altify Max, an Augmented Intelligence platform for Sales.

The sales professional, particularly the sales professional involved in complex enterprise selling, is the poster child for the knowledge worker. Like many other knowledge workers, enterprise salespeople do not produce anything physical. They think for a living, and the quality of that thought, the foundation of knowledge on which the thinking is based, the context and timeliness of their actions, and the data they use to formulate their sales strategies are the core ingredients that predict success. The team behind Max focused initially on the enterprise selling domain, an area in which the company had particular domain expertise, given that it was the day-to-day focus of its business.

---

[26] The author was the founder of Altify and is now the company's chairman.

> If Google Maps can provide directions to guide salespeople to meetings with their customers, shouldn't there be an Augmented Intelligence application that helps them to navigate all the twists and turns in the road to winning a sale.

Throughout the 1980s and right up to the present day, companies have invested heavily in training their sales teams on how to be more effective in enterprise selling. Most of these companies, like Miller Heiman, Sales Performance International, and CEB are deep in knowledge, but light on automation, and all lack any kind of intelligent software support. According to ATD, the market for sales training and sales methodology in 2015 was $20 billion but, although there was typically a high quality of knowledge disseminated in the classroom or online through eLearning, the efficacy of the training was sub-optimal. This is because there has been no effective technology deployed to operationalize the new way of working that adoption of the sales methodologies would require. Given that most of the companies did not have a technology background, this is not overly surprising. Building enterprise class software is not a trivial task.

From 2013 to 2016 venture capital firms invested large amounts of capital in lots of companies that targeted the sales performance market with product offerings using AI or Predictive Analytics. These companies provided the technology but did not have the core knowledge of the sales methodologies. The problem with the 'knowledge-less' AI in most black box sales solutions is that the black box doesn't 'understand' complex enterprise sales, and reductive pattern matching or Machine Learning on its own oversimplifies, and can actually impair, progress.

Applying 'Big Data' techniques to enterprise sales doesn't work well. Enterprise Sales is a Small Data problem, not a Big

Data problem. There is not enough consistent data for an individual salesperson to draw accurate conclusions from patterns – and the individual seller is a key variable. There is not enough homogenous training data for the machine to learn. Secondly, as we know, any functioning AI system must first be taught the intelligence and the knowledge. It can't learn the basics on its own. If Google Maps did not have maps with knowledge of all the places in the world on which to base its routing algorithms, it could not give you directions. It is the same in enterprise sales. You need a map or a blueprint to start with. The problem, therefore, that the Max team set out to solve was to provide a framework that could infuse an application with enough knowledge to guide the salesperson on how to avoid a mistake in a sales process and plot the course for success.

The Inner Workings of the Max Project

Earlier, I listed the core components of an Augmented Intelligence application: Knowledge, Data, Context, Reasoning and Notifications. Each of these apply equally well in Augmented Intelligence applications for sales professionals. The Max approach could be applied to any domain area but, sticking to the axiom of narrow domain specificity for effective Augmented Intelligence applications, the focus initially was on the Sales domain and specifically the various sales personas. Altify had acquired a sales methodology business a number of years prior to this project, so the team had great access to domain expertise. That solved the Knowledge problem.

Figure 102: ALTIFY MAX: INSIGHTS – OPPORTUNITIES

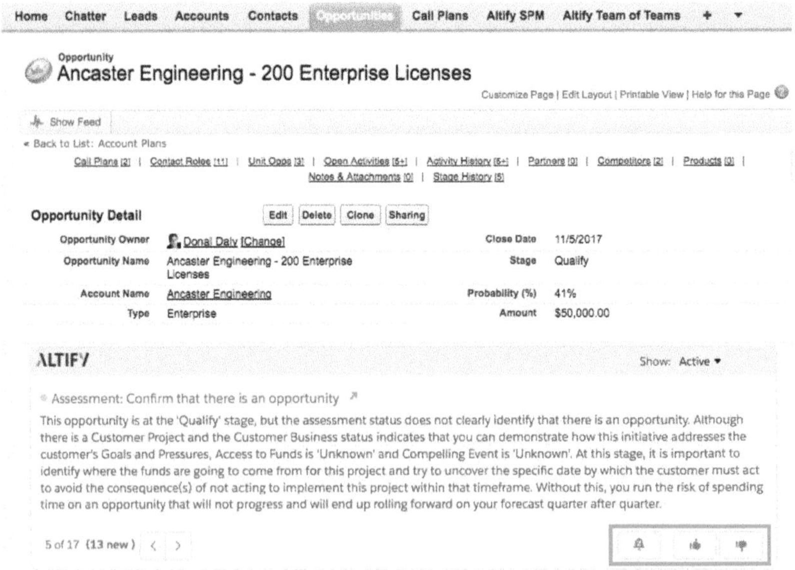

Joe the Salesperson: As Joe is working a sales opportunity, Max monitors the critical data and events in the deal. When something of importance happens, Max assesses the impact, notifies Joe of the need to act, and prescribes the action Joe should take to progress the opportunity (**Figure 102**).

Laura the Sales Manager: As Laura is busy managing her sales team, Max is keeping an eye on her sales forecast, her pipeline and her team's key deals. Max notifies her to schedule a deal review for an important deal to keep it on track, or points out when her sales forecast is at risk and recommends corrective action.

Max instantly identifies warning signs, and notifies Laura so that she can mitigate risk earlier in the sales process.

> **Sales Forecast Risk: Large deal ($450,000) needs attention.**
> Your sales forecast for the quarter has increased by $200,000 but the level of risk has increased. Joe Johnson's Ancaster Engineering opportunity has increased from $250,000 to $450,000, but this is more than 3 times the average deal size for Joe Johnson. There are 62 days remaining in the quarter. That is 52 percent of their average sales cycle. The opportunity is at Requirements stage in the funnel. Access to the buyers looks weak. There is a good understanding of the business problem. No decision criteria have been identified. Click here to schedule a deal review with Joe Johnson.

Ken in Sales Operations: Ken, informed by Max, sees opportunities to improve the team's performance. Using the Max Insight Editor, Ken can enhance the knowledge in Max to provide smarter guidance to the sales team to proactively and consistently get better results. Ken can tailor Max to his unique business and sales process by customizing or extending the supplied knowledge and insights.

There can be hundreds of moving parts in a long, complex enterprise business sale. Max could now analyze the data in Salesforce, and the inputs to other applications in the Altify

Platform, to allow the salesperson to make the most informed decision possible, while coaching them with prescribed guidance on what they should do next. The Max team examined all of the data gathered by the CRM and Altify platforms and reduced it to a set of **Insight Signals** on which Max could act.

In complex enterprise sales environments, there are many different considerations that determine the likelihood of winning a deal:

- The customer's urgency to act
- The degree to which the seller is engaged with the decision makers
- Budget allocation or access to funds for a purchase
- How well the seller's product addresses the customer's needs
- The relative preference of the buyer for a particular solution
- The level of risk perceived by the customer
- Whether the seller is selling a proven or new product
- The degree to which a solution is differentiated from the competition
- Whether the buyer is from an existing or new customer
- The speed at which the sale is moving through the sales process.

Each of these considerations, and many others, were coded into Max as Insight Signals and made available to the domain experts to build **Insights**. Insights are the directions or guidance that the salesperson needs to take the next action to progress the sale. The Max team and the domain experts, both within Altify and within the early customers, reported that the catalyst for creating impactful Insights was the Max Insight Editor capability.

Once the Insight Signals had been created, the domain experts could iteratively and incrementally pour knowledge into the system. Then they would test the Insights against a representative set of sales opportunities to see what advice would be presented to the salesperson in different situations. In its first release Max contained 50 core Insight Signals and 200 Insights that catered for the most common twists and turns in an enterprise sale. Many more have since been added.

Figure 103: ALTIFY MAX INSIGHT EDITOR – RULES, ADVICE AND CONTEXT EDITED IN A SIMPLE GUI

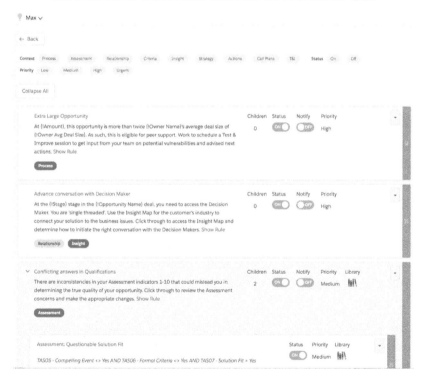

Situations always change in sales and Max has to cater for the fact that the advice provided has to change based on the Context of a sale. If a salesperson, working on a large sales

373

opportunity in their Salesforce CRM, suggests that the opportunity is in the final stage of the sales process, or in the last sales pipeline stage, but that key decision makers have not yet been identified, then Max can highlight the vulnerability and advise on actions that the salesperson might take to progress the deal or reevaluate the situation. That advice would not be relevant or appropriate for new sales opportunities where the salesperson may not have had the time yet to uncover information about the decision makers. Also, depending on the size of the sales opportunity, various sales channels, or the geographic location of the salesperson or customer, different Insights would be more or less applicable.

The Max team developed a general purpose expert system rules engine on the Salesforce platform to conduct the Reasoning on the Insight Signals. In a similar way to Google Maps, Max looks at where the salesperson is at any point in a sales process. It always understands the destination – the salesperson is trying to win the deal. Then Max plots a map to get from here to there. Using all the knowledge that has been built into the system, time and time again Max identifies risks and vulnerabilities in sales opportunities that many sellers would miss. In the first release of Max, it provided Notifications through email, Salesforce Chatter, and directly within the Opportunity Record on the Salesforce system, where the salesperson would go to add and update details of their deal.

A lot of thought and effort went into the logic for Notifications. The team recognized that they needed to ensure that every time the seller received a notification it would not be unduly repetitive, it would relate only to the few most important and urgent opportunities and it would be immediately actionable from the notification itself.

Closing the loop

Figure 104: ALTIFY MAX: INSIGHTS – FEEDBACK LOOP

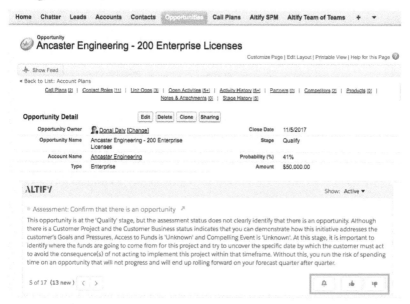

The final step in the initial Max project was to close the loop. The team built a learning engine to measure the efficacy of the Augmented Intelligence application as applied in each scenario. If Max could highlight which Insights were most frequently relevant, it could deduce competency gaps. Measuring how often a user engaged with each Insight, either by acting on it directly or by 'liking' it in the same way that they like a post on Facebook, Max could infer which Insights were deemed to deliver most value. By measuring the impact on a sale from each Insight that was used by the users, Max could distil the most valuable Insights from the rest and guide the domain experts to refine and improve the efficacy of the system.

Figure 105: ALTIFY MAX: CLOSING THE LOOP

INSIGHT LIBRARY	Advance Conversation with Decision Maker... Forecast Risk: Large Deal Needs Review...	MY CUSTOM INSIGHTS	1. SOMETHING HAPPENS
INSIGHT SIGNALS	Deal Size, Age, Preference, Access, Risk, Compelling Event, Decision Criteria, UBV, Competitive Strategy, Business lusses ...	MY CUSTOM INSIGHT SIGNALS	2. MAX ASSESSES IMPACT 3. MAX NOTIFIES USER(S)
KNOWLEDGE DOMAIN	Opportunity Management		4. MAX COACHES USER 5. USER ENGAGES
SALESFORCE	Example		6. MAX LEARNS

Altify Max is one example of an Augmented Intelligence platform for knowledge workers. It enables domain experts and knowledge workers to define Insight Signals and Insights, so that with applied knowledge, they can be turned into competitive advantage and business value. The word 'platform' is important. Much more than simply a faster and cheaper way to enable salespeople to perform better, the Max platform is a new model for creating and distributing Augmented Intelligence, and it is built in the cloud, native on the Salesforce platform. Now with Salesforce Einstein, Max can feed Einstein smarter data and Max can leverage a much broader set of Insight Signals from Einstein.

Sales Analytics and AI: Hindsight, Insight and Foresight

A little bit of insight at the moment of truth – the trigger point in a decision cycle – is considerably more valuable than all the data or information in the world 24 hours after the trigger point event. If I know, after the event, that I made the wrong decision, there is not a lot that I can do to change the outcome. A directionally correct insight delivered on time is better than the perfect insight delivered late.

The purpose of Analytics for knowledge workers should be to serve up the 'almost perfect' insight fast, in advance of the trigger point event, to provide some foresight into consequences of different decisions so that the decision made is both informed and timely.

Figure 106: HINDSIGHT, INSIGHT AND FORESIGHT

Hindsight	Looking back at the data, with an informed perspective based on domain expertise.
Insight	Applying knowledge, experience, to know what the data means so that you can interpret the results.
Foresight	Being able to predict outcomes and prescribe remedial action where necessary.

As we have progressed over the recent decade, and started to get benefit from the available technologies, most companies are at a point where they have a pretty good idea of what has happened in the past, assuming that the data recorded is both complete and accurate. Hindsight is, after all, 20:20. Economists are really good at hindsight, but are the poster children for horribly inaccurate forecasts. The economy is a notoriously complex beast and there are just so many factors to consider that getting it right can reasonably be considered hard. The recurrent theme that emerges from researchers who examine the inaccuracy of economists' forecasts is that the lack of insight into the current state – a blind belief that what happened in the past will just repeat itself – leads to the lack of foresight, and consequently any forecast that they come up with is not even directionally accurate. Economists must make forward-looking statements using only a rearview mirror. No wonder it is hard for them to see.

In business, predicting a sales forecast is also notoriously inaccurate. To say that forecasting is the bane of existence of most sales managers and leaders is probably a bit of an understatement. It is estimated that forecast accuracy in most sales organizations runs at about 50 percent – just half of the sales opportunities that are forecasted to close do so as projected. We might as well flip a coin.

Similar to the economists' problem, there is usually a lot of historical data for sales managers to work with. But while the hindsight that the data provides can be a guide at a macro-level, it is rarely sufficiently useful when applied to an individual sales opportunity because it is lacking contextual insight. Also, many sales processes have been designed by the selling organization to map to their own selling activities rather than to the customer's buying activities and many times these two are out of sync. In fact, all along the way, in the buying cycle, the customer is making a series of micro-decisions as a guide to the right purchase decision. Often the sales process does not reflect the actions that would need to be taken to guide the buyer to make a favorable micro-decision. No insight, no foresight.

This is where applied experience, bringing the principles of Augmented Intelligence to bear, is valuable. It is certainly more important than raw data, and requires different parts of the brain to figure out. A good designer of an Analytics model is curious, and that curiosity can find nuances in historical data, which when viewed through the eyes of experience, and enriched by the insight garnered through deep contextual knowledge, can join the dots so that the Analytics model itself is infused with insight and can deliver foresight to the human on the other side of the computer screen.

Data and the Four Stages of Analytics

We are moving to a point in the development of technology where we have transitioned from where we were learning how to use a computer to where we are helping the computer to learn about us. As we deploy Analytics to help solve business problems, we should consider how much context we can teach the computer so that it can notify us to take the appropriate action when necessary.

> Don't measure anything unless the data helps you make a better decision or change your actions. If you're not prepared to change your diet or your workouts, don't get on the scale.
>
> **Seth Godin**

Data without action is just data and has little value. Data is not actionable on its own. A human with the requisite domain knowledge can look at data and figure out what to do with it, but a system does not know this on its own unless we build in this ability. The system does not automatically know that the data is meaningful. With all the power available to us today with Analytics systems, at the end of the day, if it processes a bunch of data and tells me that the average revenue I can get from all my customers is $100,000, but a particular customer that I am interacting with has the potential to grow to $300,000, then it needs also to tell me what I should do about it. On its own, and in many Analytics implementations today, the system does not automatically notify people who need to know the insight that it has just uncovered. It does not recognize that we need to do something about it.

The answer is making that data actionable. That is about engagement. We want the system to:

- Understand the data from the past – **Descriptive Analytics**
- Deduce from that data the key signals that correlate to changes in outcome – **Diagnostic Analytics**
- Predict what will happen (based on current context) – **Predictive Analytics**
- Recommend actions using **Prescriptive Analytics**.

Now *that* is effective engagement, the apogee of good Analytics implementations. This is Augmented Analytics because it is guided by humans and processed by machines.

There are many definitions for each of the terms 'Descriptive Analytics,' 'Diagnostic Analytics,' 'Predictive Analytics,' and 'Prescriptive Analytics' that are generally similar but with enough variances that it is worth defining what I mean by each term. My definitions generally line up with those you will find in Gartner's *Glossary*, and that's as good a reference point for my reading audience as any.

According to Gartner, **Descriptive Analytics** is the examination of data or content, usually manually performed, to answer the question *"What happened?"* (or *"What is happening?"*), characterized by traditional Business Intelligence and visualizations such as pie charts, bar charts, line graphs, tables, or generated narratives. We all do a lot of this in reports and dashboards in the CRM. But, let's face it, very few people enjoy poring over reports trying to figure out what it all means, particularly if they were not involved in the design of the report, and so don't have an understanding of why the report was created in the first place. Dashboards, or other visualizations, are one step up the ladder, but if we are to empower the knowledge worker, we don't want to have to teach them how to interpret the charts.

Diagnostic Analytics helps you to understand why something happened and, more importantly, what data matters. Gartner's *Glossary* entry for Diagnostic Analytics is:

> A form of advanced analytics which examines data or content to answer the question "Why did it happen?" and is characterized by techniques such as drill-down, data discovery, data mining and correlations.

For me, the clue is in the name: Diagnostics Analytics summarizes raw data into Insight Signals that are interpretable by humans.

However, Diagnostic Analytics are not usually well instrumented, and analytics and interpretation cycles are wasted on spurious and often erroneous predictions. Deriving those Insight Signals is a core foundation to the following Predictive Analytics and Prescriptive Analytics, because without knowing which signals 'move the needle' it is impossible to predict what might happen or to prescribe what you should do about it. Diagnostic analysis can help avoid the correlation *versus* causation mistake.

Correlation *versus* causation

Two events can consistently correlate to each other but not have any causal relationship. An example is the relationship between reading ability and shoe size across the whole population of the United States. If someone performed such a survey, they would find that larger shoe sizes correlate with better reading ability, but this does not mean large feet cause good reading skills. Instead the correlation is caused by the fact that young children have small feet and have not yet (or have only recently) learned to read. In this case, the two variables are more accurately correlated with a third: age.

The part that age plays in this example is known as a confounding variable or confounding factor and is not being controlled for in the experiment. In this case, age influences both reading ability and shoe size quite directly. A confounding variable can be the actual cause of a correlation; hence analysis must take these into account and find ways of dealing with them, usually by searching them out and trying to alter this variable directly.

Correlation does not imply causation, but it does waggle its eyebrows suggestively and gesture furtively while whispering, "*Look over there*." Correlation, if disconnected from causation, is usually a distraction.

Data and the Four Stages of Analytics (continued)

If we know why something happened in the past, the theory goes that we will have a better chance of figuring out what will happen next. **Predictive Analytics** help you to understand the future. Gartner says:

> Predictive Analytics is a form of advanced analytics which examines data or content to answer the question "What is going to happen?" or more precisely, "What is likely to happen?" and is characterized by techniques such as regression analysis, multivariate statistics, pattern matching, predictive modeling, and forecasting.

Predictive Analytics provides companies with insights on what might happen in the future. It is important to remember that no statistical algorithm can 'predict' the future with 100 percent certainty. Companies use these statistics to forecast what might happen in the future.

The rapidly evolving **Prescriptive Analytics** capability allows users to 'prescribe' a number of different possible actions to take. In a nutshell, these analytics are all about providing advice on *"What to do next?"* Gartner's take:

> Prescriptive Analytics is a form of advanced analytics which examines data or content to answer the question "What should be done?" or "What can we do to make ___ happen?"

Prescriptive Analytics builds on Predictive Analytics. In addition to the prediction of what will happen, Prescriptive also suggests actions you can take to take advantage of the predictions, by recommending one or more possible courses of action.

Figure 107: THE FOUR PHASES OF ANALYTICS

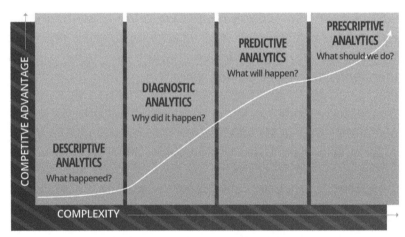

Avoiding the Pitfalls – Plugging the Gaps with Humans

Many organizations that are investing heavily in Analytics, and hiring data scientists to slice and dice the data, appear frustrated. They undeniably have more data than they had before, and in most cases (because there has been a focus on the data) the quality has improved. The data scientists and software tools are rarely a significant cause of the frustration, but they find themselves spending more time and money while failing to garner significantly better insight.

Now that technological advances have made it possible to accumulate colossal amounts of data at an increasing rate, it has become almost axiomatic that the answer to everything is in the data. But, in fact, it is not. Companies are making big bets on Big Data and Analytics – Big Data Analytics (!) – without the qualitative assessment that is required to apply deep domain expertise. That has the potential to lead to big decisions being made with misplaced confidence. Here are some guidelines to avoid the most common pitfalls.

Starting with Questions: One of the most common misunderstandings about Analytics is that, if you look at data hard enough, you will find insights. Staring at daily dashboards in the hope that insights will miraculously reveal themselves is often overwhelming, confusing and unsuccessful.

Successful Analytics start by identifying the question you're trying to answer from the data. For example, if website conversion – enticing the user to take a specific call-to-action from your website – is an issue, instead of studying your website data hoping to find reasons for low conversion, narrow down your efforts to a specific question. In this case, it might be: *"What are the leading indicators that we should measure in the website traffic that can help us to increase conversions from 23 percent to 26 percent?"* This approach allows you to focus on finding actionable drivers of conversion that can have impact.

Another question that might be used by a sales manager who wants to increase revenue in his sales team is: *"What can the data tell me about the average value of each sales opportunity that we work, the win rate for each member of my team, and how long it normally takes us to win a sale?"*

These are things that all sales managers want to know and using hypotheses to narrow the data set needed generates secondary questions to further refine the insights, such as: *"When we win a deal, how often have we engaged with all of the customer's key decision makers?"* or *"What are the attributes of customers who have most frequently purchased Product X?"* or *"Of all the sales opportunities that we pursue, are we winning the larger or smaller deals?"*

The primary hurdle that people must overcome is how to know what questions to ask. That is more of a heuristic experience based challenge than it is a pattern recognition or data analysis problem.

What do you want to know? Why do you want to know it? What will you do with the answers? These are all good questions to start with.

It's About the Business, Not (Just) the Science: Analytics for salespeople should be about knowledge, and founded in deep sales domain expertise. Analytics should not be viewed as an IT project, but as a business project, focused on a narrow domain area – bigger is not always better – to help the sellers to better perform the tasks they have to execute every day. Without the right business context, it is hard to know what questions to ask – so, in that case, any answer should do – but, of course, that doesn't work. It is understandable, though that, if there is too much of a separation between the people with the business knowledge and the people with the Analytics tools, then success is less likely. This is because a tool is just a tool and, if you don't have business expertise, domain knowledge, experience and a 'nose' for what's right, then you can't apply any human qualitative input – and that makes it hard to connect the dots.

What are the important business outcomes that you want to impact? The answer to that should drive your Analytics focus. You might start with the Key Performance Indicators in your sales business and work back from there.

Building Trust: It's extraordinarily hard for people to change from making decisions based on personal experience to making them from data – especially when that data counters the prevailing common wisdom. But upsetting the *status quo* is much easier when everyone can see how it could contribute to a major goal. With a potential big reward in sight, a significant effort is easier to justify, and people across functions and levels are better able to support it – for example:

- *"How can we reduce the sales cycle for our enterprise deals?"*
- *"What changes do we need to make to ensure that the deals we focus on and forecast are actually the ones that we can win – in line with the forecasted size and timeline?"*

If you focus on the benefit that such insights would deliver, you have a better chance of getting people on board with the project in the first instance.

Equally important, though, is the need to build trust in the outputs, the insights, the predictions and the prescriptions. If one of your quantitative experts develops an ingenious algorithm that pulled in all pipeline and sales data, historical sales forecasts and actual results, to suggest future sales behavior, the system should also explain the 'why' behind the recommendations. For the users to trust the algorithm and the results it promises, they have to understand, in so far as is possible, the sequence of 'thinking' that was used to derive the result. I call this the 'Thinking Chain.'

Here is an example of a Prescriptive Analytics notification and the associated thinking chain:

> **Sales Forecast Risk: Large deal ($450,000) needs attention.**
> Your sales forecast for the quarter has increased by $200,000 but the level of risk has increased. Joe Johnson's Ancaster Engineering opportunity has increased from $250,000 to $450,000, but this is more than 3 times the average deal size for Joe Johnson. There are 62 days remaining in the quarter – 52 percent of their average sales cycle. The opportunity is at Requirements stage in the funnel. Access to the buyers looks weak. There is a good understanding of the business problem. No decision criteria have been identified. Click here to schedule a deal review with Joe Johnson.

The final step in building trust is to close the loop. Allow users to give feedback on the insight or advice by using something akin to a Facebook 'Like' to indicate if they found the insight useful.

It is equally important to measure the efficacy of each insight. Which insights were presented most frequently, and what measurable difference occurred when the insight was acted upon? As your project progresses you will learn about which insights the users think are most valuable and which are actually moving the needle in your business. Bring your users on this journey. It will help you to build a foundation of trust, a prerequisite for any effective organizational change.

Objectivity and Confirmation Bias: The purpose of any analysis should be to get to the objective truth, the insights that will allow you to determine the actual factors that drive the results, rather than spurious correlations that might lead you to specious predictions.

Once you have uncovered those deterministic factors you can begin to develop some heuristics or rules of thumb that are based on experience and are empirically true. These rules must pass the *"Do I believe it?"* test. Using common sense – which unfortunately is not necessarily all that common when faced with copious amounts of seemingly correlated data – you can test your assumptions to develop a meaningful prediction or forecast in a systematic way rather than on an *ad hoc* basis.

Assiduous application of this approach will get to a level of accuracy that is much greater than average and will trend towards higher precision over time. Of course, there will always be exceptions, situations that you have not considered or experienced in the past and being open to this possibility will improve the way you assess the results of your analysis. Always question and focus on the rules or process being applied. Sometimes you will get it wrong, but that's OK. Rather than being disappointed in getting it wrong, you can rightly be pleased that you have got it as right as you could. While it may seem counterintuitive, the paradox is that, by focusing more on the process than on the results, you are more likely to get better results.

When something doesn't fit into our established way of thinking we usually blame the something instead of questioning our way of thinking. Trying to fit a square peg into a round hole, you might blame the peg, when maybe the problem is with the hole. So, when the results of your Analytics efforts result in an outcome that you didn't expect, you need to be open to it.

We should be cautious with confusing the unfamiliar with the improbable. Just because we didn't expect it doesn't mean

DIGITAL SALES TRANSFORMATION

that it can't happen. A scenario that we have not yet considered might look strange, but should not be summarily dismissed. A reaction of *"Wow, I never saw that coming. I never looked at it that way before"* is much more valuable than *"See, I knew it all along. I was right!"* You've learned a lot more in the first of these two scenarios.

Where Do I Go from Here?

There are many different opinions on the value and threat of AI. But while polarized positions still exist, there is enough evidence of advancement in AI, of its impact on our lives, and on the lives of others, that there is a strategic imperative to respond. This, I feel, is no longer a matter of opinion.

As one of my college professors used to say: *"We are all entitled to our own opinions, but we are not entitled to our own facts."*

The facts are clear:

1. AI is impacting your personal and professional life today, and the impact will only increase in the short term and medium term.
2. AI is getting smarter. (Most of the time we don't notice.)
3. All AI systems need to be taught about the domain to which they are being applied. This is a critical, but often overlooked, aspect of AI.
4. Big Data works when you truly have Big Data, but only when you know the big questions. Small Data matters too and that fact is particularly relevant to sales professionals today.
5. (AI + Humans) is greater than the sum of the parts. Knowledge remains a core.

AI systems for Sales are certainly getting smarter, but only when the task to which they are being applied can be reduced to a codified set of signals that they can understand. AI can help with easily defined tasks that can be reduced to binary signals. For all others, the knowledge must be embedded into the system.

This is a good time to think about what you should do next:

1. Embrace the arrival of AI (particularly the Augmented variety) as a positive force for the enablement of sellers.

2. Decide what tasks currently being undertaken by your salespeople, such as data collection, data processing, scheduling, reporting, can be offloaded to the machine.

3. Look at your most value add activities – those that require the application of expertise, such as strategic sales, marketing strategy, and customer engagement – and consider how these activities would be better if augmented with core domain knowledge. Solving this problem will deliver rapid competitive advantage.

4. Before embarking on any Analytics or Big Data project, consider first the questions that you need to answer that will move the needle in your business.

5. Remember that most value add tasks for knowledge workers are not great candidates for mere data analysis. In most cases the datasets are too small. Your return will be much greater if you can figure out how to apply knowledge to the small quantity of data that you have to gain insight.

AI is just the next step in automation – though it is a very significant step. The efficacy of any project will be dependent not just on technology or technical feasibility. The costs of the project, the value of the work, the scarcity or otherwise of the skills needed will all need to be considered. In the context of the work that sales professionals need to do, you will get greater return from investing in the humans – augmenting the seller with Augmented Intelligence – rather than delegating the thinking to the machine. After all, sellers think for a living, and we will benefit by making that thinking more informed.

The next four chapters paint a picture of your Digital Sales Transformation journey in a nutshell, helping sellers to think, and to learn how to build and deploy a Customer

Engagement Model that is Customer First, and technology enabled.

Note: Many of the technology examples used in the chapters that follow are based on my experience of working with Altify and partnering with Salesforce. It's not meant to be partisan – the principles are universally applicable – but it's the framework that I know best and have seen work.

CHAPTER 13:
SALES PROCESS

Implementing a Sales Process

Developing a sales forecast generally isn't much fun, but getting it wrong means that you are not only spending time doing something you don't like – but worse, you're still not getting any benefit. An inaccurate forecast points to a weakness in your sales process.

An effective sales process, mapped to the customer's buying process and consistently executed, provides clarity and visibility on your business and gives you greater control over your destiny. It is an early warning system; it shows where you are strong and identifies actions that need attention. If you define and use a sales process well it will bring you an uncommon freedom to focus on what you have to do today, without the interminable stress that accompanies uncertainty.

In *Chapter 3: Digital Sales Transformation | Part 2: Customer Engagement Model*, the strategy for engagement at Customer Impact Level 1 was stated as:

> ALIGN WITH BUYING PROCESS TO ACCELERATE SALES
> Design sales process, mapped to the customer's buying process and implement a framework for accelerated sales velocity, consistent visibility and management.

Implementing a Sales Process is the 'how' to deliver on that strategy. I will now go through the Goal, and Objectives and Methods for Sales Process.

Figure 108: SALES PROCESS – OVERVIEW

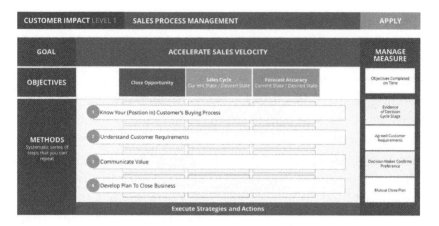

Sales Process Goal

The Goal of implementing a Sales Process is to Accelerate Sales Velocity. That doesn't just mean shortening the sales cycle. While shorter sales cycles are generally desirable, there are other factors at play. Win Rate obviously matters. Running eight deals quickly only to win one is not very sensible. Deal Size also matters – you want to maximize the value of each deal that you close. In this context Sales Velocity means the revenue that you can achieve in any given period. If instead of winning five deals of $20,000 each in a quarter to generate $100,000 in revenue, you can achieve $120,000 by winning four $30,000 deals in the same period, then that seems like a sensible idea.

From the overall sales team's perspective however, the value of a buyer centric sales process goes beyond metrics that relate just to opportunities. A repeatable sales process provides the team with a defined, systematic and measurable way to sell and makes sure every salesperson knows the buying signs that occur when you are winning. The result is an increase in productivity, shorter onboarding for new sellers, more accurate sales forecasts, greater organizational alignment – all supporting functions can contribute more effectively if they know where the seller is in a given sale – and because your sales activities map to the customer's buying activities, customers have a better buying experience.

Sales Process Objectives and Methods

There are three core objectives to be achieved when implementing a sales process for the sales team:

1. Close the opportunity
2. Reduce sales cycle duration (current / desired state)
3. Improve sales forecast accuracy (current / desired state).

I will deal with the first two now, and the third later in the chapter.

The methods to apply to be successful are:

1. Know your position in the customer buying process
2. Understand customer requirements
3. Communicate value
4. Develop a plan to close.

Here's a spoiler. It's all about having a buyer centric sales process.

Summarizing the methods (which come to life in the sales process outlined below):

1. It is first necessary to understand where the buyer is in his buying process so that you know the next action to take. You can determine this by seeking evidence in each stage in the sales process as detailed below.
2. To provide evidence that you can meet the customer's needs you must have a clear and joint understanding, with the customer, of their specific requirements (see *Chapter 9: Know Your Customer First*). See *Requirements* stage in the sales process below.
3. As the customer progresses on their journey from awareness of their requirement to the selection of a supplier, your job is to communicate the value that your solution provides so that the decision maker can

develop preference for you as their chosen supplier. (See *Chapter 10: Create and Communicate Value*). See *Evidence* stage in the sales process below.

4. Then you need an action plan to close the business. See *Acquisition* stage in the sales process below.

According to *Inside the Buyer's Mind*, only two-thirds of sales organizations claim to have a sales cycle aligned with their customer's buying cycle. Those buyer centric sellers have a win rate that is 22 percent greater and a sales cycle that is 22 percent shorter than those who have not implemented this discipline.

The Structure of a Sales Process

A sales process guides the sellers on the next best actions to move an opportunity from the first stage in the pipeline through the various buying gates to the last stage in the pipeline.

In my example I have a six-stage pipeline, so there are six stages that map the seller's activities to the customer's buying activities. The stages are:

1. Target
5. Qualify
6. Requirements
7. Evidence
8. Acquisition
9. Verbal order and close.

In each stage you need to have verifiable evidence, from the customer's perspective, that you are aligned with the buying cycle and that you are making sufficient progress that means you can advance to the next stage. I refer to the steps in each stage – the questions you need to answer and the evidence you must find – as *Qualifiers*. Depending on the complexity of the buying process, each stage will contain a number of qualifiers. You might have one process for your larger deals that might contain 25 qualifiers (as in the model here), and perhaps a second process for smaller deals with just 12 qualifiers.

In the **Target** stage, you just want to be sure that you are working with a company that fits the criteria defined by your Ideal Customer Profile as described in *Chapter 5: The Ideal Customer Profile*.

So the Qualifier here is:

1. Does the company meet the criteria of your Ideal Customer Profile?

Qualify is self-explanatory. Here you want to ensure that there is a valid opportunity that merits allocation of time and resource to pursue.

In this stage the questions you need to answer are:

2. Have you evidence from the customer that this is a priority project?
3. Have you evidence of the pressure the customer is facing or the problem they are trying to solve?
4. Have resources (people) or funds ($) been identified to this project by the customer?
5. Have you confirmed a target start date by which the project needs to get started?

In **Requirements**, you can determine how well the customer understands what he needs, whether his need is Unknown, Known or Active, as described in *Chapter 9: Know Your Customer First*, how deeply the problem impacts the customer's organization, what the buying process is, and whether the customer has a vision of the benefits a solution such as yours might deliver.

This stage is the best opportunity to shape the need, develop the requirements, and guide the customer along your chosen path, assuming you can show potential business benefit to be gained from purchasing your solution.

So now:

6. Do you have a confirmed buying process?
7. Have you engaged with the key players?
8. Is there a clearly documented description of the business problem and requirements that is agreed between you and the buyer?
9. Have you confirmed that you have a good solution fit for the customer's need?

10. Is there a committed date by which the customer has to act?

11. Has the customer committed resource to the buying project?

When you are in **Evidence**, as the customer is collecting proof, gathering data and evidence that your solution can satisfy his needs, you're investing a little further in rounding out his requirements and testing whether he can visualize how your solution is his best choice. To achieve that, your time is spent in creating and demonstrating value, working jointly with the customer to arrive at the best solution. Your activity should be focused on highlighting your competitive advantage through the creative application of your product or service. You must demonstrate that you can meet the buyer's needs better than your competitor. You will begin work on establishing his return on investment from purchasing your product, though that may well only be finalized in the *Acquisition* stage.

At this stage, you should understand the hierarchy of influence in the customer's organization, and have agreed with each influencer his motivation and 'hot buttons.' You must be clear about how you can meet the needs of each of these influencers.

Now that you have invested considerable time working with the customer, you are entitled to know all the decision criteria that will be applied to the evaluation. Use the techniques outlined in the Problem Discovery Model in *Chapter 9: Know Your Customer First,* to determine whether the project is at risk, from budget cuts or competing projects. Most importantly, you must clarify the customer's compelling reason to buy.

Confirm the answers to these questions:

12. Have you confirmed that you can meet the need for each buying influencer?

13. Has the decision maker confirmed that you are the preferred supplier?

14. Is the budget allocated, authorized and available?

15. Have you re-confirmed that this is a priority project?

16. Are competitive issues understood?

17. Has customer confirmed a compelling reason to buy?

18. Are all decision criteria well-understood?

19. Is the personal motivation for each buying influencer known?

When you get to **Acquisition** you need to stay particularly close to the customer and your frequency of interaction should increase. From the customer's perspective, this is the time of highest risk – he is about to commit his company to a purchase decision – so you must act accordingly.

Thus far, the customer has been engaged with you, outlining his needs and, determining whether your solution can meet those needs. You should once again ensure that the customer is satisfied that you are the best choice. You should be clear that he understands his costs, and your entire value. You may need to return to some of the 'proof points' already established, making sure of your competitive position, testing once more that the value you bring is well-understood, and that it meets the requirements of the customer.

Then ask yourself:

20. Has all legal / procurement / technical due diligence been completed?

21. Have you agreed and submitted final commercial terms and all necessary legal documents?

22. Are the necessary implementation team resources (for both supplier and customer) aligned and in place?

23. Has a mutual closing plan (with dates) been agreed with the customer?

In **Verbal Order and Close**, there are only two tests: Has the buyer given you a verbal order and did you get a signature? Are you sure that you will get the deal and a signed contract? The only reason you should lose now is if there are unreasonable contract terms required by the customer, or there has been a material change in circumstances. By understanding the complete buying process from the outset, you should have been able to identify this earlier and hopefully will have addressed it.

And so the last two questions are:

24. Has the decision maker given a final commitment to buy?
25. Have you received a signed contract and purchase order?

In this example you will see that I designed the sales process to be objective and evidence based and to reflect the customer's buying cycle.

It seems logical to me to link the selling cycle to the customer's buying cycle. Then the selling actions are obvious, as outlined in the process above.

According to the *Business Performance Benchmark Study*, for the 65 percent of sellers who map their activities to the buyer's activities the attendant benefits are significant: a Sales Cycle that is 22 percent shorter accompanied by an increase in Win Rate of 22 percent, as shown below.

Figure 109: THE BENEFITS OF A BUYER CENTRIC SALES PROCESS

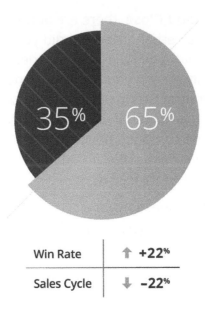

Win Rate	⬆ **+22**%
Sales Cycle	⬇ **−22**%

Making It Scale

When I first got involved in the sales effectiveness industry, early this century, two things struck me. The depth of thinking that was applied to sales process and methodology was impressive, clearly based on research and experience. Even though I had started and run four companies before that, and I thought I knew a bit about sales, there were concepts that I had not considered. The second thing that I was surprised by was the (almost) complete absence of technology support to guide sellers through their sales process or methodology. This was one of the reasons why I started Altify.

When you embed a sales process in software (integrated into your CRM) it is so much easier to use and measure. When a seller interacts with an intelligent sales process they can see progress and immediately know what to do next. The sales manager can review the opportunity updates as they happen, removing the need for weekly deal updates. Different sales processes can be automatically presented to the seller based on the attributes of the deal so no time is wasted. Existing data in the CRM can be used so that the salesperson does not have to duplicate data entry. And, as I will describe below, because sales process software can measure and learn from all the sales cycles executed through the software, the guidance can get smarter and the system can provide objective and intelligent deal probability and forecast close dates.

Figure 110: AN AUTOMATED SALES PROCESS IN SOFTWARE

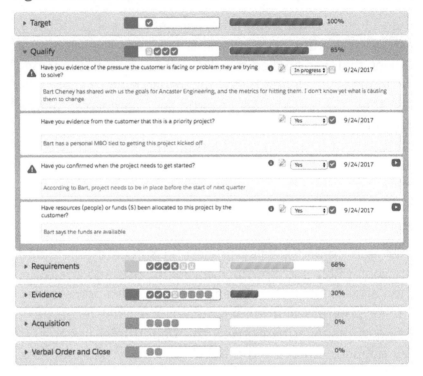

Improving Forecast Accuracy

We have hit two of the three objectives that were outlined earlier. You have seen that applying the process will increase your ability to close the deal and will also reduce the length of the sale cycle:

1. Close the opportunity ✔
2. Reduce sales cycle duration ✔
3. Improve sales forecast accuracy.

The third objective is *Improve sales forecast accuracy.*

By the very fact of applying a buyer centric sales process you will already have more clarity and a greater sense of where you are in the deal, and the evidence allows your judgment to be more accurate. However, it can get better.

By leveraging a sales process algorithm in software you will get an objective measure of closure probability and close date.

JP Knapp is an Area Vice President at Vocera Communications and a steward of sales effectiveness solutions for his company. He is an avid supporter of using sales process to guide his sales team to accelerate sales velocity and improve their forecast accuracy.

A Practitioner's Perspective
JP Knapp, AVP Vocera Communications

The 5th largest deal in company history closed exactly on the day it was predicted eight months earlier. Sales Process Manager helped us see firsthand the accuracy of calculated close dates and value of having the knowledge built into our sales process.

While you may already know your Sales Cycle – the number of days it typically takes to close a deal – you can achieve greater accuracy on your sales forecast if you can define the duration for each stage. By implementing a smart sales process within your CRM you can measure how long it takes across all of your deals to move from one stage to the next, for a particular sales motion, and then use that to inform the likely forecast date.

In my example I designed a sales process for a $50,000 deal. My hypothetical sales cycle is 84 days long, and based on historical analysis of previously closed opportunities, I have determined how many days it usually takes in each stage of the process. I have also learned the probability of winning the deal based on stage progression.

Figure 111: SALES STAGE DURATION / WIN PROBABILITY

Stage	Duration (Days) From - To	Days to Close	Win Probability %
Target	0 - 3	84	12
Qualify	4 - 16	80	24
Requirements	17 - 36	67	38
Evidence	37 - 58	47	62
Acquisition	59 - 70	25	80
Verbal Order and Close	71 - 84	14	94

If you do not have sufficient empirical data to document the specific duration and win probability for each stage, you can begin by assessing how long you think it might take to complete all the qualifiers in a stage. Then, over the period of a few sales cycles, use your sales process software to learn the actual results.

If it usually takes two weeks from the time when all commercial terms are agreed to get contracts signed and for the customer to raise a purchase order, then set the duration of your *Verbal Order and Close* stage to be 14 days.

Similarly, as you consider all the qualifiers that have to be completed in the *Requirements* stage, you can estimate the elapsed time to learn about the buying process, engage with key buying influencers, and determine that your solution fits the customer's needs. In my example I have set this time as 20 days.

Acknowledging that not everything will necessarily happen in a linear manner, you should know that if you have not completed the qualifiers in the *Evidence* stage, it is unlikely that you will close this deal in less than 25 days, the start of the *Acquisition* stage. If there are only 10 days left in the quarter it is really unlikely that you can close an opportunity that is still in *Evidence*.

Some organizations use weighted pipeline measures to calculate a sales forecast. The theory goes that, if you add up all the opportunities in your pipeline, multiplied by the probability of closure of each deal, the aggregate is your forecast. I am not a fan of this approach. You don't close a percentage of a deal; you either close it or you don't.

Ten opportunities each with a win probability of 10 percent does not equal one deal that is closed – that has a 100 percent win probability. While the math might say the two are equal, clearly they are not.

To explain this more clearly, I have built out two forecast tables here for a salesperson with a $100,000 quota for the quarter, working six opportunities, with 30 days remaining in the quarter.

Figure 112: WEIGHTED PIPELINE APPROACH

Opportunity	Value	Probability %	Weighted Value
1	$20,000	80	$16,000
2	$48,000	38	$18,240
3	$100,000	12	$12,000
4	$12.000	80	$9,600
5	$32,000	94	$30,080
6	$60,000	38	$22,800
Total	$272,000		$108,720

This might give you a great sense of confidence, but it may be misplaced. My recommendation, particularly as you get to the later part of the quarter is to use a *Guided Forecast*; at its simplest a combination of calculated *Win Probability*, and *Days to Close*. Start by setting a Win Probability threshold (say 75% – anything below this doesn't get into your forecast) and then check whether the 'Days to Close' value is less than the remaining days in the quarter.

Figure 113: GUIDED FORECAST APPROACH

Opportunity	Value	Probability %	Days to Close	Forecast	Value
1	$20,000	80	25	Yes	$20,000
2	$48,000	38	67	No	$0
3	$100,000	12	84	No	$0
4	$12.000	80	25	Yes	$12,000
5	$32,000	94	14	Yes	$32,000
6	$60,000	38	67	No	$0
Total	$272,000				$64,000

For example, in **Figure 113**, applying the two screens drops Opportunity 2 from the forecast, since it doesn't meet the Probability threshold (actual probability 38% is less than 75%) and, with only 30 days left in the quarter, there's unlikely to be enough time to close it.

The results in **Figures 112** and **113** are quite different. The weighted approach does not provide any guidance on which opportunities to focus for the quarter and totally ignores the temporal aspect of the sales process. Because the weighted value suggests that he will close $108,720, the seller will feel comfortable that he can make his $100,000 quota, but it seems that without additional effort and focus this is unlikely to be true.

Consider on the other hand what happens with the Guided Forecast approach. The seller will first double down to make sure that he is following the sales process to ensure that he wins deals #1, #4 and #5, to lock in the $64,000 in revenue and then he identifies from the remaining three deals where he can apply extra effort to try to accelerate one (not all) of the remaining opportunities to make up the $36,000 gap to quota. It will be hard, but at least now he knows where to focus and that gives him an increased chance of getting there.

There may be other factors that you add into your Guided Forecast. These might include selling to an existing customer *versus* a new customer, a tenured *versus* a novice seller, seasonality in your business, and historical performance of the individual seller. You can learn the impact of these factors from empirical data once you are tracking the actual performance in software.

Figure 114: FORECAST GUIDANCE

Taking a Guided Forecast approach will provide an objective measure of Win Probability and Close Date and will help you determine the actual deals that can make up your forecast. In **Figure 114** you can see that the system is proving its intelligent guidance on Win Probability (41 percent) and Close Date, which is 31 days later than the seller's expectation.

Designing Your Sales Process: 7 Principles

There are seven principles to apply when designing your sales process:

- Customized to the buying cycle
- Sales tools in context at each stage
- Many simple and complex processes
- Benchmarks and insight
- Team visibility for sales manager
- Informs sales forecast visibility
- Integrates with CRM system.

Customized to the buying cycle

In most cases, customers know every step they want to take in the buying cycle. They have a business problem to solve, alternatives to consider, decision criteria they deem critical, and a procurement process that is understood. In short, they have a plan, with hurdles and obstacles you have to scale.

Ensure that your sales process maps to the customer's buying cycle and that the qualifiers you use at each stage seek out verifiable evidence of progress from the customer's perspective.

Sales tools in context at each stage

At each stage of the buying process, salespeople need to employ just the right tools, at the right time, to advance the sale to the next stage in the process. The sales process is a collection of micro sales events, each crafted to move closer to the eventual goal – closing the deal. For each qualifier consider what messaging, insights, and sales tools will best help the seller to successfully complete that qualifier with the customer.

Many simple and complex processes

It is unlikely that one sales process will be sufficient for your business. Sometimes you are pursuing a brand new customer. In other cases, you may be dealing with renewals, or expansions in an existing account. The software you use should be smart enough to know the type of opportunity and intelligently present the right steps for each sales process type. This ensures you have the right sales effort, sales activities and outcomes for the appropriate buying process. Also, the different stage durations and win probabilities in each process will better inform the sales forecast.

Benchmarks and insight

Benchmarking delivers many advantages for companies looking to improve the performance of their sales organization. When deploying a sales process initiative, ensure that you have built in capability to:

- Record a current-state assessment, or benchmark, that goes beyond the typical lagging indicators of win rate, quota achievement, deal size, or market penetration. You should be looking for measures of early qualification, the velocity through each stage of the sales cycle, and indicators of where deals are most commonly getting stalled or lost.
- Develop a foundation or framework for sales productivity improvements that are truly transformative. You know where you are starting from, so you see what you have to change. (See the *Pipeline* section in *Chapter 16: Sales Performance Management*.)
- Learn more about the cadence of your sales organization as it gathers data on more sales cycles.

Team visibility for the sales manager

All sales managers need readily available visibility in the sales process activities of their team and both the absolute and relative behavior and performance of each salesperson on the team. If the sales organization is adopting a sales process to increase sales velocity, then it must provide an easy-to-use tool to enable the sales manager to monitor the team's application of the processes, and the consequent impact on revenue performance, by providing the following data:

- What deals being worked on by the team are critical for this quarter?
- Where is each deal in the sales process?
- Where should we be focused?

These answers should be informed by a sales manager's view of the operation of her team's sales process. The sales manager is the critical link. If you can leverage your sales process initiative to increase her visibility into the sales team, you will strengthen that link and improve overall performance of both manager and seller. (See *Chapter 16: Sales Performance Management*.)

Informs sales forecast visibility

Salespeople spend about 2.5 hours each week on sales forecasting, and for most companies, the accuracy of sales forecasts leave a lot to be desired. The good news is that there is a very strong causal connection between sales process and forecast accuracy.

To maximize the impact of your sales process on the accuracy of your sales forecast, there are two things to consider:

- Does the sales process incorporate intelligence that objectively monitors the close date of the sale? If you have built in the sales best practices, and your sales process can learn about the rhythm of your business, then it should be smart enough to help predict the close date of the opportunity. It should also identify for the salesperson the difference between their opinion of when the deal will close, and a projected close date based on past behavior of winning sales cycles.

- Does the sales process provide the sales manager with insight into deal vulnerabilities and risks in the forecast? It should be able to answer these very important questions: What's in the forecast? Are any of the reps counting on unusually large deals to make the quarter? Are all deals being worked? What's closed? What deals are forecasted? Which deals are moving quickly, and where are the opportunities that are stalled?

Your sales process should give those 2.5 hours back to the salesperson, improve the accuracy of the forecast for each opportunity, and provide the sales manager with insight to help her understand what she needs to do to make or exceed the quota for the team.

Integrates with CRM system

This one should be a 'no-brainer.' Let's say you use Salesforce as your CRM. If that is the case, you are already asking your sales team to enter their opportunity information into Salesforce. If that is where your opportunity information is held, then that is where the sales process must live. That way it can intelligently react to the attributes of the opportunity, like the size of the deal, or the products included in the opportunity record, to present the right process for that opportunity.

Conclusion

Over the years I have seen great companies develop wonderful sales processes. I observed two primary pitfalls:

- Many times sales processes were developed with an inward looking lens – measuring the actions taken by the seller, instead of the evidence received from the customer. (To be fair these do not fall into the 'wonderful' category.)
- The second reason for failure was an attempt to deploy the sales process to the sales team without software to support the deployment.

At the start of this chapter I said that an effective sales process, mapped to the customer's buying process and consistently executed, provides clarity and visibility on your business and gives you greater control over your destiny. That is true, but it can only happen when it is Customer First, in software, and tied to the pipeline and forecast management systems.

CHAPTER 14:

OPPORTUNITY
MANAGEMENT

Implementing Opportunity Management

Winning strategic sales opportunities is the lifeblood of every enterprise B2B salesperson. These are the deals that matter – the ones that pave the way to President's Club. The scorecard at the end of the quarter tells its own story. Either you got there – or you didn't. No place to run.

The truth for most enterprise sellers though is that they don't win that many deals. Average deal value is usually at least six figures. Quota is perhaps one to three million if you are in a high margin business like software. In lower margin segments enterprise sellers will have higher quotas and larger deals. But the truth remains the same. To make your revenue target you need to win less than a dozen deals per year.

Looking at it from the other side of the table: the customer is not making too many purchases either – at least not of this magnitude. That's because the impact on the customer's organization is significant and there are only so many material projects that can be consumed at any one time.

I believe that in this context salespeople are knowledge workers. The best salespeople combine empathy, creativity and experience to solve problems and are more successful when the interests of the customer guide them. It's no longer about waging war against the customer, but being a partner that gains network value from the relationship.

But you still have a target. The best way to achieve it is to select the deals that matter – solving problems for customers that you can solve better than anyone else. This is not purely a numbers game – it is more about quality than quantity.

In *Chapter 3: Digital Sales Transformation | Part 2: Customer Engagement Model*, the strategy for engagement at Customer Impact Level 2 was stated as:

BUILD RELATIONSHIPS THROUGH VALUE CREATION TO WIN

Enable sellers to qualify opportunities, build relationships, connect solutions to customer business problems, and create value and position competitively. Implement a deal management framework with increased visibility and collaboration for higher win rate and larger deals.

Opportunity Management is the 'how' to deliver on that strategy. I will now go through the Goal, and Objectives and Methods for Opportunity Management.

Figure 115: OPPORTUNITY MANAGEMENT – OVERVIEW

CUSTOMER IMPACT LEVEL 2	SALES PROCESS MANAGEMENT	APPLY
GOAL	WIN THE OPPORTUNITIES THAT MATTER	MANAGE MEASURE
OBJECTIVES	Maximize Opportunity Result (Desired State)	Objectives Completed On Time
METHODS Systematic series of steps that you can repeat	1 Know Your Customer's Business / Opportunity	Insight Maps Validated by Customer
	2 Build Relationships	Key Player Coverage & Preference
	3 Assess Opportunity and Competitive Landscape	Positive Answer To 4 Key Questions
	4 Set Strategy	Mentor Validates Win Strategy
	5 Create and Communicate Value	Key Player Can Articulate Business Value
	Execute Strategies and Actions	

Opportunity Management Goal

The Goal of Opportunity Management is to *Win The Opportunities That Matter.* The average win rate for enterprise B2B sales is 21.7 percent, and the average cost of lost deal pursuit for a seller carrying a million dollar quota is $218,000. This is the stark reality. At the end of the day, there are only two reasons why you lose:

1. You should not have been there in the first place (poorly selected or poorly qualified), or
2. You were outsold (poor deal strategy or execution).

Effective opportunity management helps you to mitigate the underlying causes of losses to win the opportunities you choose to pursue.

Opportunity Management Objectives and Methods

There is just a single objective to be achieved with opportunity management:

1. Maximize the opportunity result.

That does not mean that the purpose of opportunity management is just to win larger deals, though that of course is desirable. Maximizing the opportunity result might mean qualifying out of the opportunity quickly. As we know, earlier failure is better than late failure. Maximizing the opportunity result could also include developing relationships in the account for future opportunities, closing a small deal now to expand later, winning a marquee account to give you a foothold in a new market, or just simply maximizing the value of this particular deal.

To deliver on the Goal of Opportunity Management: *Win the Opportunities That Matter*, the following methods apply:

1. Know the customer's business / opportunity
2. Build relationships
3. Assess the opportunity and the competitive landscape
4. Set strategy
5. Create and communicate value.

Know the customer's business / opportunity

As I said in *Chapter 9: Know Your Customer First*, Most customers don't care how much you know, until they know how much you care. As explained in *Chapter 9*, it is really important to know what problems the customer has to resolve, and what process is broken or doesn't exist. I will not repeat the contents of that chapter, but I do want to stress one very important point: *Broken is better than Better.*

Your customer's project to fix something that is stopping them performing a critical business task (*aka* something is broken) will always take priority over a project to improve a process that even partially works (*aka* make it better). I stress this point, because as I was discussing the Customer Insight Map construct – Goals, Pressures, Initiatives and Obstacles – with a sales consultant, she suggested to me perhaps I change the name of Obstacles to Requirements. I recoiled in horror! OK, that was a little melodramatic – but I wanted to make this point clearly: *Broken is better than Better.*

When someone describes their aspirations in terms of Requirements they usually talk positively in terms of what they want to achieve. That's all good, but it rarely creates urgency, and often means that the problem is not really well-understood, and that the impact of not achieving the aspiration is not quantified.

For example, when someone says that they want to eat healthily, we all smile and nod and wish them well. But if this is expressed as avoiding a second heart attack, resolving the problem becomes more critical.

Similarly, when a seller says they want to sell consultatively, you recognize that as a good thing to do. On the other hand if the aspiration is articulated negatively as inability to convey value that leads to competitive losses, now you know what problem you have to fix. Broken is better than better.

Presenting this story visually in a Customer Insight Map (**Figure 116**) will enable you to validate with the customer that you understand their business and the business problem they need to solve. *Validation with the customer needs to be restated. It is important and is your key measure of progress.*

Figure 116: THE CUSTOMER INSIGHT MAP – 3

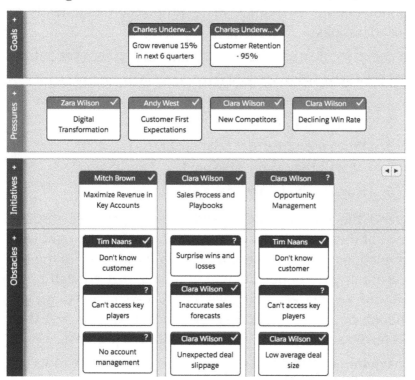

You cannot be positioned well in an opportunity unless you know enough about the customer's business so that you can identify how implementing a project using a solution such as yours will resolve their business problem. Don't forget to consider how the customer is prioritizing the resolution of their problems. (Hint: Broken is also much more urgent than Better). Review *Chapter 9: Know Your Customer First* for guidelines on how to discover what you need to know.

Build relationships

In *Chapter 6: Relationships: The Buyer's Perspective*, I talk about the mutual authentic engagement between buyer and sellers. Relationships that are founded on trust and respect, and guided by shared values in pursuit of shared goals, are the foundation for a mutual value proposition that leads to closed business.

In *Chapter 7: A Structure for Building Relationships*, I set out the five key relationship questions:

1. Who matters?
2. How do they think?
3. What is your current relationship?
4. What is the relationship gap?
5. How do you bridge that gap?

Spend the time to understand how to progress through each of these questions so that you can attain the right level of relationship and preference (for you) with each of the key players in your opportunity. If you have met enough times with the key players, and have had successful meetings, you should be able to uncover evidence that you are their preferred supplier. This is a key measure of progress.

I have found that it is useful to use smart software tools like a Relationship Map (**Figure 117**) to visualize the interconnections of rank and influence.

In this Relationship Map, you can quickly get an overview of your relationship status in the opportunity. The map displays the organization structure, but also identifies where you have support (green bars) and who is against you (red bars). You can also see, using the green *Lines of Influence*, the internal relationships. Other attributes on each individual on the map indicate whether the people in the map are in the Inner Circle (Controls Outcomes) or the Political Structure (Make Things Happen) as I defined in *Chapter 7: A Structure for Building Relationships*.

Figure 117: THE RELATIONSHIP MAP – 3

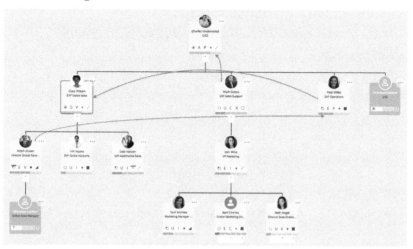

Think about this: if you have to win 10 deals in a year, and your win rate is average (21 percent) then you need to work about 50 opportunities. Then if the average number of people involved in each buying committee is 6 to 10, then you need to stay on top of your relationships with 300 to 500 people. It is definitely easier if you lean on software to help.

Based in Geneva, Switzerland, Marc Parizot is a sales director with Honeywell Aerospace. He describes himself as a life-long student of sales best practices and customer centricity. From my interaction with Marc, I think he has a lot to teach us all. Marc kindly agreed to share his viewpoint on Relationship Maps.

A Practitioner's Perspective
5 Benefits of Relationship Maps
Marc Parizot, B&GA Sales Director at Honeywell Aerospace

In my business, which is a combination of customers in both in B2B and B2C environments, we're facing the following challenges:

- A significant number of opportunities that a single salesperson has to manage in parallel

- A decision making process – at the customer – with an increasing number of people being involved which makes it complex

- A need for immediate reliable information leading to ability to forecast the wins.

There is a common denominator to these challenges = People.

My sales team is tasked to investigate and behave as Sherlock Holmes – less gut feeling and more 'evidence' based inputs. Such an approach ultimately results in an ability to identify the real opportunities that are worth pursuing.

In order to gather the evidence, the team tries to get as deep as possible into the customer's organization to identify the decision makers and influencers. Then, they also need to know who is a supporter and who is a non-supporter and / or enemy, who is neutral, and identify the people for whom we can't tell.

Easy to say, slightly more challenging to do properly ... especially when you couple it with the high number of opportunities you have to manage and a request from your manager to forecast.

This is where we have found technology to be an essential tool.

We use the Relationship Map to get a visual representation of both power and influence in an account. This is, in my opinion, the absolute foundation of any deal. In many cases, the salesperson tends to build the map in her head. This might work when you have a handful of simple deals. In most of the cases, it doesn't work. When you take into account that any input to the deal assessment should come from a 'person' at the customer, it is critically important to have a robust structure helping you to build and develop the relationship map in order to have it under control.

430

We use the Relationship Map to:

1. Capture what we know for sure
2. Identify the unknown and the gaps
3. Do a proper analysis of the situation
4. Use the embedded AI based coaching to advise us on the right relationship strategy
5. Take actions – which could involve other persons than the opportunity owner.

We need a core methodology to approach how we develop our relationship strategies for each of our key opportunities. But if we had not deployed software to bring it to life we certainly would not have had as much success as we have had. I just don't know how in today's world you can win without this combination.

Assess the opportunity and the competitive landscape

Now that you know the customer's business and the role that the project plays in resolving a business problem for 'the people that matter,' you're well-equipped to determine how, or if, you want to continue with your pursuit of this opportunity.

In *Chapter 3: Digital Sales Transformation | Part 2: Customer Engagement Model* I introduced the idea of structured opportunity qualification, and the four key questions to consider, reprised here for your convenience, are:

1. Is there an opportunity?
2. Can we compete?
3. Can we win?
4. Is it worth winning?

Deploying this assessment framework guides you to continuously assess whether the deal is worth pursuing and where you may have vulnerabilities that you need to address. Don't forget that sometimes the truth changes. Without continuous assessment, it is hard to know if you are still on track.

Figure 118: FOUR KEY QUESTIONS

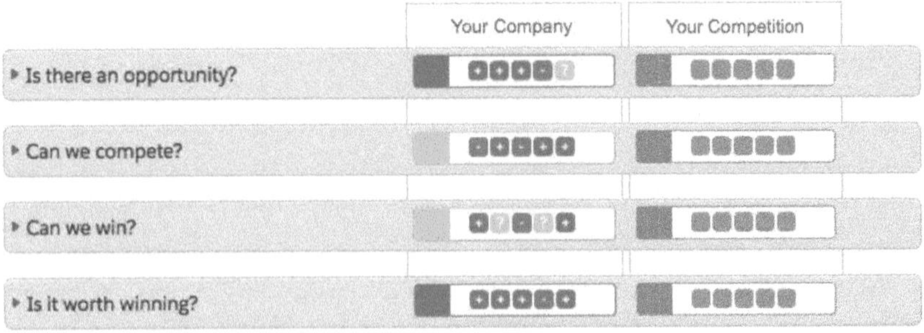

When you deploy your opportunity management system in software, it is easy for the salesperson to use and easier for all to share and collaborate. Also, by leveraging AI in a smart system, you can check for inconsistencies in your answers and point out where you might be contradicting yourself.

Customization / personalization is another key benefit of software. Some readers will recognize this assessment approach as the Target Account Selling Assessment or TAS 1-20. (I purchased the TAS business from Oracle in 2006). The important point, however, is not that you use this particular assessment framework – or that you apply all 20 questions to every opportunity type – but that you consistently use some method. *As with all sales methodology components, the best one is the one that is used regularly and uniformly for opportunities of similar profiles.* When you use a software application that is integrated with your CRM (where you enter your opportunities) you get the immediate benefit of measurement and collaboration.

The TAS method is one that has worked well for me (and over a million sellers around the world) so I will describe now in more detail the sub-questions behind each of the four key questions.

Is there an opportunity?

You need to assess whether the customer has a compelling reason to solve a business problem. You don't always need to have an identified budget for the project at this stage of qualification, but your customer must have access to funds if the project's ROI calculation merits the investment.

Figure 119: IS THERE AN OPPORTUNITY?

1	**Customer Project**	A project sponsored by a key player has been approved and resources are assigned. You can articulate, from the customer point of view, what this project will achieve and you understand where this project fits in terms of the customer's other projects.
2	**Customer Business**	You have a strong understanding of the customer's business (their Goals, Pressures, Initiatives, and Obstacles) as it relates to this opportunity and a key player has confirmed your insight.
3	**Customer Financial Condition**	The customer's financial situation is compatible with the customer project. After reviewing the organization's financial situation (how they are performing in the marketplace, and against their targets and competition), you judge that the organization has a strong financial condition and this project will continue to support their performance or the organization is in a stressed financial condition and this project could remedy performance issues.
4	**Access to Funds**	The requisite funds for the project have been allocated or a key player has confirmed that, if you put the right business case together he will be able to find the money.
5	**Compelling Event**	A key player (who owns the Pressures) has confirmed that there is a pressing need for change by a specific date to avoid consequence(s) of inaction or to get the anticipated payback.

Can we compete?

Can you provide unique business value to the customer with a solution that fits their needs – from the perspective of most of the key buying influencers?

Figure 120: CAN WE COMPETE?

6	**Formal Decision Criteria**	You know the specific criteria and process that the key players will use to evaluate alternatives. A key player has confirmed the solution capabilities, legal requirements, and / or financial criteria and which criteria matter most and the milestones and deadlines in the customer's decision process.
7	**Solution Fit**	The solution is capable of meeting the critical requirements of the project – as described by the customer. The key players have acknowledged that your solution relieves the pressure and meets their most important requirements.
8	**Sales Resource Requirements**	You expect you can win this opportunity with the same (or lower) sales effort, compared with similar opportunities.
9	**Current Relationship**	A key player has confirmed that you have a competitive advantage, based on their experience with you either in this company, as an incumbent supplier, or in a similar project in a previous company.
10	**Unique Business Value**	A key player has confirmed that your solution delivers business value in a way that uniquely differentiates you from the competition.

Can we win?

This is all about the relationships you have in the deal. You cannot win unless someone who matters in the customer organization is working on your behalf. That way you can assess the informal decision criteria and make sure you are aligned politically with the people that matter.

Figure 121: CAN WE WIN?

11	**Inside Support**	A key player has confirmed that they want you to win and has done something to indicate their support (for example, revealing information to help you win, or actively selling on your behalf in their organization).
12	**Executive Credibility**	You or another person on the team can regularly access one or more of the relevant key players at the executive level.
13	**Cultural Compatibility**	The customer's culture closely resembles your company's culture or you and your team can adapt to their culture.
14	**Informal Decision Criteria**	A key player has shared the intangible, subjective factors that could affect this decision and you can leverage these to your advantage.
15	**Political Alignment**	The key player(s) who own the Goal(s) and/or Pressure(s), want you to win and demonstrate their support by influencing the outcome to ensure you win – for example, by creating a sense of urgency and/or changing the criteria or process

Is it worth winning?

Is the return from the deal worth the effort? This can be determined by matching the cost of sale to the strategic value of the opportunity, the short term and long term revenue, and the likelihood of the customer being successful. Don't forget that last part – it's critical to long term repeat business.

Figure 122: IS IT WORTH WINNING?

16	Short Term Revenue	You expect the customer's initial order to be the same size as (or larger than) the average opportunity size for your business, and the initial order is expected within a normal sales cycle.
17	Future Revenue	The expected lifetime value of the business generated by this opportunity is greater than or equal to the average lifetime value for a customer in your business.
18	Profitability	The profit from this opportunity is greater than or equal to the average profit on an opportunity in your business.
19	Degree of Risk	The level of risk in this project, for you or the customer, is no greater than your normal projects.
20	Strategic Value	The opportunity is strategically important for your company – for example, the customer is a marquee player in the market (and will be a reference), or the customer has agreed to be the first to purchase a new offering.

The key thing to remember about opportunity assessment is that it is not a one-time event. Consistent assessment helps you to continuously monitor your opportunity health, identify where there might be risk or vulnerabilities, and where you might have a significant competitive advantage or challenge.

To paint a picture of the competitive landscape you combine your knowledge of the active competitors in the opportunity with your knowledge of the questions in *Can we compete?* That might seem fairly obvious, but until you know that you have a good Solution Fit, which maps to the Formal Decision Criteria, you cannot assess whether you can provide Unique Business Value to the customer. You will see that, as with any good assessment framework, there are interconnections between the questions.

A smart AI powered Opportunity Management system will keep track of any inconsistencies for you.

You will remember the **Customer Value Question**: *What problems does the customer have that you solve better than anyone else?* This is where this question meets the Truth Test: *"Yes, if I were the customer, with those business problems, then I would definitely want to buy what I have. It's the best thing for them to do."*

If you can truthfully answer the Truth Test in the affirmative, then you should be in a good place. You should consider how well you can facilitate the customer's business outcomes and deliver the value that is required, and of course understand how well are you aligned to the players that matter.

Set strategy

Strategy sets direction, and dictates actions and behaviors. Without strategy there is no context about the actions that you will subsequently take. Everything we have done so far informs the strategy that we adopt, and consequently the actions that we must take. Our knowledge and understanding of the customer's business as it pertains to this opportunity, the relationships we have with the people who matter, the competitive landscape and the overall assessment of the opportunity all provide a wealth of knowledge with which to make an informed decision.

Remember the objective of opportunity management is to maximize the opportunity result. So, the first question to answer is, to paraphrase Joe Strummer – the singer with the 1970s English punk rock band, The Clash (really showing my age now) – "Should I stay or should I go?"

The right answer might be to walk away and spend time on more worthwhile opportunities. The other two options are to:

- **Actively Pursue** (sometimes called an Attack strategy – the nomenclature is a little bellicose for me), or
- **Position for the Future.**

If you choose to *Actively Pursue* it means that there is an active opportunity, where you can compete, you think you can win, and the opportunity is worth winning. However this does not singularly mean that you present your solution as the complete answer to the question your customer's requirements describe. If you have a good Solution Fit, and the customer has agreed that you have Unique Business Value, then you need to assess whether that combination meets all the requirements and that you are well-positioned to compete effectively across the spectrum of needs.

Alternatively, you might find yourself in a situation where there are unstated needs that you believe the customer should consider that point to problems that you solve better than anyone else. In that case you will need to change the rules and move the goalposts so that the customer evaluates you and your competitors against a new set of criteria. You can only be successful with this strategy if you have identified one of the key players who understands that the new capability that you have added into the mix is truly of value to the customer's company, and that person will need to champion the perspective for you.

If your Solution and Unique Business Value only meet part of the customer's needs, then it is still valid to pursue the opportunity. In this case, however, you must accept that a competitor might fulfill the remaining requirements.

If you are not in a position to win today, you may want to *Position for the Future*. This might be applicable in a situation where you are the incumbent and you are protecting your position from the competition. Using your past success with past projects and current or past relationships in the account will support this approach. You need to rely heavily on communicating the value that you have delivered in the past. This is a time to expand your relationships and continue to articulate your business value.

Another scenario where you might want to *Position for the Future* is when there is no Compelling Event and your primary competitor is No Decision. Assuming that you believe there is potential for a future opportunity, you must continue to build relationships and develop greater understanding of the customer's business until a Compelling Event occurs naturally, or through your work to develop an Unknown Need as described in *Chapter 9: Know Your Customer First*. If there is a Compelling Event but you are not in a position to compete, you could try to delay things if you believe you will have a better solution for the customer in the near-term future.

You know that you have a winning strategy if your Mentor – the person inside the customer's organization who is selling on your behalf when you are not there – validates that your strategy is a winning strategy.

Create and communicate value

In *Chapter 10: Create and Communicate Value*, I explored in depth the importance of value creation and value communication, so I won't go into detail here. I am surprised sometimes though by sellers who do themselves a disservice by understating the value that they have delivered in the sales process or in previous projects. Once your key players can articulate the business value that you can provide – you know you have succeeded in communicating value.

If you are not confident that you can answer "Yes" to all of the 20 questions in the assessment for your company's position (see **Figures 119, 120, 121**, and **122**), then either there is information that you have yet to uncover, or there are areas where you need to convey a value message to the customer.

There is a simple acronym (PRIME) that you can use as a guide to check whether these are Actions you need to take. You should ask yourself if you need to:

- **P**rove your value
- **R**etrieve missing information
- **I**nsulate against the competition
- **M**inimize your weakness
- **E**mphasis your strengths.

You should not forget, when crafting your messaging, that you may also need to craft messaging to combat the competition's strengths.

Conclusion

Use the Customer Insight Map to collaborate with the customer on the problems that need to be resolved and help your customers visually connect where your solution can help solve their business challenges. As you identify key players you can develop your relationships by aligning with the customer on their business problems. The Relationship Map should be your guide to navigate the organization and get to the centers of influence and power. A solid assessment process helps you to figure out whether there is a deal worth pursuing and how you should go about it. Then decide on the strategy to pursue and execute.

There are only so many opportunities that an enterprise B2B seller can pursue. This Opportunity Management framework will help you select those where you should focus and increase both your win rate and deal size. Planning takes time, but as the saying goes:

> The beauty of not planning is that failure comes as a complete surprise and is not preceded by a period of worry and depression.

It is better to plan.

CHAPTER 15:
ACCOUNT
MANAGEMENT

Implementing Account Management

When I wrote *Account Planning in Salesforce* in 2013 I started by posing a question:

> Do you need a different approach when you are selling to big companies just because they are big?

What's the matter with just using the very same methods that have worked in smaller companies? Are there really considerations that are so dramatically different that they call into question the basic techniques that succeed elsewhere?

The answer is both "Yes" and "No." Yes, you need a different approach, but no, you do not need to throw out techniques that succeed elsewhere. The core principles of *Know your Customer's Business*; *Build, Elevate, and Expand Relationships*; and *Create and Communicate Value*, apply to both Opportunity Management and Account Management. The factor that drives a need for an 'industrial strength' account management process can be captured in one word: *scale*.

A large company is usually a collection of small, interrelated commercial activities, organized by function or geography, specialism or purpose, competitive forces or market dynamics. When approaching any such ecosystem, a deliberate design is demanded.

The reality is that most (though not all) account planning and management efforts start from one opportunity in one division or business unit of the account. You've found your first deal. Now you want to expand your footprint by delivering value to more business units, or by selling more solutions from your product portfolio to that first business unit. As you make progress, this account now becomes a material source of revenue and the dynamics shift to value co-creation and long term business partnership. Your perspective shifts from a deal-oriented lens to a strategic vision. The account is in fact a marketplace, but one where your success or failure is clear for everyone in the market to see.

Your greatest fear will be customer defection – but the force driving your actions should be customer success. As you build relationships across the organization, deliver the desired customer outcomes, and communicate the value that you are delivering, the customer looks to you as their Trusted Advisor, and you seem to achieve your cross-sell and up-sell targets without strain. That's how you keep your competitors at bay.

I cover the principles of Account Planning and Management in this chapter and throughout other chapters in this book. For a fuller treatment of the topic, I'd suggest reading *Account Planning in Salesforce*.

In *Chapter 3: Digital Sales Transformation | Part 2: Customer Engagement Model*, the strategy for engagement at Customer Impact Level 3 was stated as:

> CREATE COMMON VISION TO GROW IN LARGE ACCOUNTS
> Craft an integrated approach to elevate and expand relationships, understand the customer's business, create, measure and communicate customer success. Implement an integrated framework for the account team to build pipeline and close revenue in existing accounts.

Account Management is the 'how' to deliver on that strategy. I will now go through the Goal, and Objectives and Methods for Account Management.

Figure 123: ACCOUNT MANAGEMENT – OVERVIEW

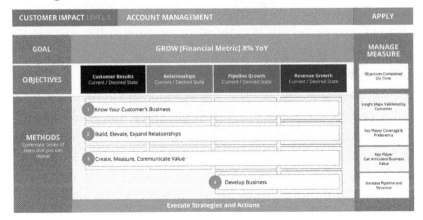

Account Management Goal

The Goal of Account Management is to Grow [Financial Metric] X percent Year-on-Year. I used [Financial Metric] instead of Revenue, Profit, Market Share or Customer Retention, as you can have more than one goal. It is important however to be clear as to what you want to achieve.

There are many benefits to account management. The *Account Planning Book of Evidence*[27] reports:

- Win rate improvement in existing accounts (60 percent)
- Increased understanding of customer's business (72 percent)
- Better customer loyalty (55 percent)
- Average deal size is 14 percent greater
- Sales cycle is shorter by as much as 26 percent.

All of these improvements together have a dramatic impact on the overall velocity of revenue achievement – but that only happens when a rigorous account planning and methodology is applied and is supported by technology.

---

[27] Research report by Altify: *Effectiveness of Account Planning on Enterprise B2B Sales*: **https://www.altify.com/account-planning-book-evidence-2016/**.

Account Management Objectives and Methods

There are four core objectives to be achieved when implementing account management:

1. Document (positive) customer results
2. Grow relationships
3. Grow pipeline in the account
4. Grow revenue.

When you have documented customer success you are in a good position to grow relationships because, by delivering value, you build credibility. That helps to build pipeline, and when you close some of the opportunities in the pipeline, you grow revenue.

To deliver on the Goal of Account Management and achieve these four objectives, the following methods apply:

1. Know the customer's business
2. Build, elevate and expand relationships
3. Create, measure and communicate value
4. Develop business.

If you read *Chapter 14: Opportunity Management*, you will notice certain similarities. You've learned much of this already. But, as I said earlier, the difference between account and opportunity management is really just a matter of scale. You need a wider aperture on your lens.

Before you get into the specific methods below, make sure that your focus is on the right accounts. Review *Chapter 5: The Ideal Customer Profile*.

Know the customer's business

In *Chapter 9: Know Your Customer First* I described how to uncover what is going on in the customer's business.

The work to be done at the account level is similar to that in Opportunity Management, but it covers the account as a whole, and not just one opportunity within the account. When your focus is limited to an opportunity you are typically involved in one project to meet a single Goal. At the account level, just like there is an organizational hierarchy, there is also a hierarchy of Goals. You need to understand the hierarchy of Goals, Pressures and Initiatives all the way up and down in the customer's organization.

In the example below you will see that Goals distributed through the organization are connected to the higher or wider overall company goals.

The CEO of a SaaS company has set a company goal to:

INCREASE REVENUE BY 50%

Then she delegated 'sub' Goals to her lieutenants:

- **Increase new business revenue by 40%**
  (Goal owned by the Chief Sales Officer)
  - Expand in APAC to achieve $20m in new ARR
    (Goal owned by President APAC)
  - Grow North America new ARR to $80m
    (Goal owned by VP Sales America)
- **Reduce customer churn to 5% to increase retained revenue**
  (Goal owned by Chief Customer Officer)
  - Achieve 97% customer retention in EMEA
    (Goal owned by VP Customer Success EMEA)
  - Achieve 95% customer retention in North America
    (Goal owned by VP Customer Success North America)
- Etc.

Once you understand how Goals flow through the organization you can build interconnected Customer Insight Maps that link these Goals and associated Pressures and Initiatives. You need to understand how the overall vision impacts each of the business units (and executive leaders and teams) to build one common shared vision with the customer – the core element of your Account Management strategy.

You know you are making progress when the various business leaders can validate the Customer Insight Map that pertains to their area of the business.

Build, elevate and expand relationships

In the account you are operating in a closed marketplace. The downside is you don't have a lot of room to screw up. The good news however is that, if you have delivered on your previous promises, and the customer does not find you difficult to work with, expanding your relationships and getting introductions to new business leaders will be much easier than if you are trying to penetrate a new account.

The principles and practices outlined in *Chapter 6: Relationships: The Buyer's Perspective* and *Chapter 7: A Structure for Building Relationships* are critical to know when you're investing with a customer to build a vision of mutual success. With an account perspective, you will likely find that you need to leverage your executive team to get to the executives in the customer's organization. *Chapter 8: The Executive Sponsor: Their Role in Large Accounts* is your guide to leverage this oft-underutilized resource.

Create, measure and communicate value

At this point in the book I hope I have sufficiently explained the need to communicate value. A structured approach to doing that is explained in *Chapter 10: Create and Communicate Value*.

To be effective at communicating value in a large account you really need to understand the business, the people and the issues that are concerning them. They will always want to know the success their company has achieved in working with your company in the past, and you will lean on the relationships you have developed to support that message.

The key metric to measure to know if your value communication is working is the ability of the key players in the company to articulate your business value and / or the value they have received from your solutions.

Develop business

Using the three methods above, we have hit two of the four objectives that were outlined earlier. When you know the customer's business, developed your relationships, and communicated value, you should have achieved two of the objectives: documented customer results that you can share, and a stronger base of relationships.

1. Document (positive) customer results ✔
2. Grow relationships ✔
3. Grow pipeline in the account
4. Grow revenue.

It is time now to leverage the power of the last method *Develop Business* to Grow Pipeline and Grow Revenue.

Let's say there are three different Solutions that you sell.

1. Servers for storage
2. Printing services
3. Security consulting services.

And there are three business units or divisions that you have identified:

1. Acme US
2. Acme EMEA
3. Acme APAC.

Figure 124: THE WHITESPACE MAP – DETAIL (BLANK)

		What you Sell		
		Servers	Printing	Security
Where you Sell	Acme US			
	Acme EMEA			
	Acme APAC			

Ideally you want to achieve complete penetration for all your Solutions across each of the three business units. As you close opportunities and identify qualified opportunities to pursue you can plot them on the map.

Figure 125: THE WHITESPACE MAP – DETAIL (UPDATED)

	Servers	Printing	Security
Acme US	$100,000	$80,000	White Space
Acme EMEA	White Space	White Space	$56,000
Acme APAC	$23,000	White Space	White Space

In **Figure 125**, I have added four opportunities to the map. There are still five areas where there is whitespace.

When dealing with a large account in the real world, things are a little bit more complicated than this simple view. You rarely start from a blank sheet of paper. There are probably more than three Solutions in your arsenal, and there will probably be a greater number of business units in the account.

Using a software application integrated with your CRM is the easiest way to track all the data to give you a one-screen picture of what is going on in your account and where you have opportunity to expand.

Figure 126: THE WHITESPACE MAP IN SOFTWARE

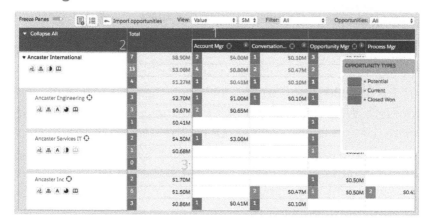

There are three main areas on the Map:

- **Solutions:** The columns on the map represent the solutions you are selling to the account. This is *what* you are selling.
- **Units:** On the left of the map is the list of business units within the account. This is *where* you are selling.
- **Opportunities:** Your goal is to identify, create, and win opportunities at each intersection of solutions and units.

To identify whitespace you should plot all won and active opportunities on the map and then see what other areas are left to explore.

Figure 127: THE WHITESPACE MAP – DETAIL (UPDATED 2)

	Servers	Printing	Security
Acme US	$100,000	$80,000	White Space
Acme EMEA	White Space	White Space	$56,000
Acme APAC	$23,000	White Space	White Space

For example, if Acme US had a need for Servers that resulted in a $100,000 opportunity for you, then you should ask yourself: What is it about their business requirement that might be similar in EMEA? Does the fact that there is a demand in EMEA for Security Consulting Services provide any insight into the needs in the US or APAC? What Goals in EMEA or APAC might be positively impacted by the Printing Services solution that you have?

Mapping your opportunities in the manner I described is the best way I know to explore whitespace and to focus on creating new opportunities to grow pipeline. When the customer says: *"Aha, I never thought of that – I think that could really help our company,"* then you know you might be on to something and creating opportunities that you can win.

In the end, the results speak for themselves. Billy Martin of Salesforce, one of the most effective practitioners of Account Planning and Management that I know, tells a great story about Salesforce's journey to drive value with its customers.

A Practitioner's Perspective
Benefits of Account Planning / Management
Billy Martin, Senior Director, Global Sales
Enablement Programs, Salesforce

What's cool about this is when you get these teams together and they start collaborating, you get opportunities, true opportunities in the CRM that are generated out of this process that never existed before. They just weren't even on the radar screen.

We generate pipeline reports out of these sessions that are like $20m and $30m worth of pipeline that just didn't exist before. And if we could keep our numbers up, if our typical close ratio is 20 percent or 30 percent, that could be really impactful to the business. This comes because of the way the methodology helps those teams to think differently about those accounts or about their portfolio.

Right now, we're tracking about 50 percent of our pipeline for marketing cloud through the software. How much of that will we close? We hope all of it, but the cool thing is that it's being tracked in a very strategic way. The software gives us a full view of a customer across all the different products. It's brought a new level of visibility that we didn't have before and it gives us a better view of the full whitespace.

The ultimate goal from our perspective is that we have one plan. We use one tool. And the account execs can tell one story. And that story is: "How am I gonna make my number? How am I gonna be successful as an account executive?"

About those Objectives ...

You will remember in *Chapter 14: Opportunity Management* I described PRIME Actions. In Sales Process, one of the last steps in the process was to create a mutual close [action] plan with the customer. Every strategy requires action. When your scope of activity is at the account level – increased scale, and a longer term perspective – you need a little more structure to how you organize your actions. I find it helpful to think about this using three components:

- **Objectives:** What you are trying to achieve
- **Strategies:** The approach you are going to use
- **Actions:** The tasks to be undertaken.

Combined, these Objectives, Strategies and Actions (OSAs) describe your plan for engagement with the account.

Our four objectives for Account Management are:

1. Document (positive) customer results
2. Grow relationships
3. Grow pipeline in the account
4. Grow revenue.

Below are two examples of OSAs that we could use for the third and fourth objectives:

- **Grow Pipeline Objective:** You should have a Pipeline Objective wherever there is whitespace. This is how you identify future opportunities.
- **Grow Revenue Objective:** Your Revenue Objective should be to close the qualified opportunities that are currently in your pipeline.

Your **Pipeline Objective** summarizes the specific areas in the account that you want to pursue, based on the potential opportunities you have identified. The strategy that supports your pipeline objective describes how you will grow pipeline. The actions you identify are the major steps you need to take in order to execute your strategy and achieve the objectives.

Of course, you will need to apply the necessary resources to carry out the tasks. Review *Chapter 11: Create and Communicate Value at Scale: Account Based Marketing* **and** *Chapter 8: The Executive Sponsor: Their Role in Large Accounts*.

Figure 128: PIPELINE OBJECTIVE, STRATEGY AND ACTIONS

Business Unit	Acme EMEA, Acme APAC
Pipeline Objective	Build additional pipeline of $250,000 in the account by end of Q2.
Strategy	Map the capabilities of the Servers and Printing Solutions to the business issues for Acme EMEA and Acme APAC. Brainstorm new possible initiatives based on experience in Acme US, leveraging existing relationships.

Action	Resources	Date	Owner
Review Customer Insight Maps for EMEA and APAC	King, Analysts	6/11	Eric King
Brainstorm solution fit and possible initiatives	Account Team	6/30	Eric King
Collaborate with US (Servers, Printing), APAC (Servers) to gain insight on results delivered	Customer, King, Market Analyst	7/11	Eric King
Document customer results (US, APAC)	Marketing	7/13	Marketing
Identify EMEA Key Players	Eric King	7/15	Eric King
Get introduction to EMEA from US/APAC supporters	Eric King	7/22	Eric King
Create presentation to capture hypothesis and possible business impact	Account Team, Marketing	7/30	Eric King

The **Revenue Objective** relates to opportunities that you want to close. You need to consider the strategy that will describe your approach, the actions that need to happen, with the associated resources that are required.

Figure 129: REVENUE OBJECTIVE, STRATEGY AND ACTIONS

Business Unit	Acme EMEA, Acme APAC
Revenue Objective	Close additional revenue of $200,000 in the account by end of Q3.
Strategy	Combine current open opportunities into a single enterprise agreement for all solutions to accelerate buying cycle and grow deal size.

Action	Resources	Date	Owner
Work with individual business units to drive demand	King, Support	8/30	Eric King
Communicate value of Enterprise License to Acme HQ	Executive sponsor, King	9/30	Eric King
Create new opportunity to include the three opportunities	King	8/30	Eric King
Use Opportunity Management to pursue and win new deal	King, Account Team (inc. executive sponsor)	10/21	Eric King

The two example OSAs above outline the strategy you have chosen and the specific actions to be taken, with defined resource and target timelines. Account management and planning is a team sport. Everyone needs to know his or her role. I can't see how you can assign, track, update and collaborate as a team on this without software, so I think having your OSAs managed within an application is essential so that everyone a clear picture of responsibilities and inter-dependencies.

Conclusion

The key thing to remember when working with a large account is that it is a long game. But a long game is played in short parts. If you know where you are going in the account – you have a clear strategy and a common vision with the customer – you should consider every move that you make in the account in that context. When you are working an opportunity, know that your actions will advance or damage your account strategy. The actions of your Customer Success team must be informed by the strategy. Marketing's role needs to follow the account strategy playbook. Everyone on the same page!

You will need multiple Customer Insight Maps to gain agreement on the overall business problems. Make sure they follow the Goal hierarchy.

Relationship strategies will be broad as you leverage the resources of your organization to achieve your desired level of relationship in the account. The Relationship Maps should be your guide to navigate the organization and get to the centers of influence and power. Value communication must be your constant companion.

The first three core methods position you to effective develop business:

1.   Know the customer's business
2.   Build, elevate and expand relationships
3.   Create, measure and communicate value.

Whitespace is your framework to see how you can fill your pipeline with deals you can win by applying the methods described in *Chapter 14: Opportunity Management*.

Remember, the customer said: *"Partner with me,"* so as you agree the common vision with your customer, make sure that your OSAs plot the journey to that destination.

CHAPTER 16:
SALES PERFORMANCE MANAGEMENT

Implementing Sales Performance Management

Front line Sales Managers have the toughest job in sales. They are the last link between the company and the sales team's interaction with the customer. For a company to be successful, the sales management function must perform. But sales managers are pulled in so many different directions, by so many people, it can be hard for them to find the time to focus on effective sales performance management.

Think about all the tasks a sales manager has to balance: hiring, enablement, coaching, closing deals, running the sales forecast, managing the pipeline, supporting HQ information requests, and conducting the Quarterly Business Reviews ... and that's when she's not traveling to visit the corporate office, meet her team, or meet customers.

In *Chapter 3: Digital Sales Transformation | Part 2: Customer Engagement Model*, for each of the Customer Impact Levels we identified the required behaviors and practices of the sales manager.

These behaviors and practices, listed in **Figure 130**, combine to present the sales manager's role in supporting her team as they engage at each of Customer Impact Levels.

Figure 130: THE BEHAVIORS AND PRACTICES REQUIRED IN THE SALES MANAGER'S ROLE

LEVEL 1 SALES MANAGEMENT

Manage team to the sales process
Collaborate on call plans
Use sales process stages for forecasting
Manage pipeline quality
Measure effectiveness and productivity

LEVEL 2 SALES MANAGEMENT

Level 1+
Coach to deal management framework
Collaborate in deal reviews
Use opportunity health / progress for forecast
Institute forecast and pipeline cadence
Collaborate with supporting functions

LEVEL 3 SALES MANAGEMENT

Level 1, Level 2+
Collaborate on account plan and review
Measure customer success results
Engage executive support in formal program
Support relationship strategies
Measure pipeline and revenue growth in account

Haiden Smith is VP Business Development at syncreon. The motto of Haiden's alma mater, Rhodes University in the Eastern Cape of South Africa, is: *Where leaders learn*. In his 20+ years in sales leadership, Haiden would say that he had learned to lead, and leads people to learn. His sales leadership style is a blend of learning and coaching, and he is intrigued to see how advances in AI technology can help him learn more effectively and coach more wisely.

A Practitioner's Perspective
Benefits of AI for Sales Management
Haiden Smith, Vice President Business Development
– Automotive America, syncreon

Donal puts it perfectly: "There is nothing more fulfilling than watching a sales manager collaborate with her team, coach deals, motivate and guide individual sellers to fill competency gaps to improve."

With our fast paced and data rich environment today, managing our time and having the ability to distinguish between good and bad deals early on will enable the sales manager of yesterday to be the effective sales coach moving forward. Big data and the ability to use the data and provide real-time analytics is the first step.

If we can enhance that with AI prompts and coaching based on both the data analytics and industry best practice from multiple industries and disciplines, real-time and in the salesperson's hand … we then enable not only our salespeople to be more successful, but our sales managers to be coaches, enablers and success factors in the teams' improved success rates.

You can't replace sales managers with AI, but you can certainly enable them to apply themselves effectively to drive success.

Sales Performance Management is 'how' you bring it to life.

Figure 131: SALES PERFORMANCE MANAGEMENT – OVERVIEW

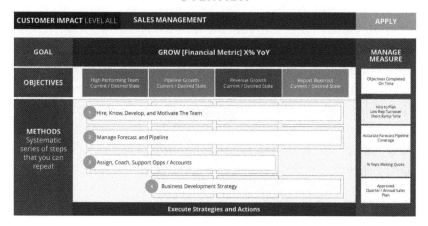

Sales Performance Management Goal

The main Goal of Sales Performance Management is to Grow Revenue year-on-year. There may be supplemental goals to increase margin or improve sales productivity but the purpose at the end of the day is to maximize the revenue from the sales team. Every sales manager has a quota for her team and through a combination of management and coaching intervention, implementation of sales process or methodology, and effective business management, her job is to make or exceed quota.

Sales Performance Management Objectives and Methods

There are four core objectives to be achieved by the front-line sales manager:

1. Build, maintain, or improve a high performing team
2. Grow pipeline
3. Grow revenue from closed opportunities
4. Report and plan business.

To deliver on the *Goal of Sales Performance Management* and achieve these four objectives, the following methods apply:

1. Hire, know, develop and motivate the team
2. Manage pipeline and forecast
3. Assign, coach, support opportunities and accounts
4. Business development strategy.

Hire, know, develop and motivate the team

The sales manager first needs to hire the right people, ensure their onboarding is effective, their compensation is competitive, and that they are motivated and coached to perform to their maximum ability. Motivation, coaching and onboarding are part of overall sales management and a function of supporting the team with good processes and practices as outlined elsewhere in this book.

You will know you are successful if you have hired to plan, and have low rep turnover and short ramp time. Hiring and compensation are two big topics that could fill up a full book so I don't cover them in detail here.

Manage pipeline and forecast / Assign, coach, support opportunities and accounts

Once the right team is in place, the sales manager has to manage the achievement of her sales forecast while she guides the team to grow the pipeline. I have combined these two methods within the following section *5 Key Sales Performance Management Questions* as they are best explained by looking at them together.

5 Key Sales Performance Management Questions

Sales management is a complex and multi-faceted role. My goal in this chapter is to cover the primary areas of sales performance. I describe how the sales manager can quickly and materially impact performance by following specific best practices and by leveraging technology.

Even though structured coaching is recognized as being a true driver of sales productivity, most sales managers don't offer coaching on a regular basis. The theory is great, but in most cases, it is not working in practice. The math illustrates this phenomenon better. Let's assume that the sales manager has eight people on her team, each working six material opportunities, with an average sales cycle of 90 days. That's 48 opportunities in her universe, at any one time. Even if she tries to coach just half of these opportunities effectively each month, spending two hours per opportunity, she quickly runs out of time.

Some sales teams have considered sales analytics as a solution to resolving some of the sales managers' challenges. When these approaches fail, it is usually not because they don't know or can't see the answers in the data; it is more often that they have not adequately considered the questions.

When you bring it back to basics, there are only five questions the sales manager needs to answer to run the sales business:

1. What's the best cadence for how I manage my sales team?
2. How can I understand the sales performance KPIs in my business?

3. Can I reduce risk and avoid surprises to make my sales forecast?

4. Are there enough real deals in my pipeline? Where are the risks?

5. QBR: What happened to my forecast / pipeline last quarter?

The goal is to help you to get the best sales performance possible from your team, crush your quarter with real-time insights and coaching, gain visibility into the sales forecast and sales pipeline and identify where there are risks and how you might overcome them.

A Day in the Life of a Sales Manager

We follow Kelly, a B2B sales manager working for JKHiggs, with a pretty expansive sales territory covering most of the Mid-west of the United States. With nine sellers on her team, there are two top performers who she knows she can count on every quarter. At the bottom of the list are one struggling long term seller and two new salespeople. Sandwiched in the middle are her core performers, who typically deliver about 70 percent of their quota.

Kelly's like most sales managers in similar positions. In addition to having a clear revenue goal, she has also been tasked with some supplementary goals:

- **Make the Number Every Quarter:** No surprise here; most sales managers are consumed with making the number. JKHiggs is in a rapidly expanding market and striving for an ambitious market leadership position. JKHiggs has one very strong competitor, and there is concern that unless momentum is maintained, the opportunity will be lost.

- **Increase Rep Productivity:** Not every company uses this metric, but Kelly is also measured on yield / head, therefore she is encouraged to maximize the productivity of her team. She also needs visibility on the balance of team performance, so that she might lessen her dependency on the two top performers.

- **Build / Coach the Sales Team:** Kelly and her manager recognize that ramp-up time for new salespeople is long. To maintain a low attrition rate, and to maximize her sales results, she knows she needs to invest in developing the team.

- **Provide Accurate Sales Forecasts and Annual Revenue Guidance:** Kelly needs to provide accurate short term sales forecasts and indicative medium term revenue outcomes. One critical measure of excellence, from the CEO's perspective, is the ability to understand risk, and have confidence in future business. This responsibility belongs with Kelly.

- **Present Quarterly Reviews and Strategic Outlook:** JKHiggs is on a fast growth path and needs to consistently learn what is working in the business, so it can course-correct as needed, and make the right strategic investments. Kelly needs to be able to explain deviations in her sales forecast every quarter, and provide insight into developments in her sales pipeline from the start of the previous quarter.

Though not all sales managers will have the same goals as Kelly, the pressures – the 'why' she needs to achieve these goals – will be similar across most B2B sales organizations.

What's the best cadence for managing my sales business?

Effective sales managers balance short term, current revenue activities (typically represented by the current sales forecast), with future business pursuits (represented by the pipeline). When most sales managers wake up every day, they are concerned about the deals on the table today. Good sales managers triage the opportunities, focusing where they can win and applying resources accordingly, while at the same time securing their future business by working on the pipeline.

Neither of these goals will be achieved unless the team is performing. While Kelly is working on forecast and pipeline to the right cadence, she needs to stay on top of the key sales performance metrics for the team, all the time. Then, every quarter, she will need to prepare for her QBR. She needs to find her rhythm. Here is what the cadence might look like in Kelly's business:

- **Every Day | Understand the KPIs:** To improve the operations of the sales business, Kelly, our front line sales manager, needs to first understand the KPIs that matter for the business; things like Number of Deals, Average Deal Size, Win Rate and Sales Cycle. She can benchmark her team's performance, on an aggregate and individual basis. She needs real-time visibility into their actual and historical KPIs and an understanding of how these are evolving over time. She might not use these every day, but she needs to have them as a reference point as she interacts with her team, coaching them to improve. She needs to consider their empirical strengths and weaknesses, to give her a compass to guide their direction.

- **Every Week | Manage the Forecast:** Any business practice is most effective when it is regular and consistent. People get into a rhythm, know what to expect and what they need to do for productive engagement. Kelly's meetings should focus on issues arising from what is changing in her *Must Win* deals, managing risk to short term revenue, and seeing what has impacted her forecast. We all know that a forecast is a moving target. Kelly needs to know where she stands, real-time, or else seeing the way forward is nearly impossible.

- **Every Month | Manage the Pipeline:** Unless there is a healthy pipeline, Kelly's business is in trouble. Pipeline management is too rarely treated as urgent, even though the strength of the pipeline is one of the most critical indicators of future sales. Kelly must institute a regular monthly pipeline review to ensure the health of the business going forward.

- **Every Quarter | Report on and Plan the Quarter:**
  From Front Line Sales Manager (FLSM) to seller or FLSM to CSO, the value in regular Quarterly Business Reviews (QBRs) is the insight into past performance, to drive change in process or behavior, and to improve next quarter's performance. Unless Kelly has an effective rear-view mirror, to assess what happened to her pipeline and forecast in the previous quarter, she will be exposed at her QBR, and won't have insights from which to learn from past experiences. Her forward-looking view will be hazy at best.

Every day | Understand the KPIs

There are only four factors that impact how much you sell. I use a term called the Sales Velocity Equation: a function of (A) the number of sales opportunities you work, (B) the average deal value, (C) your win rate and (D) the length of the sales cycle. Simply put: You want to increase A, B and C, and reduce D. If you increase A, B and C by 10 percent and reduce D by 10 percent, then you increase your sales velocity by 47 percent. Go on, do the math – it works out.

Figure 132: THE SALES VELOCITY EQUATION

$$V = \frac{\# \times \$ \times \%}{L}$$

OPPORTUNITIES   DEAL VALUE   WIN RATE

SALES VELOCITY

LENGTH OF SALES CYCLE

If Kelly can accurately calculate these four factors for each of her team, then she can quickly highlight weaknesses that need to be addressed.

Simple, right?

Yes, but maybe not quite as simple as it looks. Let's look at why, using Win Rate as an example.

Let's say one of the sellers on Kelly's team worked the four deals listed here, and at the end of the sales pursuits, achieved the following results:

- Deal A: $20,000 – **WIN**
- Deal B: $10,000 – **WIN**
- Deal C: $40,000 – **LOSS**
- Deal D: $30,000 – **LOSS.**

He won Deal A and Deal B, and lost Deal C and Deal D. Win two. Lose two. That is a 50 percent Number Win Rate.

However, when we add the values of the deals, we get a different result. The aggregate of A and B is $30,000, where C and D together add up to a value of $70,000. On a value basis, this translates to *Value Win Rate* of 30 percent.

Even if Kelly's company JKHiggs had a system that highlighted both Number Win Rate and Value Win Rate – what does it mean, and what can Kelly do about it? Is she supposed to check the ratio for each seller, dig into the underlying data to try and understand what is happening – and then consider the selling behaviors she should change in each case, before finally assessing the impact on the value of her pipeline?

In this case, the interpretation is straightforward. If the Number Win Rate for Kelly's team is significantly higher than the Value Win Rate, then the team is winning the small deals, and losing the bigger deals. That's a problem and points to a value-selling challenge, rooted in poor understanding of the customer's business and how to apply JKHiggs' solutions to drive benefit for the customer.

Figure 133: MEASURING VALUE AND NUMBER WIN RATE

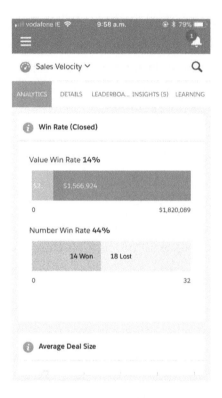

But it doesn't stop there. What does it say about the future potential revenue from the pipeline, if the team can't win any of the big deals? It should call into question whether the pipeline is a true reflection of future business potential.

When I ask a sales manager their 'typical' deal size they might answer $100,000. But if I follow up with "What is your average transaction value?" they will often look at me askance and question if I am serious. But I couldn't be more serious. If indeed my 'typical' deal size were $100,000, then it would not be unusual for that to be followed with an additional $20,000 for some complementary service or product. Now my average transaction size is $60,000, the sum of the two transactions, divided by two. The CRM doesn't understand 'typical,' it understands 'average,' so when your sales data is infected with a few very small transactions or a very large deal, analysis based on averages is of questionable value.

Furthermore, most companies only measure the *Won Cycle*, but it is equally important to measure how long it takes to lose deals: a long lost cycle means wasted resources, and potential problems in sales process or qualification practices. Comparing Won Cycle *versus* Lost Cycle gives great insight to the effectiveness of sales process execution.

Figure 134: MEASURING WON AND LOST SALES CYCLES

To understand business performance you should measure:

1. Sales cycle for won deals
2. Sales cycle for lost deals
3. Value win rate
4. Number win rate
5. Average deal size for won deals
6. Average deal size for lost deals.

Whatever system you use to inform your sales performance, KPIs should be configurable such that you can exclude anomalous data. For example, if your typical deal is $50,000 with a sales cycle of 90 days, you may want to exclude any deal under $10,000 or deals that have sales cycles less than 10 days. These quick deals are probably small add-on opportunities and should not be included in the analysis of your typical performance.

Similarly, if you put your opportunities into the CRM as soon as they are created by Marketing or by Business Development Reps before they are fully qualified, you may want to measure the KPIs for qualified deals only. Make sure that your system allows for that.

Every week | Manage the forecast

You will remember that Kelly's first and fourth goals are *Make the Number* and *Provide Accurate Sales Forecasts and Guidance.* As a front line sales manager, Kelly understands that these two goals are wholly interconnected.

An ineffective or inefficient forecasting process often involves an unproductive weekly call trying to figure out the forecast number. To change the focus of the process, I prefer to call it a Revenue Outlook call, rather than a Sales Forecast call. The purpose every week should be to figure out how to make the number, with clarity on the current state (where we are today), focusing on the deals that can be closed in period, keeping on top of what is changing every week, and seeing risks early, so that effective action can be taken.

For most sales managers, there are four obstacles to overcome to get this forecasting right.

1. **Hard to sssess Current State *versus* Quota / Target:** This metric should be the easiest thing for Kelly to get right, but often it's harder than it should be. Setting targets needs to be contextual and account for a flexible approach to setting the team's quota, by individual or in aggregate. It should support different periods, different types of revenue. When the targets have been set, Kelly should be able to see what is won, what is expected and what other deals are possible to close in the period. If Kelly doesn't have an accurate real-time view she won't know how to direct her team.

2. **Changes are hard to see:** If Kelly's team is working all the 48 opportunities I referenced earlier, how hard do you think it is for Kelly to keep on top of all the changes week-to-week? The weekly call becomes a 'details update' exercise, rather than a deal or pipeline strategy session. Kelly needs a system that concentrates her attention on changes to deals and brings these changes to her attention in real-time. She needs to be aware of any material value change in her key deals. Then she can lock in on the impact and coach the team to take corrective measures.

3. **No early warning of deal risks to forecast:** How many times would you say Kelly has heard: "*I never thought that deal was actually going to come in this quarter, it's just so much bigger than any other deal I've closed, so of course it was going to take longer!*" Do you think she would then bang her head against the wall, mumble incoherently and wonder how that deal ever

made it into the forecast or why someone did not raise a red flag to alert her of the risk? Now it's too late to try to pull other deals forward; she misses her number *and* the forecast is proven inaccurate. If Kelly looks for nothing else, she should be crying out for an early warning system on her most important deals.

4. **Difficult to determine where to focus:** Not all deals are equal. If one of Kelly's sellers has 10 deals he is working, how does he know where to prioritize his efforts? If his win rate is 30 percent, then he should expect to win three opportunities, but what if he reduced his span of attention to just seven deals, then would the extra time applied to those seven deals help him to win four out of seven, instead of three out of 10?

    It is not easy to apply a qualitative lens to a list of opportunities, and sorting by value or pipeline stage is not necessarily the best guide. The deals that come to the top of the list need to be further assessed for risk. The best way for Kelly to prioritize her team's efforts is to combine risk, opportunity health, dollar value, strategic value, and pipeline stage.

Of these four obstacles you will learn that the first two are easily resolved with technology and – yes, I know you figured this out yourself – the second two are easily fixed with Sales Process and Opportunity Management.

The bottom line is that not only must Kelly make her number, she must do so with a level of predictability that makes her secure in her forecast. Every week she needs to be able to plot a roadmap from her current position to her desired future destination, aware of the pitfalls along the way. If she is going off track, signposts along the way that provide guidance on how to get back on track will increase her chances of success.

Applying technology to forecast management

There are many tools available to help with forecasting, that report the numbers for reps, managers, and regions. Many solutions allow for managers and executives to apply judgment to the forecast on a roll-up basis so the company can aggregate opinion to come up with an overall forecast. These are valuable but don't provide much guidance to sales managers. Kelly needs to manage, not just report, the forecast; she must maximize performance, not just measure results. Kelly needs a manager's console that presents current state (*versus* quota) and a way to uncover risk.

Figure 135: REVENUE OUTLOOK – CURRENT STATE

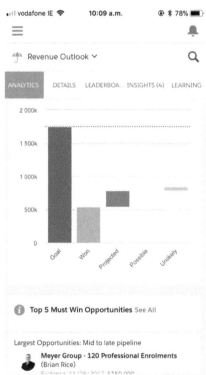

If Kelly has the right application she can quickly monitor the performance of her team against quota, her top 5 deals for the quarter, the deals that are at risk, and deals she needs to focus on for next quarter – all from her phone while she is on the road. Now she knows where to focus.

Next, she needs to assess what changed from last week's forecast call. Salesforce's opportunity trending reports can help with this and she can have her operations team create reports that will guide her in that exercise.

Alternatively, she can use a specialist application to view the changes on a week-to-week basis for each of her sellers.

Figure 136: WHAT CHANGED IN MY REVENUE OUTLOOK?

	Date From: 9/24/2017		Date To: 10/1/2017				
> **Won** From:	**$364,106** To:		**$907,049** Change:			$542,944	
Opp Name	Owner	Was	Amount	Value Change	CloseDate	Adjustment
Key Success Path Checkpoints	Greg D	Projected	$128,800	$128,800	8/31/2017	
RM 450	Jack R	Projected	$123,000	$0	9/13/2017	
Services	Jack R	Projected	$48,950	$48,950	10/31/2017	
_Aug17 Services cl	Katarina H	Did not exist	$44,076	$44,076	8/24/2017	
> **Projected** From:	**$2,972,251** To:		**$8,533,783** Change:			$5,561,532	
> **Possible** From:	**$7,088,227** To:		**$6,231,035** Change:			-$857,192	
> **Other** From:	**$19,198,200** To:		**$18,484,666** Change:			-$713,534	

In this application, she can see for each seller, and each forecast category, the changes in any of the deals. It tracks value change and stage movement and is a quick way for the rep to answer the question: *What changed in your forecast since last week?*

Then she can look at the details of the deals and have the system identify status and risk.

Kelly can also benefit from the embedded AI in the application to gain further insights into risk in her forecasts. The following are examples of insights that are automatically delivered to Kelly:

$3,698,050 OF PROJECTED VALUE IN UNUSUALLY LARGE DEALS: 37 DAYS REMAINING: You are relying on large deals to make your goal but there is only 37 days left in the period. Ensure that you are working these deals in order to get them over the line. These opportunities typically progress more slowly and are more complicated than your average size deals. You might want to schedule a deal review with the team to make sure you have a solid strategy to win. You can view these opportunities here.

$1,013,500 POSSIBLE VALUE IN LARGE DEALS: Even though these are Possible (not Projected) these large deals will have a material impact on your revenue. Ask yourself and your team to identify why you might lose, continue to build inside support with the buyer and confirm (triangulate) solution fit, unique business value, competitive threats, and the compelling event. You can view these opportunities here.

PIPELINE INCREASE: $3,856,195: Pipeline growth is a combination of opportunities added to the pipeline, opportunities removed from the Pipeline (Won and Lost), and change in the value of open opportunities in the pipeline. Your pipeline has grown by $3,856,195 in this period. There was $8,920,626 added to the pipeline; Won $868,626 and lost $4,195,805. Both Won and Lost are removed from the pipeline. You can view the net change in your pipeline here.

Now Kelly knows where she needs to intervene, on which deals to focus her coaching energy today, knowing that some are less urgent. She knows the risks and vulnerabilities in her business. Knowledge breeds confidence.

Every month | Manage the pipeline

Every sales manager wants a good and 'honest' pipeline. They care about the integrity of the data, and they worry constantly about whether they can depend on the information to secure future business.

Managing the pipeline effectively takes a lot of discipline and focus – and that's not easy. In addition to the fact that it is hard to assess the current state of the pipeline, or to see changes in pipeline stage or value, there are other common challenges that sales managers like Kelly face in staying on top of this critical practice:

1.   **Lots of dead wood in pipeline:** Even if the total value of the pipeline is on target – assuming there is a target for every seller – that doesn't mean Kelly is safe. Sometimes the pipeline is full of deals that are not being worked actively, or are lost, only they have not been marked as closed / lost. This practice is dangerous because it delivers a false sense of security. Kelly needs to look for opportunities that have been in the pipeline for more than twice her typical deal sales cycle. These deals are unlikely to be won. She also needs to assess whether all the opportunities are actively being worked. I consider a deal to be *stalled* if it has not been updated in more than 30 days. When a deal has not been touched in 60 days, I consider it *inactive*. Lack of activity often happens because the deal has in fact been lost – but just has not been closed out in the CRM.

2.   **Traditional weighted pipeline is misleading:** As I described in *Chapter 13: Sales Process*, multiplying the pipeline by the probability of closure gives an

inaccurate estimate of pipeline value. Nine deals at 10 percent is not equal to one deal at 90 percent. Secondly, if you have a $1.2m quota and a 25 percent win rate, then traditional thinking might suggest that you need a 4X pipeline for a total pipeline value of $4.8m. But if you have a sales cycle of a month, and an average deal size of $10,000, then having $4.8m in your pipeline is nonsensical. More discernment is required to get to the right pipeline value target, and consequently, an assessment of what is needed to make the number.

3. **Hard to identify pipeline health:** A healthy pipeline comprises what I refer to as a healthy mix of Rocks, Stones and Pebbles. *Rocks* are the big elephants and it's OK to have some in the pipeline, but dependency on just a few larger than normal deals is risky. *Stones* are the average size opportunity, the deals the team knows how to sell and deliver, and the basis upon which the sales quotas have been set. *Pebbles* are the smaller deals, and while they might grow into larger opportunities later, they still soak up a lot of sales resources.

   In addition to deal size, Kelly should be aware of any deals that are moving more slowly through the funnel than usual. Deals that have been in the system more than twice the average sales cycle will typically not close. Finding the Rocks and the very slow deals helps identify outliers that need extra focus, if she is to minimize risk in the deal mix.

Kelly can be successful in her pipeline management if she can remove the deadwood from her pipeline, identify vulnerabilities and shortfall, differentiate between qualified and non-qualified deals, and get a clear picture of how opportunities are moving through the funnel.

Every month she needs insight – actually, let's call it foresight – a look into the future health of her business based on a quantitative calculation and a qualitative judgment of every deal, every seller, every risk.

Applying Technology to Pipeline Management

As with forecasting, there are many tools to help with pipeline management. You should use all the reports available in Salesforce (or other CRM) to get as much insight as possible. In addition to those reports, Kelly can also gain great insight from smart applications that quickly provide insight into risks in the pipeline.

Figure 137: PIPELINE MANAGEMENT – 2

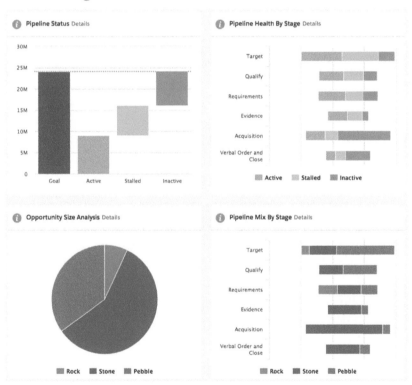

You can see in **Figure 137** above that Kelly can see the Pipeline Status for each seller and know whether they have sufficient value in the pipeline to make their quota in future periods. In addition, not only can Kelly see the total pipeline value measured against the pipeline goal, but she can also see whether the deals in the pipeline are being worked in Health By Stage, and if the seller has a healthy mix of Rocks, Stones and Pebbles in Size Analysis and Pipeline Mix.

Kelly can also leverage intelligent insights to understand what is going on in the pipeline.

The first three pipeline insights for Kelly are:

GOAL: $24,000,000. PIPELINE: $24,118,853. Your Pipeline Goal is $24,000,000. Total actual Pipeline is $24,118,853 representing 100 percent of Goal. Active Pipeline value is $10,907,866, Stalled $6,576,323 and Inactive $6,634,664.

ALERT: ACTIVE PIPELINE ONLY 45 percent. Your overall pipeline is ahead of the Goal of $24,118,853 – well done. However, only $10,907,866 is Active. You need to review Stalled and Inactive opportunities to make sure your pipeline value is accurate. Keeping an Active pipeline is of paramount importance in ensuring future revenue. You can view these opportunities here.

OPPORTUNITY SIZE ANALYSIS. Good mix of deals. Experienced sales professionals will understand that relying on a small number of big deals is risky, and they will balance their opportunity portfolio with smaller deals in order to keep the numbers moving, in case the big rock falls off the cliff. You seem to be working on a good mix of large deals, average deals and smaller opportunities. Well done.

Business Development Strategy

We have covered two of the four methods that reflect the daily, weekly and monthly cadence of Kelly's business. Now as she reflects on the past quarter and considers how her business development strategy might need to change, she will probably do this in the context of a Quarterly Business Review.

Every quarter | Report on and plan the quarter

Many sales organizations conduct a Quarterly Business Review in order to align stakeholders on future strategy. The key is to not just look in the rear-view mirror and conduct a post-mortem on the quarter that just passed, but also to look ahead and amend or remodel the strategy for the future. World-class sales organizations commit to this process and have a steady QBR cadence.

Unfortunately, many QBRs are ineffective, and without accurate and up-to-date historical and future data, the outcomes are rarely worth the effort. Sales managers like Kelly arrive at the meeting full of trepidation, if they had a bad quarter, or bursting with braggadocio if they crushed their number.

It is important to use the QBR to foster a rhythm of continuous improvement. The QBR is a wonderful opportunity to share viewpoints and hypotheses with everyone working together. Key wins and losses should be discussed in detail, and there should be an exchange of views on pipeline growth, forecast attainment, and forecast accuracy. Every sales meeting should be an opportunity for the team to get better. The QBR is a great place to share ideas. Don't just focus on the negative. Structure the meeting so best practices and key wins are discussed in detail.

Answering the question at the top of this chapter: *What happened to my forecast / pipeline last quarter?* is just a small part of the challenge that sales managers like Kelly face. But it is a critical question to be able to answer because it speaks to how well she understands the business. I have seen too many sales managers wilt in front of executives when the historical data they presented was incomplete or out-of-date. *"Oh, I'm sorry, I think the operations team must have pulled that report last week, and maybe things have changed since"* is not a response that instills confidence.

Kelly must know what happened in her historical business if she is to have any credibility with her leadership. She needs to be able to use historical and future performance data to drive the conversation, with both lagging and leading indicators, insights gained, and best practices learned. Armed with this informed perspective, Kelly will now be able to manage the discussion and gain alignment on how the team will make next quarter.

Conclusion

At the start of this chapter I set out the Goal of Sales Performance Management as *Grow financial metric x percent year over year* and listed the four key objectives to be achieved by the front-line sales manager:

1. Build, maintain, or improve a high performing team
2. Grow pipeline
3. Grow revenue from closed opportunities
4. Report and plan business.

How do you know how you are doing? Check these off:

1. Accurate sales forecast
2. Pipeline coverage (to make future revenue targets)
3. Higher of reps making quota (target 70 percent+)
4. Approved quarterly (annual) sales plan.

My approach to describing how you might achieve those goals was by living vicariously through the challenges of Kelly, our sales manager from JKHiggs. We guided Kelly to answer the *5 Key Sales Performance Management Questions* to run her sales business:

1. What's the best cadence for how I manage my sales team?
2. How can I understand the sales performance KPIs in my business?
3. Can I reduce risk and avoid surprises to make my sales forecast?
4. Are there enough real deals in my pipeline? Where are the risks?
5. QBR: What happened to my forecast / pipeline last quarter?

Now that Kelly is equipped with the practices and technology to answer these questions she can get on with her business. However, it is important to remember that while Front Line Sales Managers are the critical link in any sales organization, the job of closing deals and building pipeline remains with the individual seller. The manager must however be intimately familiar with all the principles in this book, particularly *Chapter 9: Know Your Customer First*, *Chapter 7: A Structure for Building Relationships* and *Chapter 10: Create and Communicate Value* so that they can coach and develop the sales team to excel at these practices.

CHAPTER 17
FINAL WORDS

There is a lot of change going on in the world. You can get depressed and throw your hands up in despair wondering how you will cope, or you can embrace the opportunity that change brings. Change is good. It's also often hard. But to succeed in business and life, you must run toward it. Life is not a straight line.

I started this book outlining the **Customer Impact Architecture**, walking in the customer's shoes to get inside his mind. If you want to be successful you must again reflect on the fact that the impact on a customer of a bad buying decision is typically greater than the impact on a salesperson of a lost deal. Taking that to heart forces you to think about the customer, how he wants to buy, and what impact he expects from the deployment of your solution. It leads you to learn more, to discover, to find ways to create and co-create value. Your goal as a salesperson is to make your number. That's clear. But in this Customer First world, you must put the customer first. Any other approach is short term at best, and not the path to sustained success.

I asked you to consider the **Customer Value Question**: *What problems does the customer have that you can solve better than anyone else?*

The answer to that question prompts a natural follow up. The Ideal Customer Profile should be your compass that guides your go-to-market strategy, the careful selection of targets that leads you to the true north, selecting customers where you can grow revenue through the creation of mutual value.

As we moved though the book I focused a lot on the three core principles that underpin any effective sales transformation:

- Know your customer first
- Build, elevate and expand relationships
- Create and communicate value.

If you do nothing else you must invest the time to become proficient in each of these methods and behaviors. This will be time well spent. Understanding the people and their problems, and how to engage in business conversations that convey your value, are the elements that will help you to weave your own tapestry of success, each thread carefully selected and each stitch purposefully completed.

Too many times I have seen well-intentioned and enlightened sales professionals struggle with the conflict between making their number and making the customer successful. My principal message to you is that these seemingly conflicting goals can in fact be wholly aligned. If you know how to execute on the appropriate customer engagement strategy that maps to the impact on the customer, you will both win.

In the final section of the book, *Chapters 13* to *16*, I described the methods that you can apply to guide your journey. In fact, this is where it all ties together.

Figure 138: THE DIGITAL SALES TRANSFORMATION ARCHITECTURE MODEL

It starts with the customer – as it should. Then I mapped the methodology to the each of the buyer's statements: "Help me buy," "Guide me," and "Partner with me" – all on a foundation of a structured approach to sales performance management.

The accelerator of course is the technology and, as you saw, each impact level has the requisite technology layer, AI strengthened as appropriate, to equip you with the full Digital Sales Transformation capabilities required.

Even as I write this, I know the world continues to change. It's an ever-evolving story. We are constantly buffeted by the winds of change, the torrent of innovation, disruption and global transformation. I hope that this book has provided you with some ideas and tools so that you can decide how the story ends. You can embrace the change, put the customer at the center, and use the turbulence to write the epilogue to your personal narrative.

I am reminded of a quote from the ex-CEO of the former leader in the mobile phone industry:

> We didn't do anything wrong, but we still lost.

And as Mike Rosenbaum said in the *Foreword*:

> There are always countless reasons why it's hard to change. But I urge you to get started. Now. Today.

Thank you for taking the time to read this book. I await with great anticipation to hear your stories of success. I wish you well.

Thank you,
Donal

INDEX

ABOUT THE AUTHOR

In 1986 Donal Daly started his quest to improve human performance with his first Artificial Intelligence software company. In 2005, he founded Altify, his fifth company, to improve sales performance through software and he is regarded as the catalyst for global advancement in sales transformation. Donal is author of multiple Amazon bestsellers including *Tomorrow | Today: How AI Impacts How We Work, Live and Think*, and the seminal publication *Account Planning in Salesforce*. His ideas, books, and speeches have inspired people around the world to perform better. He can be found at **donaldaly.com**.

OAK TREE PRESS

Oak Tree Press develops and delivers information, advice and resources for entrepreneurs and managers. It is Ireland's leading business book publisher, with an unrivalled reputation for quality titles across business, management, HR, law, marketing and enterprise topics. NuBooks is its ebooks-only imprint, publishing short, focused ebooks for busy entrepreneurs and managers.

In addition, Oak Tree Press occupies a unique position in start-up and small business support in Ireland through its standard-setting titles, as well as its training, mentoring and advisory services.

Oak Tree Press is comfortable across a range of communication media—print, web and training, focusing always on the effective communication of business information.

OAK TREE PRESS
E: info@oaktreepress.com
W: www.oaktreepress.com / www.SuccessStore.com

Lightning Source UK Ltd.
Milton Keynes UK
UKHW020854120319
338972UK00007B/41/P